# The Derbyshire Miscellany

# The Derbyshire Miscellany

## Michael E Smith

# Contents

# Contents

# Acknowledgements

Several people have helped me in writing this book. I should like to express my particular thanks to the following:

Nick Smith for advice and assistance with digital photography.

The staff at DB Publishing for their advice, support and encouragement and for bringing the work to fruition.

The staffs of the following libraries without whom the research could not have been completed:

Chesterfield Library
Derby Local Studies Library
Ilkeston Library
Nottingham University Library (Hallwood and King's Meadow sites).

# Introducing Derbyshire

**Derbyshire is an East Midland county which borders Nottinghamshire, Staffordshire, Leicestershire, Yorkshire and Cheshire.**

It is roughly 58 miles long from North to South and 34 miles in breadth at its widest point.

It covers an area of 262,860 hectares.

Around 80% of land in Derbyshire is used for agriculture, 11% is urban and industrial and approximately 8% is used for other purposes such as woodland, parks and golf courses.

A substantial part of the Peak District National Park lies within Derbyshire .

The city of Derby is a unitary authority but remains part of the ceremonial county of Derbyshire.

In addition to the city of Derby the county contains eight towns with a population of over 20,000. These are Belper, Buxton, Chesterfield, Dronfield, Glossop, Ilkeston, Long Eaton and Swadlincote. Other important towns include Alfreton, Ashbourne, Bakewell, Clay Cross, Matlock, Ripley and Heanor.

Nine tenths of Derbyshire is drained by the River Trent, which in turn is fed by the rivers Derwent, Dove and Erewash.

Derbyshire is well served by both road and rail. The M1 motorway flanks the eastern side of the county and provides easy access to the north and south. The A50 corridor gives access to the M6 and the north west. Chesterfield and Derby have regular and frequent rail services to London, Birmingham, Sheffield, Leeds and Manchester. Matlock and Belper have direct services to London.

Derbyshire has a diverse economy which includes agriculture, engineering and service industries. Notable manufacturing companies include Rolls-Royce, Toyota and Bombardier.

Derbyshire County Council is the largest employer in the county with over 37,000 employees.

The average house price in Derbyshire in 2012 was £137,235. The average price for different types of house within the county was as follows:

Detached house £225,837
Semi-detached £116,207
Terraced house £90,230
Flat/Maisonette £129,434

Derbyshire is divided into ten constituencies for the election of Members of Parliament to the House of Commons.

Derbyshire Constabulary is made up of 1,972 uniformed and plainclothes police officers supported by 344 special constables, 171 Police Community Support Officers (PCSOs) and 1,409 support staff. It has an annual budget of almost £25 million. The force is organised into three divisions, each headed by a Chief Superintendent, also known as the Divisional Commander. The divisions are: High Peak and the Derbyshire Dales (B Division), Chesterfield, North East Derbyshire, Amber Valley and Bolsover (C Division) and Derby, Derby South and Erewash (D Division). Divisions are further divided into a series of policing sections led by a Section Inspector. Local policing is complemented by a range of support units which operate across the force area including a dog section, scientific support department and the North Midlands helicopter unit. The headquarters of Derbyshire Constabulary is at Butterley Hall near Ripley. The work of Derbyshire Constabulary was overseen by an independent body called the Derbyshire Police Authority but this has recently been replaced by a directly elected Police and Crime Commissioner.

Derbyshire Constabulary receives around 2,390 calls a day and deals with approximately 61,000 crimes each year.

Derbyshire Constabulary Male Voice Choir was founded in 1956. Over the years it has achieved some notable success and has, through its concerts, raised thousands of pounds for charities. It has appeared alongside some famous names including John Hanson, Russ Conway, Ken Goodwin and Shane Richie. In April 2012 the choir was invited to take part in a special Jubilee concert at the Palladium and helped to raise over £1,500 for the local air ambulances.

The Church of England Diocese of Derby was founded in 1927. It is part of the Province of Canterbury and covers roughly the same area as the County of Derbyshire. Its diocesan bishop is the Bishop of Derby who has his seat at Derby Cathedral. He is assisted by the Suffragan Bishop of Repton. The current Bishop of Derby sits in the House of Lords.

**Bishops of Derby**

| | | |
|---|---|---|
| Edmund Pearce | 1927 – 1936 | Previously Master of Corpus Christi |
| Alfred Rawlinson | 1936 – 1959 | Previously Archdeacon of Auckland |
| Geoffrey Allen | 1959 – 1969 | Previously Principal of Cuddesden College |
| Cyril Bowles | 1969 – 1988 | Previously Archdeacon of Swindon |
| Peter Dawes | 1988 – 1995 | Previously Archdeacon of West Ham |
| Jonathan Bailey | 1995 – 2005 | Translated from Dunwich |
| Alisdair Redfearn | 2005 – Pres | Translated from Grantham |

The University of Derby was created in 1992 and was the only school of higher education in the country to be upgraded directly to a university. The main campus is at Kedleston Road on the edge of Derby but it also operates from several sites throughout the city. Another campus is located at Buxton in the north of the county. The university offers single and joint honours courses in a wide range of areas including arts, business, health, science, technology, computer gaming and leisure industry-related subjects. Around 30 courses are available online. The University is engaged with regional businesses through its award-winning, University of Derby Corporate b2b division and has several initiatives in place to boost student employability including over ninety incubation units.

Derby College is a further education centre which operates from a number of sites in and around Derby. It offers a range of courses including vocational training, foundation degrees and continuing professional development.

Chesterfield College was created in 1984 following the merger of Chesterfield Technology College with the College of Art and Design. In 1993 it became the first associate college of Sheffield University and now offers foundation degrees in a number of subjects including construction, electrical and electronic engineering and early years education.

The NHS is currently undergoing a period of reorganisation and restructuring. NHS Derby City and NHS Derbyshire County are the local Primary Care Trusts (PCTs) for Derby and Derbyshire with responsibility for health care across the whole area. The task of the PCTs is to ensure that the right health service and support are available for local people. This means finding out what the local population's health needs are, then making sure that the total budget of over a billion pounds is wisely spent.

NHS Derby City serves over 280,000 people registered with the thirty GP practices in the city. NHS Derbyshire County is the eighth largest PCT in the UK and covers a population of approximately 750,000 in over ninety practices. NHS Derby and NHS Derbyshire County work together as a single cluster with a single Chief Executive and senior team.

In January 2012 Derby became one of the first fifty places in the UK to pioneer a new British Heart Foundation 'Heart City' status offering people practical steps to improve heart health.

NHS 111 is a new Health Service telephone number being piloted in Derbyshire. It was launched in the Chesterfield, Bolsover, Bakewell and Matlock areas on October 25th 2011.

BBC Radio Derby began broadcasting officially on 29 April 1971. It serves an area including most of Derbyshire as well as the areas around Burton-on-Trent and Uttoxeter in Staffordshire. Its output is manly speech based, featuring news, sport, weather, travel, interviews and discussion combined with music and competitions. Most of its listeners are aged over 45 although its sports and weekend programmes attract a wider audience.

The area around Chesterfield and North Derbyshire is served by BBC Radio Sheffield.

The north-western parts of the county including Glossop, Chapel-en-le-Frith and Whaley Bridge are served by BBC Radio Manchester.

Independent radio stations which serve parts of Derbyshire include Ram FM and Peak FM.

The *Derby Telegraph* was first published in 1879 as the *Derby Daily Telegraph*. It is now owned by Northcliffe Media and is the county's most important and widely read newspaper. It has an average daily circulation of over 37,000 and is published from Monday to Saturday each week.

The Derbyshire Times is a weekly newspaper which was founded in 1854. It is published in five editions and claims to be read by over 108,000 people.

Derbyshire Building Society was founded in 1859 and grew to become the ninth largest building society in the country. It was acquired by the Nationwide Building Society in December 2008 and now trades as a division of Nationwide.

Derbyshire Archaeological Society was founded in 1878 as an archaeological and natural history society to foster and encourage interest in the past life and natural history of the county. There are now four sections: the Archaeological Research Group, the Architectural Section, the Industrial Archaeological Section and the Local History Section. The Society is one of the major county bodies consulted by planning authorities on matters concerning archaeological sites and historic buildings.

The National Trust has four significant properties in Derbyshire; Hardwick Hall, Kedleston Hall, Sudbury Hall, and Calke Abbey. It also owns a number of areas of countryside including the Longshaw Estate, Mam Tor, the High Peak Estate and Dovedale National Nature Reserve.

English Heritage cares for a number of properties in the county including Hardwick Old Hall, Bolsover Castle, Peveril Castle, Sutton Scarsdale Hall and Wingfield Manor. Ancient monuments in its care include Arbor Low and the Nine Ladies Stone Circle.

People living in parts of Derbyshire have their own distinctive dialect. This is particularly noticeable in the areas around Chesterfield, Swadlincote and the Erewash Valley. The author D. H. Lawrence used the dialect of the Erewash Valley in some of his novels.

East Midland Trains is the main provider of passenger rail services in Derbyshire and has its headquarters at Pride Park, Derby. It operates fast regular trains to and from London St Pancras International as well as services to Sheffield, Nottingham, East Midlands Parkway and Leicester. Local services include the Derwent Valley Line which travels through the picturesque and historic landscape between Derby and Matlock.

The M1 motorway runs north-south through Derbyshire connecting the county with London, Leicester, Northampton and other towns and cities.

The major bus operators in Derbyshire are Arriva Midlands and Trent Barton. Other companies providing services in the county include Midland General, Hulley's of Baslow, Notts & Derby and Stagecoach in Chesterfield.

Derbyshire is served by the East Midlands Airport just outside the county in Leicestershire. It was originally owned by a consortium which included Derbyshire County Council.

The county boasts two professional football teams; Derby County FC and Chesterfield FC.

Derbyshire County Cricket Club was founded in 1870. Its home ground is the County Ground at Derby but occasional matches are still played at Queen's Park, Chesterfield.

Derby has the highest proportion of people who do not have any formal qualifications. A Report by the Centre for Cities think tank, published in 2012 ranked the city bottom out of 64 towns and cities. Researchers found that 30,600 people, or 19.5% of the city's total population who were able to work had no qualifications.

The average weekly wage in Derby in 2012 was £440.

There are over 300 parks and open spaces across Derby covering almost 700 hectares of land.

Derbyshire features in the writings of some of England's best known authors including Jane Austin (*Pride and Prejudice*), Sir Walter Scott (*Peveril of the Peak*), George Eliot (*Adam Bede*) and D H Lawrence (*Sons and Lovers*).

## Approximate Distances from Derby

| | |
|---|---|
| Aberdeen | 473km/294 miles |
| Aberystwyth | 184km/114 miles |
| Bangor | 181km/113 miles |
| Bath | 182km/113 miles |
| Berwick-upon-Tweed | 319km/198 miles |
| Birmingham | 57km/35 miles |
| Blackpool | 145km/90 miles |
| Bodmin | 435km/270 miles |
| Bournemouth | 247km/153 miles |
| Brighton | 252km/157 miles |
| Bristol | 180km/112 miles |
| Burton-upon-Trent | 17km/11 miles |
| Buxton | 48km/30 miles |
| Cambridge | 134km/83 miles |
| Cardiff | 198km/123 miles |

| | |
|---|---|
| Carlisle | 240km/149 miles |
| Chelmsford | 187km/116 miles |
| Cheltenham | 121km/75 miles |
| Coventry | 57km/36 miles |
| Doncaster | 71km/44 miles |
| Dover | 276km/171 miles |
| Edinburgh | 355km/221miles |
| Falmouth | 396km/246 miles |
| Fleetwood | 151km/94 miles |
| Glasgow | 373km/232 miles |
| Gloucester | 129km/80 miles |
| Halifax | 94km/58 miles |
| Hull | 119km/74 miles |
| Kendal | 177km/110 miles |
| Leicester | 39km/24 miles |
| Leeds | 96km/61 miles |
| Lichfield | 35km/22miles |
| Lincoln | 71km/44 miles |
| Liverpool | 116km/72 miles |
| Llandudno | 163km/101 miles |
| London | 183km/114 miles |
| Luton | 137km/85 miles |
| Manchester | 81km/50 miles |
| Newcastle-upon-Tyne | 229km/142 miles |
| Northampton | 86km/53 miles |
| Norwich | 190km/118 miles |
| Nottingham | 22km/14 miles |
| Oxford | 131km/82 miles |
| Penzance | 420km/77 miles |
| Peterborough | 91km/57 miles |
| Portsmouth | 236km/147 miles |
| Preston | 125km/77 miles |
| Sheffield | 51km/32 miles |
| Stockport | 70km/44miles |
| Stoke-on-Trent | 48km/30 miles |

| | |
|---|---|
| Southampton | 225km/140 miles |
| Sunderland | 221km/137 miles |
| Swansea | 223km/138 miles |
| Taunton | 240/149 miles |
| Telford | 71km/44 miles |
| Torquay | 310km/193 miles |
| Wakefield | 85km/36 miles |
| Weymouth | 265km/165 miles |
| Wolverhampton | 58km/36 miles |
| York | 118km/74 miles |

*Derby Townscape*

# The Peak District

**The Peak District is an upland area of great natural beauty. It lies mainly within Northern Derbyshire but also includes parts of Cheshire, Greater Manchester, Staffordshire and South and West Yorkshire.**

The Peak District is conventionally divided into two areas; the White Peak and the Dark Peak.

The White Peak is the lower, southern part of the Peak District. The area takes the form of a limestone plateau about one hundred feet above sea level. It is well drained and dissected by both dry valleys and river valleys. The soils are poor and calcareous, creating grazing land for both sheep and cattle. Much of the area is divided into fields by dry stone walls.

The Dark Peak is the higher, wilder part of the Peak District. The rocks of the area are gritstone and shale which means that in winter the soil is almost always saturated in water. The Dark Peak contains large areas of heather moorland which is used to rear grouse. Thousands of years of erosion have created the famous gritstone edges which are popular with climbers.

On 17 April 1951 the Peak District became Britain's first National Park.

When the Peak District Park was created its boundaries were marked by distinctive signs made from abandoned millstones, one of the Peak District's traditional industries.

The Peak District National Park covers an area of 1,438 square kilometres.

Over 17 million people live within 50 miles of the Park.

Around 40,000 people live within the boundary of the Peak National Park.

Over 80% of the population of the Peak District National Park live in Derbyshire.

The Peak District is sparsely populated with a density of 0.26 people per hectare compared with a national average of 3.77.

About 10% of the population live in Bakewell, the largest settlement and the only market town.

Over 98% of the people living within the Peak District regard themselves as White British.

Over ten million people visit the Peak District National Park each year.

The Pennine Way, the Trans Pennine Trail and the Pennine Bridalway pass through the Peak District National Park and are accessible to walkers, cyclists and horse riders.

A recent survey of how visitors travelled to the Peak District found that 85% travelled by car, 9% came by coach, 3% walked, 2% came by bus or train whilst only 1% cycled.

The Peak Park Planning Board has two main duties:

To conserve and enhance the natural beauty of the area
To provide and promote facilities for the enjoyment of the National Park

More than 90% of the Peak District National Park is privately owned.

The biggest private land owner in the Peak District is the National trust which owns 17,507 hectares (12% of the National Park).

As a result of the Countryside and Rights of Way Act of 2000 there are now over 500 square kilometres of open access land in the Peak District National Park.

Around 360 million years ago most of what is now the Peak District lay under a shallow tropical sea. The fossilised remains of marine creatures can be seen in the limestone rocks of the White Peak.

Around 326 million years ago sands, gravels and mud were deposited on top of the limestone to form the gritstone and shale of the Dark Peak.

Arbor Low near Youlgreave is a late Neolithic henge monument. It was built around 2500 BC and consists of a circular bank 249 ft in diameter and 7ft high with an internal ditch around 30ft wide and 6ft deep, enclosing a central area. There are entrance causeways at the northern and southern ends. The stone circle comprises more than 40 recumbent limestone slabs with three lying at the very centre. These central stones form a 'cove' close to which a skeleton was found during excavations in 1901-2. Arbor Low is linked to the Bronze Age barrow of Gib Hill 350 yards away by an earth ridge.

A number of Iron Age Hill forts may be seen in the Peak District. The most impressive include Man Tor, Carl Wark and Fin Cop. Recent excavations at Fin Cop have discovered evidence of a battle which may have resulted in the massacre of women and children.

The limestone uplands of the Peak District were first farmed by Neolithic people around 6,000 years ago. These early farmers cleared woodland to rear sheep and cattle and grow crops such as pulses, beans, wheat and barley.

Around 86% of the Peak District National Park is classified as farmland. There are around 2,000 farms of which half are very small.

Cattle outnumber people in the Peak District by nearly three to one. Sheep outnumber people by more than ten to one.

In the Dark Peak farmers raise small herds of beef cattle in a handful of tiny fields with a few stone barns for shelter.

Black and white Friesian dairy cattle are a common site in the White Peak although there has been a decline in the number of dairy farms in recent years.

Agricultural and country shows are held annually in the Peak District at places such as Bakewell, Hayfield and Hope.

Farmers Markets are held at Bakewell, Buxton, Castleton, Hathersage, Matlock, Whaley Bridge and Wirksworth. They provide an ideal opportunity for people to buy food and local products direct from local farmers, food producers and craftsmakers.

The Peak District National Park looks after more than 150 small areas of woodland covering about 500 hectares.

Many of the former lead mining sites in the Peak District have been colonised by rare lead tolerant plants such as leadwort and yellow mountain pansy.

The Rowan or Mountain Ash is found frequently in the Peak District. It grows on a wide range of soil types but is most common on the moist acid soils of the Dark Peak.

Bloody Cranesbill is one of the most striking plants of the White Peak. It takes its name from the colour of its stems.

Cloudberry is a mountain plant found in parts of the Dark Peak. In Victorian times it was more common than it is today when the fruit was collected for sale.

Butterbur is a plant of stream and riverside. It is abundant on the banks and shallow waters of the Dove, Wye and Derwent.

Moorland plants such as cotton grass, bilberry and cloudberry can be found in the Dark Peak and the area is also home to wild red deer and mountain hares. Upland birds such as red grouse, curlew, ring ouzel, merlin and peregrine falcons are also regularly observed here.

The development of the heather moors of the Peak District started over 2,500 years ago as a result of wetter climate and deforestation.

Today heather covers around 20% of the Dark Peak moors, where it is managed for the rearing of grouse. These birds need young growth for best feeding but older growth for nesting and cover for the young. This is achieved by the controlled Spring-time burning of selected areas.

Birds of prey are a common sight in the Peak District and include the common buzzard, kestrel, barn owl and little owl.

The National Park Warden Service was established in 1954 with one full-time warden and a handful of volunteers. The service was later expanded and renamed as the Ranger Service. Today the Ranger Service is divided into fourteen areas each managed by an area ranger, There are a further five full-time Rangers, a Pennine Way Ranger and over 300 volunteer Rangers.

The Peak District Mountain Rescue Organisation was formed in 1964 to co-ordinate the activities of all mountain rescue teams in the Peak District. The civilian mountain rescue teams based at Buxton, Derby, Edale, Glossop, Kinder, Oldham and Woodhead are all members of the organisation as well as the Peak District Area of the Search and Rescue Dog Association, the RAF Mountain Rescue Team based at Stafford and the Derbyshire Cave Rescue Organisation.

The Tissington Trail is a bridalway and walk/cycle path which runs for about thirteen miles from Parsley Hay in the North to Ashbourne in the South. The Park Authority operates cycle hire from both ends of the trail. It was opened in 1971 and utilises the former railway line connecting Ashbourne with Buxton.

The High Peak Trail is a seventeen mile trail for walkers, cyclists and horseriders which runs from Dowlow near Buxton to High Peak Junction, Cromford. Opened in 1971, it follows the track of the former Cromford and High Peak Railway.

The Peak Park Planning Board operates a number of information centres. A purpose-built information centre was completed at Edale in 1966 and is now open every day except Christmas Day and Boxing Day. Other visitor information centres can be found at Bakewell, Ashbourne, Buxton and Castleton. A mobile information centre visits agricultural shows and well dressing events throughout the summer.

Well Dressing is a popular and distinctive feature of many Peak District villages. It involves decorating local wells or springs by pressing wild flowers, mosses and bark on to a wooden frame covered in wet clay to form a picture, often depicting a scene from the bible. The best known and oldest well-dressing ceremony takes place at Tissington on Ascension Day each year.

*Well Dressing at Tissington*

The highest part of the Peak District is Kinder Scout, a bleak plateau which rises above 2,000 feet. Other areas of high land include Axe Edge (1,810 ft), Mam Tor (1,790 ft) and Win Hill (1,523 ft).

The Kinder Downfall, at 98ft is the highest waterfall in the Peak District. It lies on the River Kinder, where it flows west over the edge of Kinder Scout. In certain wind conditions (particularly when there is a strong west wind) the water is blown back on itself and the resulting cloud of spray can be seen from many miles away.

The parish church of St John the Baptist is known as the Cathedral of the Peak.

Chapel-en-le-Frith is known as the Capital of the Peaks.

The Dovedale Sheepdog Trials are held in August each year at 11am.

There are around 2,900 listed buildings in the Peak District National Park that are of special architectural or historic interest. These include great houses such as Chatsworth as well as simple cottages, mills and buildings associated with the lead mining industry.

The annual Peak District Walking Festival offers guided walks with local experts on themes such as food and drink, ghosts, heritage and geology.

The Peak District has 98 kilometres of off-road cycle trails.

There are National Park Cycle Hire Centres at Ashbourne, Bamford and Parsley Hay near Buxton.

The Peak District has some of the most challenging and popular climbing routes in Europe including the internationally important Stanage Edge near Sheffield.

Fishing is popular in various parts of the Peak District. The rivers Wye, Derwent and Dove are particularly known for their rainbow trout, brown trout and grayling. Excellent coarse fishing is available lakes and reservoirs such as Ladybower and Carsington.

Caving is popular in the Peak District which is home to the highest natural cavern in the UK (Titan Cave at Castleton).

There are several caves open to the public in the Castleton area. These include Blue John Cavern, Treak Cliff Cavern, Speedwell Cavern and Peak Cavern.

*Park Life* is the community magazine of the Peak District National Park. It is published in March and October each year and provides information about how the National Park Authority is working with local organisations and communities.

The Peak District National Park contains over a hundred conservation areas. These are defined as areas of 'special architectural or historic interest, the character or appearance of which it is desirable to preserve or enhance'. Recently adopted conservation area appraisals include Castleton, Bonsall, Hathersage and Monyash.

The Longshaw Estate, a few miles to the south-west of Sheffield is an area of moorland, woodland and farmland which has been owned by the National Trust since 1931. Wildlife on the estate ranges from rare birds to hairy wood ants. Quarrying for millstones took place on the estate from the 15th-century until the 1970s and numerous abandoned millstones are still to be found in and around the vicinity of the former quarry sites.

The National Stone Centre at Wirksworth was opened in 1989. It covers an area of fifty acres about half of which is designated as a Site of Special Scientific Interest for its geological features. It contains six former quarries, four lime kilns and over 120 disused lead mine shafts. The Stone Centre aims to tell the 'Story of Stone' in the UK – its geological origins, the history of its working from earliest times, its multiplicity of uses, environmental issues and its contribution to landscape and art. The Centre also provides a wide range of professional services including design, geo-conservation, quarry history, research, site interpretation, educational advice and stone sourcing.

The Peak District was recently voted one of the UK's top tourist destinations. In a poll conducted by *Countryfile Magazine* in 2012 the Peak District came second only to Cornwall among judges and readers of the magazine, beating areas such as the Cotswolds, Yorkshire Dales and the Lake District.

The World Championship Hen Races are held in the car park of the Barley Mow Pub at Bonsall on the second Saturday in August each year. The event has won international acclaim and has featured in the national press and the BBC *Countryfile* programme.

Bonsall was also the location of one of Britain's most convincing UFO sightings. On 5 October 2000 Sharon Rowlands claimed to have observed a large luminous orb with a shimmering pink colour hovering and rotating in a nearby field. Her camcorder film which shows the object moving towards her is considered by many to be one of the best UFO films ever recorded and has been inspected by NASA.

The Peak District National Park provides the following advice to visitors in order to protect the wildlife and countryside:

- Take special care not to damage, destroy or remove features including rocks, plants and trees. They provide homes and food for wildlife and add to everybody's enjoyment of the countryside;
- Take your litter with you;
- Keep dogs on leads or under close control so they do not disturb ground nesting birds.

# Derbyshire Through Time

## Prehistoric Derbyshire

Cresswell Crags, which straddles the Derbyshire-Nottinghamshire border, is one of the most important Paleolithic (Old Stone Age) sites in Britain. Neanderthal man arrived here around 43,000 BC just before the last glaciations. At this time the area was also home to bears, bison, lions and woolly rhinoceros. After the retreat of the glaciers modern man made his home in the caves.

Stone Age hunters roamed over Derbyshire and evidence of their occupation has been found at a number of places. The chambered burial tombs at Minninglow, Five wells and elsewhere provide evidence of their religious beliefs and burial practices whilst Arbor Low near Youlgreave represents the finest henge monument in the county.

During the Bronze Age farmers began to sow patches of emma wheat and other crops in the fertile alluvial soil of the Trent Valley. Evidence of Bronze Age settlement has also been discovered at a number of sites in the Peak District. At Swine Sty on Big Moor archaeologists have identified an extensive settlement and farming site. The Peak District also contains a number of Bronze Age stone circles of which the Nine Ladies on Stanton Moor is the best known.

A bronze age log-boat was discovered in a quarry at Shardlow in 1998. It contained a cargo of Bromsgrove sandstone, which is found a few kilometres upstream at King's Mills. Tests determined that the boat was around 3,400 years old. It was conserved by the York Archaeological Trust and is now displayed in Derby Museum. In 2003 another Bronze Age log-boat was found in the Shardlow Quarry. Although it was complete and hardly damaged the decision was taken that it should be carefully reburied to preserve it for the future.

It was during the Bronze Age that burial practices began to change with individuals being buried alone, often accompanied by a pottery beaker. For this reason some historians refer to these people as 'Beaker Folk'. Such vessels have been found with both inhumations and cremations in the Peak District in places such as Stanton Moor, Gibb Hill, Eyam and elsewhere.

During the Iron Age or Celtic period much of Derbyshire was inhabited by the Coritani tribe. Their territory covered not only the present county of Derbyshire but also large parts of Nottinghamshire, Leicestershire and Lincolnshire.

Iron Age hill forts have been identified in Derbyshire at a number of places including Mam Tor, Carl Wark and Fin Cop.

## Roman Derbyshire

The Romans established forts at Buxton (Aquae Arnemetiae), Derby (Derventio), Chesterfield (Castrafeld), Brough (Navio) and Glossop (Melandra/Ardotalia). There was also a small fort at Pentrich along Ryknield Street.

The Romans mined lead in Derbyshire. The centre of the lead mining industry was at a place called Lutudarum, now believed to be a site beneath Carsington Reservoir. A number of pigs of lead have been discovered bearing references to their Derbyshire origin.

*Roman pig of lead which was discovered on*
*Cromford Moor in 1771*

Sites of Roman pottery kilns have been discovered at Shottle, Hazelwood, Holbrook, Pleasley and Derby. The wide mouthed storage jars which were mass produced here were known as 'Derbyshire Ware'. They were produced in three standard sizes and were used for the transportation and storage of a variety of foodstuffs.

## Saxon and Viking Derbyshire

Derbyshire lay within the Saxon Kingdom of Mercia whose capital was at Repton.

In the 6th-century the Saxons founded a settlement known as Northworthige or Northworthy. Over the centuries this grew into the town, and later city, of Derby.

During the 7$^{th}$ and 8$^{th}$ centuries minster churches were established at Repton, Wirksworth, Ashbourne, Bakewell, Hope, Derby and Chesterfield.

Monastic annals record that King Ethelbald was buried at Repton in 757 AD.

A Saxon helmet was discovered at Bentley Grange, near Monyash in 1848. Made from iron and horn and decorated with a bronze and silver-gilt boar, it is one of only three so far discovered in the whole of Britain. The Bentley Grange Helmet and other artefacts found at the site are displayed in Sheffield Museum.

In the early 10th-century the Vikings established a town near to and incorporating the Northworthy area, They called it Deoraby – the place of the deer. It became one of the five boroughs of the Danelaw.

In the mid 9th-century the churches at Repton and Derby were centres of pilgrimage to the shrines of Saint Wystan and Saint Alkmund respectively.

A Royal Mint was established at Derby during the reign of King Athelstan (925-41).

The Scandanavian word gata (anglicised to gate) provides evidence of Danish settlement in a number of Derbyshire towns. Examples include Sadler Gate and

Iron Gate in Derby whilst in Chesterfield we find Soutergate, Gluman Gate and Knifesmith Gate.

As Christianity spread through Derbyshire a number of simple Saxon crosses were erected throughout the county. Particularly fine examples can be seen at Eyam, Bakewell and Bradbourne.

King Edward the Confessor held a number of extensive manors in Derbyshire including Ashbourne, Ashford, Bakewell, Chesterfield, Darley, Hope, Matlock Bridge, Melbourne, Parwich and Wirksworth.

## Derbyshire and the Norman Conquest

Edward the Confessor died in January 1066 and was succeeded by Harold Godwinson. It seems likely that men from Derbyshire were present in the army which fought against William I at the battle of Hastings.

The Domesday Book, complied in 1086 provided the first detailed picture of the county.

Derby was the only town mentioned in the Derbyshire Domesday. In 1086 it had a population of around 700. The population of Derbyshire as a whole has been estimated to have been around 12,000.

Following the Norman invasion a number of motte and bailey castles were constructed in Derbyshire at places such as Duffield, Castleton, Gresley, Pilsbury and Bolsover. Some of these were simple earth and timber structures which were never rebuilt in stone.

The Normans constructed a number of stone churches within Derbyshire and substantial fragments of Norman stonework can be found in around a hundred churches across the county.

Some of the most complete examples of Norman church architecture may be found at Melbourne, Bakewell and Steetley Chapel near Worksop.

In addition to churches the Normans also founded a number of abbeys, priories and hospitals in Derbyshire. These included Dale Abbey, Darley Abbey , Repton Priory, Calke Abbey and Breadsall Priory. Later, in the early 13th-century, the Dominicans founded a friary at Derby in the area that is now known as Friargate.

## Medieval Derbyshire

In addition to Derby and Chesterfield a number of boroughs were created during the medieval period. These included Ashbourne, Bakewell, Castleton, Glossop, Heanor, Ilkeston and Wirksworth.

King John granted Derby a charter in 1204. This gave the burgesses control over their affairs, power to appoint a bailiff and a monopoly of wool dyeing.

During the conflict between Henry III and his barons a battle was fought in and around the town of Chesterfield. In 1266 two of the rebel barons, Robert de Ferrers and Baldwin Wake, confronted a Royalist army led by the King's nephew, Henry de Almaine. There was fierce fighting around the church and part of the town was set on fire by the King's men. The rebels, however, were soon put to flight and Robert de Ferrers was taken prisoner.

In 1380 Derby became the seat of Assizes for the whole county.

A number of Derbyshire landowners are recorded as having fought in the Battle of Crecy on 26 August 1346. These included Sir John Chandos of Radbourne, Sir John Curzon and Sir Robert de Twyford.

The Black Death reached Derbyshire in May 1349 and struck down large numbers of people throughout the county. In some places whole villages were wiped out.

Only a few months after the Peasants Revolt of 1381 a band of rebels attacked the Augustinian Priory at Breadsall and assaulted the prior and canons.

Leprosy was widespread in Derbyshire during the Middle Ages. Leper hospitals were established at a number of places including Derby, Chesterfield and Alkmonton.

A number of Derbyshire villages including Barton Blount and Hungry Bentley were deserted in the late 13th-century following a succession of wet summers.

During the Wars of the Roses in the 15th-century a particularly savage attack took place in the parish church at Chesterfield. On New Year's Day 1422, Thomas and John Foljambe led an attack on their rivals who were hearing mass at the time. Local landowners William Bradford and Henry Longford were killed. Henry Pierrepont and Thomas Hailsby had the thumbs of their right hands hacked off.

## Tudor Derbyshire

A number of Derbyshire men took part in the battle of Bosworth Field in 1485 which led to the death of Richard III and the founding of the Tudor dynasty.

The national ecclesiastical census of 1563 suggests that the population of Derbyshire at that time was around 50,000.

In 1586 the 'sweating sickness' killed every man in St Peter's Parish in Derby.

Mary, Queen of Scots was held prisoner in a number of different Derbyshire houses including Wingfield Manor. It was while she was here that the infamous Babington plot was hatched.

Derbyshire suffered a number of outbreaks of the plague during the 16th-century. One of the most serious occurred at Chesterfield between October 1586 and November 1587. Almost 300 people died out of a total population of around 1,200.

## Stuart Derbyshire

Charles I granted a charter to Derby in 1637. This allowed the town to elect its first mayor.

During the Civil War (1642-46) Derby was garrisoned by Parliamentary troops commanded by Sir John Gell of Hopton Hall who was appointed Governor of Derby in 1643. These troops took part in the defence of Nottingham, the siege of Lichfield, the Battle of Hopton Heath and a number of other engagements in surrounding counties. They also successfully defended the town against Royalist armies.

George Fox, the founder of the Quakers, was imprisoned at Derby in October 1650 after interrupting a church service in the town.

The plague struck the Derbyshire village of Eyam between September 1665 and November 1666 but the village has become famous because the local vicar William Mompesson persuaded the people to quarantine themselves to prevent the spread of the infection. A total of 273 people died but the plague did not spread to the surrounding villages. A heritage centre in the village tells the story of the plague.

The Glorious Revolution of 1688 was planned in Derbyshire when three conspirators, met on the isolated Whittingon Moor to plot the overthrow of King James II. The three conspirators were William Cavendish, Earl of Devonshire, the Earl of Danby and Mr John D'Arcy. A shower of rain forced them to take shelter at the Cock and Pynot alehouse and it was here that they agreed to send an invitation to William of Orange to seize the throne. A coded message was sent to William and plans were laid to raise armies in support of the invasion. In the event James II realised that his cause was hopeless and was allowed to flee the country. William and his wife Mary were installed as joint monarchs and the Earl of Devonshire was richly rewarded. Created first Duke of Devonshire and showered with other honours, he was also granted Crown Rights to the High Peak Hundred. The lucrative lead mining rights associated with this area added to his already considerable wealth and he was able to build Chatsworth House, just a few miles to the south of Chesterfield. The Cock and Pynot is now a museum and is open to the public from Easter to October each year.

Following the Act of Toleration in 1689 a number of non-conformist chapels were built in Derbyshire. One of the earliest was the Elder Yard Independent Chapel at Chesterfield. Opened in 1692, this is the oldest surviving non-conformist chapel in Derbyshire.

## Derbyshire in the 18th-Century

In 1745 the forces of Bonnie Prince Charlie entered Derby on their march south towards London. They remained in the town for only two days before deciding to retreat north into Scotland. During his stay in Derby the Prince lodged at Exeter House in Full Street.

The widespread enclosure of the open fields took place in Derbyshire in the 18th-century. Common land was lost and a number of men became landless labourers

The Derby Postman, the county's first newspaper was published for the first time in 1720 during the reign of George I.

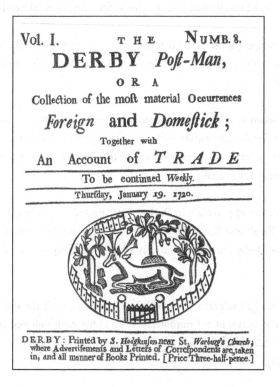

*Title page of an early edition of the Derby Postman*

John Wesley, the founder of Methodism, visited Derbyshire on a number of occasions. He made his first visit to Derby in March 1764 but was forced to leave after being shouted down.

A number of workhouses were established in Derbyshire in the 18th-century at places such as Derby, Chesterfield, Belper, Shardlow and Wirksworth.

A number of turnpike roads were constructed in Derbyshire in the 18th-century. The first road in the county to be improved in this way was part of the route between Buxton and Manchester which was authorised in 1725. A network of coaching inns was established across the county.

The first coach service from Derby to London began in 1735. It ran once a week from the George in Sadlergate taking three to four days in good weather.

Highwaymen operated in Derbyshire in the 18th-century. One of the most notorious was Pierce Cook who led a ruthless gang in the Derby area during the reign of George IV.

The canal network in Derbyshire began with the construction of the Trent and Mersey and Chesterfield canals, both surveyed by James Brindley in 1777. These were followed over the next twenty years by the Erewash, Peak Forest, Cromford, Nutbrook and Derby canals.

The manufacture of porcelain in Derby began around 1748 when William Duesbury, John Heath and Andre Planche formed a partnership. Duesbury went on to found the Derby Porcelain Company which eventually became Royal Crown Derby.

Richard Arkwright in partnership with Jedediah Strutt built the world's first water-powered cotton mill at Cromford in 1771. Other mills followed and within a few years textile communities were established at Cromford, Belper, Milford and Darley Abbey.

## Derbyshire in the 19th-Century

The population of Derby in 1801 was 10,832. In the same year Chesterfield recorded 7,330 inhabitants.

The Railways came to Derbyshire in the middle of the 19th-century. Three separate railway companies merged in 1844 to become the Midland Railway. Derby became an important railway town with locomotives and rolling stock being manufacture here.

Britain's last revolution started at Pentrich in 1817. The ringleaders were executed in Derby.

The Co-operative movement began at Rochdale in 1844. In Derby the first Co-operative store was opened in 1858.This was followed by similar stores elsewhere in the county.

A national religious census was conducted in 1851. The adult attendance at places of worship in Chesterfield was as follows:

St Mary's Church 1,445
Trinity Church 277
Primitive Methodist Chapel 580
Independent Chapel (South Pl) 159
General Baptist Chapel 55
Wesleyan Methodist Chapel 550
Elder Yard Chapel 145
Independent Chapel (Soresby Street) 293
Church of Jesus Christ and the Latter Day Saints 196
Society of Friends 41

The mid 19th-century saw the development of the first department stores. In Derby these included Thurman and Malin, Ranby's and the Midland Drapery. Chain stores followed and by the end of the century stores such as Boots, Woolworths, Lipton's and W H Smith had been established in a number of towns in Derbyshire.

Urban transport began to develop soon after the coming of the railways. Horse drawn tram services were established at Derby, Chesterfield, Ilkeston, Ripley, Swadlincote and several other places in the latter years of the century.

Following the 1870 Education Act School Boards were established to provide schools in areas where there were insufficient places provided by voluntary societies. School Boards were quickly established at Derby and Chesterfield and others soon followed. By 1875 there were twelve boards operating in the county at Bradwell, Chesterfield, Clay Cross, Derby, Dronfield, Eckington, Foston and Scropton, Long Eaton, Norton, Shirland and Highham, South Wingerworth and Unstone.

The Derbyshire Times newspaper serving the northern part of the county was first published in 1885.

Derbyshire County Council came into being on 1 April 1889. The first meeting of the Council was chaired by Sir Thomas William Evans of Allestree Hall, Derby.

## Modern Derbyshire

The population of Derby in 1901 was 62,266. In the same year Chesterfield had 39,955 inhabitants and Ilkeston 25,384.

Richard Bell, one of Britain's first two Labour Members of Parliament was elected at Derby in the 1900 General Election. The other was Keir Hardie who was elected at Merthyr Tydfil.

Rolls-Royce relocated to Derby from Manchester in 1908. It went on to grow into a major employer in the town. After the Second World War motor car production was transferred to Crewe and the Derby works concentrated on the manufacture of aero engines.

Other firms which established themselves in the town in the early years of the 20th-century included British Celanese, International Combustion, Aitons and Qualcast

The sinking of the Titanic in 1912 shocked the nation. One of the survivors was Lawrence Beesley, a schoolteacher from Wirksworth. He later wrote a book about the tragedy.

A German Zeppelin attacked Derby in 1916.

The Diocese of Derby was created in 1927. All Saints Church in Derby became a cathedral. The first bishop was Edmund Pearce.

Derby opened its own airport at Burnaston in 1938 and in the post war period Derby Airways operated a fleet of Douglas DC 3 aircraft named after the Derbyshire Dales. Regular services to places such as Glasgow and the Channel Islands were provided for a number of years, but in 1965 the East Midlands Airport was opened at Castle Donington and services were transferred there.

In 1940 spitfires and hurricanes powered by Rolls-Royce merlin engines won the Battle of Britain. The company also provided the engines for the aircraft of Bomber Command which took the war into the heart of Germany.

During the Second World War Derwent Reservoir was used by 617 Squadron to practice for the famous Dam Busters raid on German hydro electric dams.

Derby County Football Club won the FA Cup for the first and only time in its history in 1946.

Roll-Royce and Associates was established in 1959 to design and build nuclear reactors to power Britain's nuclear submarines.

Rolls-Royce went into liquidation in 1971. The government decided to take the business into public ownership and a new company Rolls-Royce (1971) Ltd was created to secure vital military contracts. The company returned to profitability in 1984 and three years later was restored to private ownership.

The 1960s saw the withdrawal of passenger services and the closure of railway stations in various parts of Derbyshire. Stations closed at this time included Ilkeston and Matlock .

Elvaston Castle and its grounds became Derbyshire's first country park in 1970.

Local government reorganisation in 1974 created a number of new and enlarged district councils and resulted in the disappearance of civic authorities such as Repton Rural District Council, Long Eaton Urban District Council and Swadlincote Urban District Council. Derby became a unitary authority responsible for all local government services within the area.

The Troubles in Northern Ireland impacted on Derby in 1992. On 14 April, in that year Sergeant Michael Newman was shot dead as he walked from the Army Careers Office to his car. Responsibility for his murder was claimed by the Irish National Liberation Army.

The latter years of the 20th-century saw the decline in fortunes of a number of important employers in Derby. A number of firms went out of business including Qualcast, Leys and Aitons. Elsewhere in the county Bryan Donkin and Robinsons at Chesterfield went out of business and at Swadlincote, Greens Pottery ceased production.

In 1989 Toyota selected Burnaston near Derby to be the site of a new factory. Production began in 1992 with a planned capacity of 200,000 vehicles per year.

Derby became a city on 7 June 1977 when Queen Elizabeth II visited the town to present letters patent to the Mayor, Councillor Geoffrey Tillett.

## The New Millenium

Staveley was chosen in 2002 to be a Pathfinder Project for the Neighbourhood Renewal Unit funded by the Office of the Deputy Prime Minister. A great deal was done to revitalise the area including projects to improve school attendance, reduce crime and encourage a healthier lifestyle.

Derby became a 'Fairtrade Town' in 2005. Other towns which obtained Fairtrade status include Ashbourne (2005), Darley Dale (2009), Bakewell (2008), Buxton (2009), Chesterfield (2009), Hope Valley (2007), Matlock (2005), New Mills (2006) and Wirksworth (2009).

Margaret Beckett MP for Derby South became the first ever female Foreign Secretary in 2006.

The QUAD building in Derby Market Place was opened on 26 September 2008. This innovative building with a steel and glass frontage houses two cinemas, art gallery, artists' studios, cafe bar and digital resource centre.

The 21$^{st}$ century saw the opening of a number of new shopping malls and retail parks in Derbyshire. At Chesterfield the Vicar Lane Shopping Centre was opened in 2000 and at Derby in 2007 a £340 million extension to the Eagle Centre was opened as Westfield Derby.

The people of Derbyshire celebrated the Diamond Jubilee of 2012 in grand style. Over a hundred street parties were held as well as other events throughout the county. Around 56 beacons were lit around the county and a picnic was held in Derby Market Place where celebrations from London were shown on the big screen. Royal Crown Derby produced a number of commemorative items including a Diamond Jubilee corgi!

Derbyshire also made important contributions to the successful London 2012 Olympic Games. Local firms contributed to the infrastructure and a number of local people participated in the opening ceremony.

Derby Council House reopened in 2012 following a massive facelift. The original facade was preserved but the interior was transformed into a light and airy space appropriate to working practices in the 21$^{st}$ century.

# Domesday Derbyshire

The Domesday Book is the first detailed record of the various settlements in Derbyshire. The vast majority of towns and villages in Derbyshire were named and surveyed in this great document and it remains one of the most useful sources of information for anyone studying the history of their area. It was complied in 1086 on the orders of William the Conqueror who instructed his commissioners to ask the following questions:

What is the name of the manor?
Who held it at the time of King Edward and who holds it now?
How many ploughs does the lord have and how many do the tenants have?
How many villagers, smallholders and slaves are there?
How many freemen are there?
How much woodland, meadow and pasture is there?
How many mills and fisheries are there?
What has been added or taken away from the estate?
What was it worth in 1066 and what is it worth now?

The return for Boyleston follows this template and is typical of the entries for Derbyshire.

## LAND OF HENRY OF FERRERS

In Boyleston Godric and Leofnoth had 2c. of land taxable. Land for 2 ploughs. Now in lordship 2 ploughs; 8 villagers and 8 smallholders who have 3 ploughs. 1 mill, 12d; meadow, 6 acres; woodland pasture 1 league long and ½ league wide.
Value before 1066, 40s; now 30s Roger holds it

The chief landowner in Derbyshire in 1086 was Henry de Ferrers, who held one hundred and fourteen manors. De Ferrrers' principal seat was at Duffield where he built a substantial castle.

The King held forty-four manors in the county which were distributed at intervals of approximately a day's march. Some of these had been royal manors in the reign of Edward the Confessor.

Most entries for the settlements in Derbyshire follow a similar pattern but there are a few which provide a little more information or are unusual in some way. These include:

A mill keeper at Morton
A smith at Alvaston
Honey payments at Hope Darley, Bakewell, Matlock, Wirksworth, Ashbourne and Parwich.
A payment of two spurs at Breaston
A ferry at Weston-on-Trent
A render of grain from the burgesses of Derby on the Feast of St Martin
Lead works at Wirksworth, Bakewell, Matlock Bridge, Crich and Ashford
A man at arms at a number of places including Bakewell, Scropton and Breadsall

Different classes of people are mentioned in the Domesday Book including freemen, sokemen, villagers (or villeins), smallholders (or bordars), censarii (rent payers) and slaves.

Freemen were free peasants with no formal obligations of labour to the lord of the manor. In Derbyshire they accounted for less than 5% of the population.

Sokemen had a status similar to that of freemen though their precise status is not totally clear. It seems that they were personally free and only owed tribute and minor labour dues to their lord. A total of 124 sokemen are mentioned in Derbyshire. Most of these are recorded close to the borders with Nottinghamshire or Leicestershire where this class of tenant was more widespread.

Villagers were the wealthiest and most numerous of the unfree peasants. They often had substantial farms of around 30 acres but owed the lord two or three days work each week. In Derbyshire they made up 65% of the population.

Smallholders or borders held much less land than the villagers and earned a living as blacksmiths, carpenters and other craftsmen. They accounted for 27% of the population of Derbyshire in 1086.

Censarii were rent payers. Only 42 are noted in Derbyshire. Almost half of these held land at Duckmanton where they were the sole recorded inhabitants.

Slaves had no property rights and could be bought or sold. Twenty slaves were noted in Derbyshire. Thirteen of these were in the fief of Henry de Ferrers and of these ten are listed at his manor of Duffield.

Previous Saxon landowners are meticulously listed. Many of these had fascinating names such as Sprot, Wulfric, Toki, Leofnoth, Wulfsi, Alnoth and Wulfgeat.

Fisheries are mentioned at Derby, Markeaton and Sawley. In addition a mill at Sudbury on the River Dove rendered six shillings and 100 eels. There was also a fish pond at Weston-on-Trent.

The five manors of Darley, Matlock, Wirksworth, Ashbourne and Parwich rendered £40 of pure silver to the King in the time of Edward the Confessor.

The Domesday Book shows that there were at least 43 churches in Derbyshire by 1086 but there were almost certainly more as five entries record a priest but no church.

Mills are mentioned in connection with at least fifty places in Derbyshire. It is difficult to be sure of the total number because mills sometimes appear in composite entries covering a number of places. These mills would have been water mills, since windmills were not introduced into England until the 14th-century.

Some of the most important settlements in Derbyshire today are mentioned in the Domesday Book including Derby, Chesterfield, Ilkeston, Alfreton and Matlock.

Bakewell Church had two priests recorded in the Domesday Book.

Derby is the only borough identified within the county. There were 140 resident burgesses and the account also mentions ten mills, four churches and a fishery. The total population has been estimated to be around 700 in 1086.

Most place names used in the Domesday Book are still recognisable today but others have changed considerably. Some of those which we might find it difficult to recognise include Herdebi (Coxbench), Werchefuuorde (Wirksworth) and Chinewoldemarescl (Killamarsh).

A full list of all the settlements which existed in 1086 together with their original names are listed below:

Abney – Habenai
Alfreton – Elstretune
Alkmonton – Alchementune
Allestree – Adelardestreu
Alsop-en-le-Dale – Elleshope
Alvaston – Aleuuoldestune
Ambaston – Emboldestune
Arleston – Erlestune
Ash – Eisse
Ashbourne – Essburn
Ashford-in-the-Water – Aissford
Ashover – Essorre
Aston (Near Hope) – Estune
Aston (Near Sudbury) – Estune
Aston-upon-Trent – Estune
Atlow – Etelauue
Bakewell – Baruue
Ballidon – Belidene
Bamford – Banford
Barlborough – Barleburg
Barrow-upon-Trent – Bareuue
Barton Blount – Barctune

Baslow – Basselau
Bearwardcote – Bereuuardescote
Beeley – Begelie
Beighton – Bectune
Birchill – Berceles
Birchover – Barcovere
Blackwell – Blachuuelle
Blingsby – Blanghesbi
Bolsover – Belesovre
Bonsall – Bunteshale
Boulton (with Alvaston) – Boletune
Boyleston – Boileston
Boythorpe – Buitorpe
Bradbourne – Bradeburne
Bradley (Near Belper) – Bradelei
Bradley (near Ashbourne) – Bradelei
Bradwell – Bradewelle
Brailsford Brailesford
Bramley – Branlege
Brampton – Brandune
Brassington – Branzinctun
Breadsall – Braideshale
Breaston – Bradestune
Bretby – Bretebi
Brimington – Brimintune
Broadlowash – Bredelauue

Bubnell – Bubenenli

Bupton – Bubedene

Burley – Berleie

Burnaston – Burnulfestune

Burton – Burtune

Caldwell – Caldewelle

Callow – Caldelauue

Calow – Calehale

Calver – Caluoure

Carsington – Ghersintune

Catton – Chetun

Chaddesden – Cedesdune

Charlesworth – Cheuenesuurde

Chatsworth – Chetesuorde

Chellaston – Celerdestune

Chelton – Cellesdene

Chesterfield – Cestrefeld

Chisworth Chiseuudre

Chunal – Ceolhal

Church – Broughton Broctune

Clifton – Cliptune

Clowne – Clune

Coal Aston – Estune

Codnor – Cotenoure

Coldeaton – Eitune

Conkesbury – Cranchesberie

Cotes in Darley – Cotes

Coton-in-the-Elms – Cotune

Cottons – Codetune

Cowley – Collei

Coxbench – Herdebi

Crich – Crice

Cromford – Crunforde

Cubley – Cobelei

Dalbury – Dellingeberie

Darley – Derelei

Denby – Denebi

Derby – Derby

Dinting – Dentic

Doveridge – Dubrige

Drakelow – Drachelauue

Draycott – Draicott

Dronfield – Dranefeld

Duckmanton – Dochemaneston

Duffield – Duuelle

Eaton – Dovedale Aiton

Eckington – Echintune

Edale – Aidele

Edensor – Ednesoure

Edlaston Duluestune

Ednaston Ednodestune

Egginton – Eghintune

Egstow – Tegestou

Elmton – Helmetune

Elton – Eltune

Elvaston – Aeluuoldestun

Etwall – Etewelle

Eyam – Aivne

Farley – Farleie

Fenny Bentley – Benedlege

Fenton – Faitune

Findern – Findre

Flagg – Flagun

Foremark Forneuuerche

Foston – Faruluestun

Glapwell – Glapewell

Glossop – Glosop

Gratton – Gratune

Great Rowsley – Gratune

Greyhurst – Greherst

Hadfield – Hetfelt

Hallam (now West Hallam – Halun
and Kirk Hallam)

Handley (nr Staveley) – Henlege

Handley (Nr Stretton) – Henlege

Hanson Grange – Hanzedone

Hardstoft – Hertestaf

Harthill – Hortel

Hartington – Hortedun

Hartshorne – Heorteshorne

Hassop – Hetesope

Hathersage – Hereseige

Hatton – Hatune

Hayfield – Hedfelt

Hazelbadge – Hegelbec

Heanor – Hainour

Hearthcote – Hedcote

Heath – Lunt

Hilton – Hiltune

Hognaston – Ochenaueston

Holbrook – Holebroc

Hollington – Holintune

Holme – Holun

Holmesfield – Holmesfelt

Hoon – Hougen

Hope – Hope

Hopton – Opetune

Hopewell – Oeuuelle

Horsley – Hosselei

Hough – Hoge

Hucklow – Hochelai

Hulland – Hoilant

Hungry Bentley – Benelene (lost)

Ible – Ibeholun

Ilkeston – Tilchestune

Ingleby – Englebi

Ivonbrook – Winbroc

Kedleston – Chetelestune

Kidsley – Chiteslei

Killamarsh – Chinewoldemaresc

Kinder – Chendre

Kirk Ireton – Hiretune

Kirk Langley – Langlelei

Kniveton – Cheniuetun

Langley (Mill) – Langelei

Lea – Lede

Linton – Linctune

Litchurch – Ludencerce

Little Chester – Cestre

Little Eaton – Detton

Little Ireton – Iretune

Littleover – Parva Ufra

Litton – Litun

Longdendale – Langenedele

Long Eaton – Aitone

Longstone – Longesdune

Lowne – Lunt

Ludwell – Ledouelle (lost)

Lullington – Lullitune

Mackworth – Macheuorde

Makeney – Machenie

Mapperley – Mappletune

Markeaton – Marchetune

Marsh – Mars (lost)

Marston on Dove – Merstun

Matlock – Maslach

Matlock Bridge – Mestesforde

Melbourne – Mileburne

Mercaston – Merchenstune

Mickleover – Ufre

Middleton-by-Youlgreave – Middeltune

Milford – Muleforde

Milton – Middeltune

Monyash – Mareis

Morley Morelei

Morton – Mortune

Mosborough – Moresburg

Mugginton – Mogintun

Nether Haddon – Hadune

Netherseal – Scella

Newbold – Neuuebold

Newton (nr Alfreton) – Neutone

Newton – Neutune

Newton Solney – Newetun

Norbury – Nordberie

Normanton by Derby – Normantune

North Wingfield – Winnefelt

Ockbrook – Ochebroc

Offcote – Ophidescotes

Offerton Offretune

Ogston – Ougedestun

One Ash – Aneise

Osleston – Oslavestone (lost)

Osmaston – Osmundestune

Osmaston by Derby – Osmundestune

Over Haddon – Hadune

Overseal – Alia Scela

Owlcotes – Caldecotes

Padfield – Padefeld

Palterton – Paltretune

Parwich – Pevrewic

Peak Cavern – Pechevers

Pentrich – Pentric

Pilsbury – Pilesberie

Pilsley (nr Bakewell) – Pirelaie

Pilsley – Pinneslei

Potlock – Potlac

Potter Somersale – Alia Summersale

Priestcliffe – Presteclive

Quorndon – Cornun

Radbourne – Radburne

Ravensholme – Rauenef (lost)

Repton – Rapendune

Ripley – Ripelie

Risley – Riselie

Rodsley – Redeslie

Rosliston Redlauestun

Roston – Roschintone

Rowland – Ralunt

Rowthorn – Rugetorn

Sandiacre – Sandiacre

Sapperton – Sapertune

Sawley – Salle

Scarcliffe – Scardeclif

Scropton – Scroftun

Sedsall – Segessale

Shardlow – Serdelau

Shatton – Scetune

Sheldon – Scelhadun

Shipley – Scipelie

Shirland – Sirelunt

Shirley – Sirelei

Shottle – Sothelle

Shuckstonfield – Scochetorpe

Sinfin – Sedenfeld

Smalley – Smalei

Smisby – Smidesbi

Snelston – Snelletune

Snitterton – Sinetrentone

Snodeswick – Estrotrewic (lost)

Soham – Salham (lost)

Somersal Herbert – Sommersale

South Normanton – Normantune

South Wingfield – Winefeld

Spondon – Spondune

Stainsby – Steinesbi

Stanley – Stanlei

Stanton (ne Newhall) – Stantun

Stanton by Bridge – Stantun

Stanton-in-the-Peak – Stantune

Staveley – Stavelie

Stenson – Steintune

Stoke – Stoche

Stoney Houghton – Holtune

Stoney Middleton – Middletune

Stretton – Stratune

Stretton Hall – Stretton alia

Sturston – Stertune

Sudbury – Sudberie

Sutton-on-the-Hill – Sudtune

Sutton Scarsdale – Sudhune

Swadlincote – Sivardingescotes

Swarkeston – Sorchestune

Taddington – Tadintune

Tansley – Taneslege

Tapton – Taptune

Temple Normanton – Normantune

Thornsett – Tornsete

Thorpe – Torp

Thulston – Torulfestune

Thurvaston – Turvesdestune

Tibshelf – Tibecel

Ticknall – Tichenhalle

Tideswell – Tidesuuelle

Tissington – Tizinctun

Trusley – Toxenai

Tunstall – Tunestalle

Tupton – Topetune

Twyford – Tuiforde

Uftonfields – Upeton

Unstone – Honestune

(Upper) Hurst – Herct

Upton – Upetune (lost)

Wadshelf – Wadesel

Wallstone – Walestune

Walton – Waletune

Walton-on-Trent Waletune

Waterfield – Watrefeld (lost)

Wensley – Wodnesleie

Wessington – Wistanestune

Weston Underwood – Westune

Weston-upon-Trent – Westune

Whitfield – Witfeld

Whittington – Witintune

Whitwell – Witeuuelle

Willesley – Wiuesleie

Williamthorpe – Wilelmestorp

Willington – Willetune

Wingerworth – Wingreurde

Winster – Winsterne

Wirksworth – Werchesvorde

Wormhill – Wruenele

Wyaston – Widerdestune

Yeaveley – Ghiveli

Yeldersley – Geldeslei

Youlgreave – Goilgrave

Measurements in the Domesday Book include furlongs, bovates, caracutes, acres, virgates and leagues. They may be calculated as follows:

Furlong – 660 ft
Caracute – No exact modern equivalent but often calculated as 120 acres
Acre – 4,840 sq yds. Originally an area of land one furlong (660ft) long and one chain (66ft) wide. This may have been the approximate area of land that an ox team could plough in a day.
Virgate – About a quarter of a caracute
League – A measurement of length, about a mile and a half

Values are expressed in a variety of terms including pounds, shillings, pence and marks. Old English currency lasted for over a thousand years until 1971 when the UK changed to a decimal currency. Prior to this the pound contained 20 shillings, each of 12 pence, abbreviated to £(ibrae), s(olidi) and d(enari). A silver mark had a value of 13s 4d, making 3 marks to £2.

Different types of land are mentioned including land for ploughs, woodland, meadow, pasture and waste. Land for ploughs is what we would now describe arable land. It was and used to grow wheat, barley, oats and beans. The average size of a Domesday plough team was eight oxen. In some entries half a plough is recorded meaning that the team was shared with another manor nearby. Pasture was where animals such as sheep, goats and horses grazed all year round. Meadows, often bordering on streams were often cut for hay and grazing. Woodland usually lay in small compact areas and was used for grazing pigs and for firewood. Waste was land that was not fit for farming for some reason.

The population of Derbyshire in 1086 has been calculated to be about 12,000 people.

Forty-seven priests are mentioned as living in Derbyshire. Two of these, Godwin and Osmer, at Derby are named individually.

**Important Derbyshire Landowners Listed in the Domesday Book**

King William was an important landowner in the county and personally held manors or a share of land in 38 different places in Derbyshire. Two thirds of the Borough of Derby remained in his hands, where he also possessed two collegiate churches.

The Bishop of Chester held only a few manors and other parcels of land in Derbyshire. At the time of the Domesday survey the bishopric was held by Robert de Limesi. He was responsible for removing his seat from the Lichfield to the much more important port and town of Chester.

Burton Abbey was a Benedictine house which had been founded by Wulfric Spoc in 1002–04. It lost much of its land after the Conquest but retained the manors of Mickleover, Appleby, Winshill, Coton-in-the-Elms, Stapenhill, Caldwell and Ticknall as well as smaller landholdings elsewhere in the county.

Earl Hugh, the Earl of Chester, contributed sixty ships to the invasion of England and was rewarded with vast areas of land, particularly in Cheshire, Leicestershire, Yorkshire and East Anglia. According to one account he was chiefly notorious for gluttony, prodigality and profligacy. In Derbyshire he held only the manor of Markeaton and the berewicks of Kniveton, Mackworth and Allestree. It should be noted that the lands which he is recorded as holding were actually in the hands of the King in 1086 owing to his involvement in the rebellion of that year.

Roger of Poitou held lands in both France and England. His English holdings included lands in Staffordshire, Essex, Suffolk, Nottinghamshire, Derbyshire, Lincolnshire and Hampshire. In Derbyshire ,however, his holdings amounted to only a handful of manors.

Henry of Ferrers fought alongside William the Conqueror at the Battle of Hastings and was rewarded with extensive lands throughout the Kingdom. He was the largest landowner in Derbyshire where he held over one hundred areas of land. He built a castle at his manor of Duffield which at the time of Domesday had a population of around 200 as well as a priest and a church. He was one of the Commissioners appointed to carry out the Domesday Survey. His grandson, Robert II founded Darley Abbey near Derby.

William Peverel is thought by some to have been the illegitimate son of William the Conqueror, but this is unlikely. He was certainly a trusted favourite and held vast areas of land throughout the kingdom. In Derbyshire he held 23 manors including Castleton (known as Peak's Arse) where he built a castle.

Walter of Aincourt held six manors in Derbyshire including Elmton which had a population of around 200 as well as a priest and a church. He had extensive holdings in Lincolnshire and Nottinghamshire.

Geoffrey of Alselin held lands in Derbyshire, Leicestershire, Lincolnshire, Northamptonshire, Nottinghamshire and Yorkshire. His manors in Derbyshire were Alvaston. Ednaston, Etwall, Egginton, Breaston and Ockbrook.

Ralph son of Hubert was an ancestor of the Freshville and Stuteville families. He held lands in Leicestershire, Lincolnshire, Nottinghamshire, Staffordshire and 30 manors in Derbyshire including Crich, Ashover and Wirksworth.

Ralph of Buron held only five manors in Derbyshire and eight in Nottinghamshire with the seat of his barony at Horston Castle, Horsley. He was succeeded by his son Hugh, who is recorded as a benefactor of Darley Abbey.

Hascoit Musard was a Breton and the founder of the baronial family of Staveley. He held lands in a number of counties including five manors in Derbyshire.

Gilbert of Ghent was a nephew of the Conqueror. He was captured during the great Northern Uprising of 1069 but apparently ransomed. He held estates in a number of counties including two manors in Derbyshire; at Ilkeston and neighbouring Shipley.

Nigel of Stafford held nine manors and two areas of sokeland in Derbyshire. His land was in the south of the county and five of his manors lay outside the current boundaries of the county. His eldest son, William de Gresley was responsible for building a castle at Gresley and was the founder of an Augustinian priory there.

Robert son of William held only the manor of Stanley in Derbyshire and only a handful in Nottinghamshire. His identity is unclear.

Roger of Bully was the founder of Blythe Abbey in neighbouring Nottinghamshire. He held only nine manors in Derbyshire compared with over a hundred in Nottinghamshire.

# Castles and Manor Houses

## Bolsover Castle

The first castle on this site was constructed by William Peverel on land granted to him by William the Conqueror. Built originally of timber it was rebuilt in stone by his son William Peverel the Second. Over the next two centuries the castle passed into the ownership of different families and various changes and improvements were made to its structure. In the 16th-century it came into the hands of Sir Charles Cavendish, son of the famous Bess of Hardwick. The original structure, now in a ruinous state, was demolished and a substantial and elegant mansion was built in its stead. Sir Charles died in 1617 but the work was completed by his heir, Sir William Cavendish. On the site of the original keep he constructed a substantial house, the 'Little Castle'. When this was completed he went on to add the Riding School and terrace range. The whole work took over 20 years to finish and was only partially complete when Charles I and his wife Henrietta Maria, paid a visit in July 1634. They were entertained in a most lavish style with a banquet and a masque specially written by Ben Johnson entitled Love's Welcome to Bolsover. During the Civil War Sir William Cavendish (created Earl of Newcastle in 1628) was appointed Commander in Chief of the King's northern army. He won a number of victories but after the disastrous royalist defeat at the battle of Marston Moor he fled the country and spent the next 16 years in exile. The castle was surrendered later in the same year but escaped demolition during the Commonwealth period. After the restoration of the monarchy the castle was repaired and once again became the home of the Cavendish family. In the 18th-century Welbeck Abbey became their principal residence. Much of the furniture and pictures from Bolsover Castle were moved there and in 1751 the terrace range was stripped to provide lead for a new wing at Welbeck. In 1755 the Bolsover passed by marriage into the hands of the Duke of Portland although by this time the only part of the castle which remained habitable was the keep or 'Little Castle'. In 1945 the castle was presented as a gift to the Ministry of Works. Now in the care of English Heritage, thousands of visitors each year enjoy exploring its fascinating story.

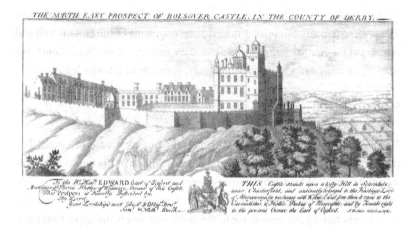

*Bolsover Castle from an 18th -century engraving*

## Codnor Castle

Codnor Castle was built by the de Grey family in the 13th-century. Initially the castle comprised a three storied keep measuring roughly 55 feet by 29 feet. It stood in the north-east corner of a large courtyard surrounded by a strong curtain wall, eight feet thick in places. In 1293 Edward I visited Codnor Castle during a progress through Derbyshire and in 1322 Edward II stayed here during his campaign against the rebellious Earls of Hereford and Lancaster. It was probably also around this time that the castle was strengthened and extended. A lower court was added and the original upper court was then adapted as the main living quarters. In the years that followed the Greys of Codnor gave loyal and distinguished service to the kings of England and played their part in many of the great events of the Middle Ages. Henry, the last Lord Grey, died without legitimate issue in 1496 and the castle at Codnor and its lands passed to the Zouch family who carried out further improvements to the South Court. Codnor remained in the hands of the Zouches for six generations until 1634 when it was sold and the family left the kingdom. Dr Neile, the Archbishop of York, and his son Sir Paule bought the estates and their descendant Richard Neile sold Codnor in 1692 to Sir Streynsham Master who is said to have been the last inhabitant of the castle. During the 19th-century the estate was purchased by the Butterley Company in order to extract the minerals beneath Codnor Park. The castle, already a ruin, was allowed to fall into disrepair. The present remains comprise a ruined keep, fragments of the curtain wall and remains of the circular wall which defended the entrance to the North Court. The keep is in a fairly dangerous state and is surrounded by a high wire fence.

## Haddon Hall

Haddon Hall was described by Pevsner as 'the English Castle par excellence' though it was never more than a fortified manor house. Although the site was originally occupied by a simple fortress most of the existing structure was built by the Vernon family. In the 14th-century the Great Hall was built and some improvements and repairs were made to the north-east Tower, the upper Court and the lower west window of the Chapel. Later still a dining room was built so that the lord could take his meals away from his dependants. Around the same period (1470–1530) the western range of apartments was added. Sir Henry Vernon (1441–1530) who was responsible for these later additions was also a favourite of Henry VII who knighted him and appointed him as Governor to his son Arthur, Prince of Wales. Legend has it that the Prince lived at Haddon for some time. The last male heir, Sir George Vernon, carried out considerable improvements to the hall. As well as embellishing and improving many of the existing rooms he carried out extensive works of his own including the range of offices at the north front and the walls of the Long Gallery. He became known as the 'King of the Peak' because of his lavish hospitality and almost regal lifestyle. On his death the Haddon estates passed to Sir John Manners who had married Dorothy Vernon. John Manners completed the Long Gallery begun by his father-in-law and laid out the terrace and the gardens. His grandson, also named John, succeeded to the Earldom of Rutland in 1641. He inherited Belvoir Castle but continued to spend much of his time at Haddon Hall. The Earls of Rutland continued to live at Haddon Hall until 1700 when the family moved to Belvoir Castle. They frequently returned for short periods but in 1740 many fittings were finally removed. The Hall remained largely uninhabited for almost 200 years but was not allowed to deteriorate. The 9th Duke was therefore able to embark on a successful programme of restoration during the early years of the 20th-century. As a result Haddon Hall stands today as perhaps the most perfectly preserved example of a medieval manor house in the whole of England.

## Mackworth Castle

Mackworth Castle might be described as 'the castle that never was'. All that remains today is a castellated gatehouse which was built around 1495. There is no evidence that a castle ever existed here although a large house platform was surveyed north of the gateway some years ago. It seems likely that this gatehouse was merely an ornate lodge which marked the entrance to a complex of buildings, workshops and outhouses. This house was probably abandoned early in the 16th-century when the owners, the Mackworth family, moved to Normanton in the county of Rutland. In the years which followed the fabric was, no doubt, dismantled by local people who would have carried away much of the timber and stone for their own use.

## Peveril Castle

Peveril Castle or the Castle of the Peak was built by William Peverel. It is not known when work on the castle began but it was recorded in the Domesday Book as the castle of William Peverel in Pechefers. It comprised at first only a stone wall around the edge of an almost inaccessible limestone crag on which it stood. Within these wall stood simple wooden lodgings for a small garrison. There is also some evidence to suggest that a domestic block (comprising a hall, solar and kitchen) and a chapel were added in the late 11th-century. The castle was seized by the crown in 1155 and its royal owners seem to have spared no expense in maintaining its structure and increasing its importance. Frequent references to Peak Castle appear in the pipe rolls (annual accounts of the sheriffs rendered to the King) and through these it is possible to trace the history of the castle in some detail. On taking possession for the crown Henry II installed his own porter and watchmen and the sum of £4. 10s. appears in the royal accounts for many years. The king was also a frequent visitor to the castle. In 1157 he received the submission of Malcolm IV, King of Scotland, here. In 1173 the King was faced with a rebellion by several powerful barons and Peveril along with other royal castles was provisioned and garrisoned. Henry II was also responsible for building the keep and repairing the curtain wall. The keep, which took about two years to build was about sixty feet high and approximately thirty-eight feet square with walls eight feet thick at the base. In 1189 Richard I granted the castle to his brother John but resumed possession of it after John's rebellion in 1194. After Richard's death in 1199 John placed his governor in the castle but in the turbulent years which followed ownership alternated between the King and the barons. Henry III was also a frequent visitor to Peveril Castle and like many of his predecessors used the castle as a hunting lodge as it stood within the Royal Forest of the Peak. To accommodate the king and his retainers a new hall was built during the first half of the 13th-century. During the 14th-century the castle changed hands on numerous occasions and eventually became part of the Duchy of Lancaster. By this time it had ceased to have any importance either as a fortification or a residence. Before long the hall and other buildings were dismantled in order to use the building materials elsewhere. In 1480 the castle was reported to be 'greatly decayed' and in 1561 its demolition was considered but rejected on the grounds that the keep served 'for the keeping of the courts' while the bailey was useful for the impounding of stray cattle. In 1609 a survey of 'decayed castells' declared that Peveril Castle was 'very ruinous and served noe use'. The present remains comprise the keep, large sections of the curtain wall and the gatehouse. It is in the care of English heritage and is open throughout the year.

## Wingfield Manor

Wingfield Manor was built in the 15th-century. Construction was begun by Sir Ralph Cromwell in 1441 but completed by John Talbot, the second Earl of Shrewsbury. When finished Wingfield Manor was larger and more impressive than Haddon Hall. It was constructed in the form of two courts; the outer court and buildings surrounding it were designed in accordance with the requirements of a fortress whilst the inner court contained the Hall, Solar, Kitchen, State Rooms and a range of apartments. John Talbot did not live to enjoy his new home for long. He was killed in the Battle of Northampton in 1460 but his family continued to reside here for the next two hundred years. Mary Queen of Scots was imprisoned here and it was during her time at Wingfield that the infamous Babington Plot was hatched. Sir Anthony Babington, who came from Dethick in Derbyshire, planned to assassinate Queen Elizabeth and place Mary on the throne of England. According to legend Babington, disguised as a gypsy, visited Mary regularly at Wingfield. The conspirators were caught and later executed. For much of the Civil War Wingfield Manor was held by the royalists but in May 1643 after a lengthy siege it was surrendered. Two years later Parliament ordered that Wingfield Manor should be dismantled. From this time on the manor house was allowed to fall into decay, a process which was accelerated in the 18th-century when parts of the house were pulled down by Imanuel Halton (the then owner) in order to provide materials for the house he was building on the opposite side of the valley. The present remains are extensive and include the entrance gateway, banqueting hall, state apartments, kitchen, buttery and crypt.

## Vanished Castles

There are also a number of vanished castles in Derbyshire. Little or nothing now remains of castles at places such as Bakewell, Bretby, Castle Gresley, Chesterfield, Duffield, Melbourne, Pilsbury and Horsley.

# Church and Chapel

Saxon carvings and architectural fragments abound in Derbyshire with good examples to be found at Bakewell, Repton, Wirksworth and Eyam.

Fifty churches are mentioned in the Derbyshire Domesday Book. Some of these would have been built before the Norman Conquest.

A carved figure of an early lead miner is to be found at St Mary's Church, Wirksworth. The figure is Saxon and came originally from the Church at Bonsall. It is known affectionately as 'T'Owd Man'.

Derby Cathedral was originally the Church of All Saints. It became a Cathedral in 1927 when the Diocese of Derbyshire was created.

The Church of Saint Wystan at Repton has a crypt which was once the mausoleum of the Saxon Kings of Mercia.

The Church of St John the Baptist at Buxton was built the 18th-century in the Italianate style with a cupola and a massive portico. It contains some very fine mosaics and stained glass.

All Saints Roman Catholic Church at Hassop was originally built as a private chapel for the Eyre family of Hassop Hall. It resembles a classical temple with an impressive pillared portico and a barrel vaulted interior.

St Mary's Roman Catholic Church in Derby was built and designed by Pugin the same architect who was responsible for the interior of the Palace of Westminster.

## Bells

The tower of St John the Baptist Church, Smalley was erected in the early 20th century to house the five bells given by the Rev Charles Kerry. They are the heaviest chime of five in any parish church in England.

Until the early years of the 20th-century a 'Passing bell' was chimed from the belfry of Tideswell Church on the death of a parishioner. A toll was made at regular intervals of two for a child, three for a woman and four for a man.

A tablet in the tower of Horsley parish church records that 'during the year 1915 there was rung in this steeple for Divine service 35,820 changes'.

Two of the three bells in St Mary's Church, Newton Solney were cast in the first half of the 17th-century and have the inscriptions 'God Save Our Church 1615' and 'God Save the Church 1638'.

When the church at Coton fell into disrepair the bells were taken to the neighbouring Lullington; so the inhabitants of Coton can still hear them when the wind is in the right direction.

St Mary's Church at Marston-on-Dove has the oldest bell in Derbyshire. It was cast by John de Stafford at Leicester in 1366 and inscribed with the words 'Hail Mary'.

## Brasses

The earliest monumental brass in Derbyshire is in Dronfield Church. Dated 1399 it is dedicated to two priests, Thomas and Richard Gomfrey. Both are depicted in mass vestments.

St Oswald's Church, Ashbourne has an ancient brass plaque marking the original dedication of the church in the 13th-century. A translation of the original Latin inscription reads: "In the 1241st year from the incarnation of our Lord on the 8th day after the Kalends of May, this church and this altar were consecrated in honour of the saint Oswald, king and martyr, by the venerable father in the Lord, Hugo de Patishul, the Bishop of Coventry". Experts believe that this brass plaque is the oldest of its kind in Britain and the second oldest in Europe.

There is an unusual Victorian brass in St Bartholemew's Church, Elvaston. It depicts the 6th Earl of Harrington (d 1866) in academic dress, holding a book in one hand and his mortar board in the other.

One of the smallest brasses in the county is in Bakewell Church. This memorial to Latham Woodruff shows him with long hair and small pointed beard of his times. He is dressed in a simple doublet with frilled collar, knee breeches and jackboots with spurs. The inscription tells us that he was a servant to the Earl of Rutland and died on 1 September 1648, aged forty.

At Youlgreave there is a small brass to the memory of Fridswide Gilbert, a spinster of that parish who died in 1604. She is depicted with hair swept back and held behind under a small bonnet. She is dressed in a low cut gown which is open at the front to expose an elaborate embroidered petticoat. On a plate below are inscribed the following lines:

FRIDSWIDE GILBERT TO THIS GRAVE
HATH RESIGNED HER EARTHLY PART
HER SOULE TO GOD, THAT FIRST IT GAVE,
ON ANGELS WINGS WENT WITH HER HART
A VERTUOUSW MAIDE SHE LIVD AND DIED
HURTFUL TO NON, BUT GOOD TO ALL
RELIGIOUS, MOSDEST, HATING PRIDE
THESE VIRTUES CROWNE HER FUNERALL

The church at Hathersage contains a number of brasses dedicated to members of the Eyre family. The earliest is dedicated Robert Eyre (d 1459) and his wife Joan (d1463). He is depicted bareheaded and dressed in plate armour. Joan Eyre, although she outlived her husband wears a horned headdress rather than a widow's veil. Her gown is high waisted and fur trimmed, and amongst the folds at the bottom is a pet dog.

Tideswell Church has a brass dedicated to Bishop Robert Pursglove who died in 1579. He is depicted in Episcopal vestments with mitre, alb, stole and chasuble and holding a crozier under his left arm. Robert Pursglove was born at Tideswell in 1504. He was appointed Suffragan Bishop of Hull in 1538 but deprived of his office in 1559 for refusing to take the Oath of Supremacy. In the same year he obtained letters patent from Queen Elizabeth I to found a grammar school in Tideswell. There are only about ten brass effigies to bishops in England and that of Robert Pursglove is the latest.

The Church of St Laurence, Walton-on-Trent contains an unusual brass memorial to Robert Morley, a former rector. It depicts him in his mass robes but minus is stole and maniple. Experts believe that a worker in stone rather than a worker in brass designed it.

## Dedications

The dedications of a number of Derbyshire churches have changed over the years. St Leonard's at Scarcliffe was once dedicated to St Giles; St Helen's at Pinxton was previously dedicated to St John the Evangelist; St Matthew's at Pentrich was originally dedicated to Saint Helen. At Mickleover, All Saints Church was once dedicated to Saint Nicholas.

The church at Peak Forest is the only one in Derbyshire and one of only two in the country dedicated to St Charles, King and Martyr. This refers to King Charles I who was beheaded in 1649.

An unusual dedication is that of St Mary and Saint Barlock at Norbury. Almost nothing is known about Saint Barlock other than the fact that he was an Irish bishop and abbot.

Dual dedications to Saints Peter and Paul as at Old Brampton, Eckington and Duckmanton are common throughout the country. According to tradition they were martyred on the same day in AD67. Saint Peter was crucified but Saint Paul, as a Roman citizen received the privilege of being slain by the sword! They share the same feast day of 29 June.

St Mary is a popular dedication in Derbyshire with a number of churches being named after her. Saint Mary is described in the New Testament as being the mother of Jesus and was the subject of particular veneration during the Middle Ages. The popularity of this saint declined after the Reformation.

There are also a number of churches dedicated to John the Baptist within the county at places such as Ault Hucknall, Buxton, Clowne and Dethick. According to the New Testament John went into the wilderness and began baptising his followers including Jesus himself, in the River Jordan. He declared that people should repent because the kingdom of heaven was coming. He is best known for the manner of his death. Having been imprisoned by King Herod Antipas he was executed because of a trick. Salome had so delighted Herod by her dancing that he promised to grant her any wish. At the urging of her mother she asked for the head of John the Baptist. This was promptly presented on a plate. The scene was painted a number of times by various renaissance artists.

There are churches dedicated to Saint Wystan at Repton and Bretby. Wystan was a Mercian prince who was murdered in AD 849.

St Alkmund is another Saxon saint with churches dedicated to him at Derby and Duffield, Alkmund was the son of King Alured of Northumbria and was martyred in 800 AD at the hands of King Eardulph.

The dedication to Saint Edmund, King and Martyr at Fenny Bentley refers to the King of East Anglia who was martyred in 869 AD.

## Fonts

There are Saxon fonts at St Michael's Church, Earl Sterndale, the Church of the Holy Cross, Morton, St Lawrence's Church Eyam, St Chad's at Church Wilne and St Leonard's at Thorpe.

The font in St Chad's Church at Church Wilne is the oldest in Derbyshire and may date back to time of St Chad himself. It is badly worn but the carving of a dragon is just visible.

All Saints Church at Ashover contains a 12th-century lead lined font, one of only about thirty in the country. On the bowl are carved a number of standing figures thought to represent the twelve apostles.

The font at Brailsford Church contains an octagonal font in the perpendicular style. The lower part of the base displays a Tudor rose.

The font in St Anne's Church Buxton dates from the Saxon period. It was used as a pig trough in the 19th-century but was restored and rededicated in 1906.

The bowl of a 12th-century font from St Michael and All angels at Taddington was used for washing glasses in the Star Inn until it was rescued in 1939.

All Saints Church at Youlgreave has a large circular font with a few animal motifs dating from around 1200.

The tub-shaped Norman font in St Mary's Church, Tissington dates from the 12th-century. It bears a number of crudely incised figures including a bird, the Agnes Dei, two beasts and two human figures.

## Windows and glass

The nave of All Saints' Church at Dalbury Lees has an early lancet window with a piece of 13th-century glass depicting St Michael.

A window in the nave of St Oswald's Church, Ashbourne contains five roundels of 13th-century glass. These depict the Massacre of the Innocents, the Presentation of Jesus, the Adoration of the Magi, Herod with the Magi and Gabriel appearing to the shepherds.

The east window in Sudbury church was presented in 1850 by Queen Victoria and the Prince Albert in memory of George Edward Anson who was the brother of the then Rector and had been private secretary to Prince Albert and Keeper of Her Majesty's Privy Purse. The glass is reputed to be the work of a German artist.

In the wall of St Werburgh's Church, Spondon is a low window, now blocked up, which is believed to have served for distributing communion to lepers who would not have been allowed into the church itself.

The church of St Matthew, Morley contains 15th-century glass from Dale Abbey. It depicts the legend of Robert of Knaresborough, the discovery of the True Cross and St Ursula.

The Church of St Lawrence, Warslow contains windows by William Morris.

The east window of St Peter's Church, Fairfield contains the first depiction of an aeroplane in stained glass. It was installed in 1919 as a First World War memorial

In 1988 a window was presented to All Saints Church, Chesterfield by the people of the town to celebrate its 750th anniversary. It depicts scenes from the history of the town from the 13th-century to the present day and confirms the important part which the church has played in the life of the town for much of its history.

*The window in Chesterfield church depicting events in the history of the town*

The church of St Michael and All Angels at Alsop-le-Dale contains a Millenium Window by Henry Haig.

A window in Ashbourne Parish Church was created in memory of two sisters who in 1901 died from burns received when rescuing their father from a lighted lamp which had exploded in his hands.

## Lecterns and Pulpits

St Peter's Church at Hope contains a carved oak pulpit dated 1652 and a schoolmaster's chair from the same period.

St Mary's Church, Tissington has a two decker pulpit dating from around 1600.

The pulpit in the church of St Michael and All Angels at Birchover was constructed in 1949. It was built from a number of different types of wood and was inspired by the Book of Ezekiel.

Holy Trinity Church at Ashford-in-the-Water has a Jacobean pulpit with carved panels.

The 13th-century pulpit in St Thomas's Church, Mellor was carved in one piece from the trunk of an oak tree.

Middleton-by-Wirksworth Congregational Church has a hexagonal pulpit dating from around 1695.

## Monuments and Memorials

Derbyshire has some of the best alabaster tomb effigies in the country including those at Ashbourne, Bakewell, Morley and Norbury. The monument to Thomas Cockayne at Youlgrave is particularly fine. Derbyshire alabaster was sent all over England to be carved into altar pieces, tombs and monuments.

The north chapel of St Oswald's Church, Ashbourne contains a notable collection of tombs from the Cokayne family as well as Thomas Banke's famous 1793 tomb for the five-year-old Penelope Boothby.

The earliest alabaster monument in Derbyshire is a wall monument in Bakewell Church. It is dedicated to Sir Godfrey Foljambe, who died in 1376 and his wife Lady Avena who died in 1383.

The tomb of Elizabeth Countess of Shrewsbury, better known as Bess of Hardwick, in Derby Cathedral is one of the most impressive tombs in Derbyshire. Commissioned and completed several years before her death it shows Elizabeth in her robes as a countess.

The Church of St Alkmund at Duffield contains an impressive and unusual monument to Antony Bradshaw (d.1614), his two wives and twenty children!

The Church of St Peter at Edensor is notable for the 17th-century monument to William, First Earl of Devonshire and Henry Cavendish. William is shown as a shrouded corpse and Henry as a skeleton. Both were sons of Bess of Hardwick.

St Wilfred's Church, Barrow-upon-Trent contains an alabaster effigy of a priest from the 14th-century.

St Mary's Church, Ilkeston contains a well preserved effigy of a cross-legged knight thought to be that of Sir Nicholas de Cantelupe who died in 1272. The Cantelupes were lords of the manor in the 13th-century.

The church of St Peter, Littleover has a 17th-century memorial to Sir Richard Harpur and his wife and children. They are depicted kneeling and facing each other at a prayer desk.

The alabaster tomb of Thomas and Agnes Beresford in St Edmund's Church, Fenny Bentley is one of only two such shrouded tombs in Derbyshire (the other being in Chesterfield). Not only are the husband and wife shown wrapped in shrouds but their 21 children are depicted around the sides in a similar fashion. It is believed that this was due to the tomb having been made about a hundred years after the death of its occupants at which time no likeness was available.

## Towers and Spires

The tower of Derby Cathedral dates from the reign of Henry VII. Since 2006 Peregrin Falcons have nested here. With a height of 178 feet it is also the highest church tower in Derbyshire and the second highest in England.

The Church of All Saints at Chesterfield is famous for its twisted spire. Several strange legends have be told to explain this phenomenon but is seems likely that the true cause was a combination of the use of unseasoned timber and the weight of the lead.

*The twisted spire of All Saints Church, Chesterfield*

All Saint's Church at Bradley has an 18th-century wooden bell turret but no tower.

St Giles Church at Marston Montgomery has a pyramidal bell cote, a rare feature in Derbyshire churches.

The tower of St Andrew's Church, Swanwick was added in 1903 as a gift from Fitzherbert Wright, who was retiring as managing director of the Butterley Company.

The tower of All Saints Church at Trusley has been leaning since well before 1824 when Samuel Butler, Archdeacon of Derby reported that it "seems sound but leans; no defect however perceptible".

The tower of St Anne's Church, Baslow supports an unusual clock-face with the name Victoria and the date 1897 on it. This commemorates the Diamond Jubilee of Queen Victoria.

A tablet in the tower of Horsley Church records that 'during the year 1915 there was rung in this steeple for Divine Service 35,820 changes ...'

The Church of Saints Alkmund and Saint Werburgh in Derby, built in 1967–72, has a fibre glass spire.

## Churchyards

St. Helen's churchyard, Darley Dale contains an ancient yew tree which is believed to be one of the thickest in England, having a girth of around 33 feet.

The churchyard at St Matthew's Church, Darley Abbey contains the graves of some of the victims of the sinking of the Lusitania in 1917.

St Paul's churchyard, Church Broughton contains 16 memorial headstones supplied by the Imperial War Graves Commission to mark the graves of airmen from overseas who died while training with the RAF training squadron based at nearby Church Broughton airfield.

Sundials made in the 1760s by John Whitehurst, the famous Derby clockmaker, stand in Morley and Thorpe churchyards.

The churchyard at Chapel-en-le-Frith has a forester's grave showing his axe and initials.

The grave of Little John, the friend and lieutenant of the outlaw Robin Hood is in Hathersage churchyard.

The partial ruins of a previous church stand in the churchyard at Ticknall. The original church dedicated to St Thomas a Becket was blown up with gunpowder but some fragments of masonry remain.

There is a stile built into the wall of Monyash churchyard.

The churchyard at Barlborough contains the mass grave of ten men who died in the Markham Colliery Disaster in 1938.

A Victorian postbox is attached to the churchyard wall at Killamarsh.

Lychgates survive in a number of Derbyshire churchyards. Examples may be seen at Aston-on-Trent, Codnor, Marston-on-Dove, Matlock, Ockbrook and Scropton.

According to local legend the last public duel in England was fought in Winster churchyard.

## Curiosities

Melbourne Church contains some interesting stone carvings including an acrobat and a grinning cat.

The parish chest in St Peter's Church, Alstonfield is over 700 years old. It is over 10ft long and has three locks.

At St Anne's Church Beeley tradition and superstition demand that at wedding services the bride and groom are not permitted to approach by the west gate and must pay coinage to leave by the narrow east gate, the wider one being used for funerals. According to local legend in 1785 one lady died on her way to be married.

St Andrew's Church, Radbourne contains some medieval benches rescued from Dale Abbey.

The Church at Kirk Ireton has an unusual ceremony known as 'roping for weddings', when the village children put a rope across the road and the bride and groom are not allowed to leave the church until a toll has been paid in silver by the bridegroom.

The oak panelling in Smisby Church is said to come from Ashby Castle.

St Michael's Church, Earl Sterndale is the only church in Derbyshire to have been hit by a German bomb in the Second World War. It was substantially damaged in 1941 but was later restored.

The church of St Mary the Virgin at Weston-on-Trent contains a parish bier dating from 1653.

An entry in the register of St Margaret's Church, Carsington and dated 29 September 1688 reads: 'Sarah Tissington died. Born without hands or arms. She learned to knit, dig in the garden and do other things with her feet.

The Bonsall Imp is a strange carving at the base of one of the pillars at St James Church. It has been described as a cross between a frog and a unicorn.

Gargoyles adorn the walls of many Derbyshire churches. Particularly fine examples can be seen at Hartington.

The church at Fenny Bentley has an aluminium ceiling in the north-east aisle. Painted by Alice M Erskine in 1895 it is believed to be one of the first buildings in England to make use of sheet aluminium.

# Derbyshire's Monastic Houses

In the Middle Ages religion played a much more important part in people's lives than it does today and thousands became monks or nuns. There were several different orders of monks though not all were represented in Derbyshire. The largest was the Benedictine Order which had been founded by St Benedict in 529AD. Benedictine communities lived a life of prayer, hard work, self discipline and good deeds, following a set of rules which Benedict himself had established. This demanded from the monks vows of poverty, chastity and obedience. The rule also set out a timetable for the monks' day which was divided into three parts; first the work of God carried out through eight daily services in church; second the work of the cloisters which included meditation, writing, translating, copying manuscripts and illuminating them; third, work in the monastic fields and gardens to provide necessary food and clothing or in the form of craftsmanship in sculpture, carving or metalwork. The Cluniacs (who established the Priory of St James in Derby) also followed a version of the Benedictine Rule but devoted much of their time to church service and prayer. There were also two orders of canons. These were priests who followed the monastic way of life but went out preaching and provided clergy for the churches which they appropriated. The Augustinian or Austin Canons wore a black habit like the Benedictine monks. They lived in comparative comfort and were well known for the generosity of their hospitality. Communities of Austin Canons were established during the Middle Ages at Derby, Breadsall, Gresley and Repton. The Premonstratensian canons were formed at Premontre in France in 1123. They followed a more austere way of life than the Austin canons and wore a white habit. These 'White Canons' established their first English house at Alnwick in 1147 and Premonstratensian abbeys were later founded in Derbyshire at Dale and Beauchief (now in South Yorkshire). The Cluniac Order was founded at Cluny in France and grew into one of the most powerful and influential orders in Europe. The small priory of St James in Derby was the only Cluniac house in Derbyshire. Military orders and communities of friars were also established and these too were represented in Derbyshire.

## Dale Abbey

A number of unsuccessful attempts were made to establish a religious community at Dale but around 1195 a group of Premonstratensian Canons from Newhouse Abbey in Lincolnshire were sent to colonise Dale. An independent abbey with Newhouse as the mother abbey was established in 1204 with Walter de Sentenay as the first Abbot. Formally this new abbey was known as the Church of St Mary of Stanley Park but this soon gave way to the more simple Dale Abbey. Under the leadership of Abbot Walter and his successors the abbey grew in prosperity and acquired lands in various parts of Derbyshire and Nottinghamshire. The abbey buildings also grew as the years passed. The main part of the church, chapter house, common room and cloisters were all constructed in the early 13th-century, soon after the foundation of the abbey but extensions and improvements were completed by a number of Abbot Walter's successors. Little is known about Dale until 1474 when the first of Bishop Redman's visitations began to record the state of the abbey during the last quarter of the 15th-century. (Richard Redman was the Abbot of Shap and the visitor-general of the Premonstratensian Order in England, Scotland and Ireland) His first visit was on 26 October 1474 and was not a regular visitation but one which was made necessary because 'public ill-fame and the clamorous report of guilt through outside brethren and our fellow canons have often cried aloud'. There is no record of the actual visitation so we are left to imagine the nature of the misdeeds which were causing such scandal. The abbot was successful in putting his house in order, however, for in 1478 Redman found 'good fame, charity and peace in head and limbs' and nothing worthy of correction by him or the chapter. He did, however find a certain laxity in the way religious observances were conducted. He forbade certain prayers which, had been introduced contrary to the custom of the order, and regulated certain feasts and ceremonies. On a more practical note he enjoined the abbot to provide suitable food and drink for the canons so as to avoid cause for grumbling. During his visitation he found 'efficiency and prosperity in temporal matters and decency, if not zeal in spiritual matters'. By 1479, however, discipline at Dale was once again in a bad state. The canons were found to be lax and careless in their observance of their Rule, kept dogs (presumably for hunting), played games for money, performed divine serviced without due reverence, ate in secular houses and ignored the rule of silence. This deplorable state of affairs, Redman attributed to the imbecility and impotence of the abbot, John Stanley, and after more than twenty years as superior of the abbey he was forced to resign. His successor, Richard Nottingham, proved to be a capable administrator but even under his leadership there were instances of immorality. During Redman's visitation of 1494, two canons were found guilty of fathering children but one of these, John Bebe, returned to Dale after a few years and succeeded Richard Nottingham as abbot in 1510. Dale survived the first phase of monastic closures but was eventually dissolved on 30 October 1538 when the abbey and all its possessions were surrendered to the crown.

## Darley Abbey

Darley Abbey was a community of Augustinian (or Austin) canons who moved from a small oratory at Derby to a new site a few miles outside the town. The building of the abbey church was completed in 1146 and was dedicated to the Virgin Mary. Over the next few years other buildings were added including cloisters, refectory, dormitories, chapter house and guest house as well as various outbuildings such as the kitchen, brew-house, bake-house, barns and workshops. By the end of the 13th-century the abbey had acquired considerable property. Its lands spread across Derbyshire and into Nottinghamshire and Staffordshire. The abbey's vast wealth came from a variety of sources. Much of its property was leased to tenants but in Derby and at several villages the canons had granges which were independent farms managed and worked by servants of the abbey and supervised by the canons themselves. Income was also received from fisheries, woods and minerals as well as fees from the churches which they held. At the start of the 16th-century over a hundred masses a year were being said for the dead and a charge was made for each. The abbey also provided hospitality for large numbers of travellers and the poor who called at the abbey gatehouse were provided with food and sometimes alms. For most of its life Darley Abbey was well administered and untouched by scandal. It suffered some financial problems in the 14th-century but these were overcome and in the Valor Ecclesiasticus of 1535 the annual income of Darley Abbey was assessed at £254. 13s. 5d. Being well over £200 in annual value Darley Abbey escaped the earlier destruction of lesser houses such as Gresley and Breadsall but on 22 October 1538 the abbot, Thomas Page finally gave way to persuasion and surrendered the abbey to the royal commissioners. As was usual pensions were granted to the abbot and his canons ranging from £50 to the abbot to £5 to the most junior canons. In addition Thomas Tupman, the schoolmaster employed by the abbey was awarded an annual grant of 26s. 8d. The abbey buildings were torn down and all that remains today is a pub called 'The Abbey' which was once probably the abbey guest house.

## Derby, the Priory of St James

The Cluniac order of monks had only one house in the whole of Derbyshire and this was the small priory with attached hospital dedicated to St James. A cell of the much larger priory at Bermondsey it was established around 1140. The priory was not well endowed but additional income was obtained from the tolls which the monks levied for passage over St. James' Bridge. Little is known of the early history of this priory but at the time of a visitation by the prior of Mont-Didier in France and the Prior of Lenton in Nottinghamshire in 1279, the house comprised only a prior and two monks. The prior was described as a worthy and good man but one of the monks was found to be living disreputably. He was expelled and sent to do penance at Bermondsey from whence another monk was despatched to take his place. Disaster struck sometime after 1325 when the priory with its church and hospital were accidentally burnt down. Royal protection was granted to the prior and his monks to collect alms for its rebuilding. The priory was almost certainly a wooden structure and this rebuilding was soon accomplished. This small priory and hospital which probably cared for only a handful of the infirm, survived until the dissolution in 1536. St James' priory, still technically a cell of Bermondsey, was surrendered and the prior, Thomas Gainsborough, was assigned a pension on the Bermondsey list.

## King's Mead Priory

The Benedictine nunnery of King's Mead was founded by the Abbot of Darley around 1160. It was situated to the west of the medieval town of Derby about a mile from Darley Abbey in the meadows by the side of Markeaton Brook. There were a number of disputes between the priory and Darley Abbey. These became so serious that in 1250 the Bishop of Coventry intervened and declared that henceforth the nuns and their property should be completely free from the control of

Darley Abbey. Records indicate that without exception the prioresses came from important Derbyshire families such as the Curzons, Gresleys and Fitzherberts. If such women did not marry their only practical alternative was to enter a nunnery, for there was no allocated place in medieval society for the aristocratic or high born spinster. If she had a genuine vocation the nunnery provided an ideal life of devotion, service and contemplation, but if not it offered at least a safe and honourable retreat. As members of the Benedictine order the nuns were expected to take part in the daily offices of the choir. King's Mead was a small and poorly endowed priory. The nuns may have done some of the housework and cooking themselves but it seems likely that the more menial tasks were undertaken by servants. The nuns spent much of their time teaching girls who were sent to the priory for a boarding education and the fees paid by the families of these girls helped to keep the priory solvent. The priory was suppressed in 1536 but by this time the number of nuns had declined to only a handful and the house was so poor that the crown must have gained little from its suppression.

## The Friary

Several orders of friar-preachers were established in Europe in the 13th-century. Their aim was to go out into the world to help the poor and diseased and to spread the word of God by means of homely and vigorous preaching. They were popular with the ordinary people and attracted both recruits and benefactions. The friary in Derby was established around the year 1230 by the Dominicans or Black Friars who had arrived in England in 1221. The friars, who numbered about thirty in Derby, went quietly about their work for over three centuries. Preaching in the market place and in local churches they attracted large congregations and when they first arrived they brought about something of a religious revival. Their greatest influence was probably with the poor in Derby. The friars spent a great deal of their time amongst the unfortunate, the destitute and the diseased and with a rough and ready knowledge of medicine many friars were able to minister to bodies as well as comfort souls. Unlike some of the religious houses in the county the friary was still flourishing at the time of the Reformation but fearing for the future most Dominican Friars had left the country by 1535. Only six remained at Derby and these finally left when the Friary was surrendered on 3 January 1539.

## Repton Priory

An Augustinian priory was established at Repton in 1172. Dedicated to the Holy Trinity and the Blessed Virgin Mary, the priory was well provided for and its original endowments were generously increased in later years. The parish church of St Wystan at Repton and its eight chapelries were all served by the canons who received in return considerable ecclesiastical revenues. Most of the 350 years of the priory's existence passed peacefully and the canons largely escaped infamous notoriety, dissention or rebuke of authority. The life of the priory was not, however, without incident. There were disputes with local landowners over fishing rights but in 1364 a much more serious incident occurred when the local villagers attacked the priory. Armed with bows and arrows, swords and cudgels they stormed the gatehouse and besieged the priory, firing arrows through the chapter house windows. There is no clear evidence to indicate what caused this disturbance but it has been suggested that it may have been instigated by a rebellious canon. During the 15th-century the priory suffered financial problems and for a period it was taken under the protection of the king in order to prevent proceedings being taken against the canons for the immediate payment of their debts. The financial affairs of the priory were placed in the hands of four members of the local, gentry and solvency was eventually restored. By 1535 the clear income of the house was £118. 8s, and in 1537 the priory was able to afford to pay a fine of £226. 13s. 4d. to the king in order to escape dissolution. This payment provided only a very short reprieve for in the following year the exemption was withdrawn and the house again condemned. The dissolved priory was granted to Thomas Thacker (Steward of Thomas, Lord Cromwell) and the buildings remained fairly intact for several years. Thomas died in 1548, leaving his property to his son Gilbert who destroyed most of the buildings in 1553. Today the site is occupied by Repton public school but fairly extensive remains of the priory are still easily visible.

## Breadsall Priory

Breadsall Priory was dedicated to the Holy Trinity and was founded in the 13th-century by a member of the Curzon family of Breadsall. Like the houses at Darley and Repton it belonged to the Austin canons. It was a much smaller establishment than either of these and the community comprised only a prior and two canons. The last prior of Breadsall, William Pendylton, had no brother canon to assist him but when the priory was dissolved 1537 he received only the very small pension of five marks a year.

## Gresley Priory

The first house of Austin Canons to be established in Derbyshire was Gresley Priory which was founded by William de Gresley during the reign of Henry I. The Gresley family and others made a number of bequests to the priory and by the middle of the 14th-century it owned land in Castle Gresley, Church Gresley, Heathcote and Lullington, the mill at Castle Gresley and the churches at Gresley and Lullington. In 1316 the priory was visited by Bishop Langton of Lichfield who ordered that pensions should not be granted from the house without Episcopal license and that no women were to be allowed within the bounds of the priory. There were no further suggestions of irregularities and we must assume that the canons went about their duties in a diligent and pious manner. The divine office was recited as in all Augustinian houses, prayers were offered up for the souls of the priory's benefactors and the canons performed the duties of the parish priests in Gresley and Lullington. Alms were given to the poor and hospitality was provided for travellers who called at the priory. By the end of the 15th-century the priory had entered a period of decline and when Prior John Smyth died in 1494 his successor was appointed by the Bishop of Lichfield as there were not enough canons remaining to elect a successor. When the priory was suppressed in 1536 there remained only the prior and two other canons who were serving their two appropriated churches as vicars.

## Hospitals

Medieval hospitals were also religious institutions. In most cases the master, prior or warden together with the brethren or sisters who formed the staff followed a definite religious rule and wore a special habit These were the hospitals of St James, St Helen and St Leonard at Derby and three others at Chesterfield, Alkmonton and High Peak. There was also a preceptory at Locko near Spondon which provided help and support for lepers.

# The Stately Homes of Derbyshire

## Calke Abbey

Calke Abbey is a baroque mansion which was built on the site of an Augustinian priory by Sir John Harpur between 1701 and 1704. His grandson, Sir Henry, lived a life of seclusion at Calke but caused a scandal by marrying his mistress; a ladies maid called Nanette Hawkins. He was killed in a carriage accident and was succeeded by his son George, who changed his name to Crewe. Sir George Crewe did a great deal to reform the workings of the estate and return the mansion to good repair. He played an active role in public life, serving as a Member of Parliament and as Sheriff for the county. He also purchased many of the paintings by British and Dutch artists which still hang at Calke. Sir George's son, Sir John Harpur Crewe devoted much of his life to the management of his estates and took a keen interest in the breeding of longhorn cattle and Portland sheep for which Calke received considerable recognition. Succeeding generations of the family played little part in public life and Calke Abbey remained trapped in the past. The eccentric Sir Vauncy Harpur Crewe banned the use of cars on the estate and refused to allow any smoking in the house. He enjoyed shooting on his estate and spent considerable amounts of money in buying rare and unusual specimens of birds, fish and butterflies from taxidermists and dealers. By the time of his death in 1924 the exhibits numbered several thousand and had spread to almost all parts of the house. His eldest daughter, Hilda Harpur-Crewe, inherited the estate and sold off part of the collection to pay death duties. When she died the house and estate passed to her nephew, Charles Jenny, who changed his name to Harper-Crewe. Like many of his ancestors he was a shy and retiring man and Calke remained one of the most impenetrable country houses in England. He died in 1981and following a spirited publicity campaign the house was taken over by the National Trust. After closing for three years so that an inventory could be carried out and conservation work undertaken, Calke Abbey reopened as a 'time capsule'. The house and stables are little restored, with many abandoned areas vividly portraying a period in the 20th-century when numerous country houses did not survive to tell their story. The parkland surrounding the house contains a 1,000 year old oak (the Old man of Calke) and is home to herds of red and fallow deer. Visitors can also explore the walled garden orangery, auricular theatre and kitchen gardens.

## Chatsworth House

The original Chatsworth House was built by the famous Bess of Hardwick who lived there from the 1560s with her fourth husband, George Talbot, sixth Earl of Shrewsbury. In 1568 the Earl was appointed as custodian of Mary Queen of Scots who was held at Chatsworth on a number of occasions. She was lodged in the apartments now known as the Queen of Scots rooms, on the top floor above the Great Hall. The Countess of Shrewsbury died in 1608 and Chatsworth was passed to her second son, William Cavendish, first Earl of Devonshire. Little changed in the House for almost a hundred years but the fourth Earl, who was created first Duke of Devonshire in 1694 decided to embark on a major building programme. Over a period of about 20 years he created a baroque palace with impressive facades, a chapel, painted hall and suite of staterooms. Some minor changes and improvements were made to the house by the fourth Duke who also employed the famous landscape architect, Lancelot 'Capability' Brown, to transform the formal gardens into the fashionable naturalistic landscape which was popular at the time. The sixth Duke, also known as the Bachelor Duke, made a number of changes and improvements to the house, the most significant of which was the addition of the north wing to accommodate his collection of books, minerals and contemporary sculpture. It also contained the dining room which was used to entertain the young Princess Victoria in 1832. She returned in 1843 as Queen with her husband, Prince Albert and was entertained by a large array of illuminated fountains. The sixth Duke also employed Joseph Paxton as his head gardener and under his direction the grounds were further improved The house had been open for people to see round since it was built but at first visitors were from the more affluent classes of society. The opening of the Midland Railway from Derby to Rowsley in 1849 however, made Chatsworth accessible to the population of the great manufacturing towns and by this time around 80,000 people were visiting the house during the summer. During the Edwardian era the house was used for lavish parties and shooting weekends and King Edward VII was a regular visitor. Little changed during the early years of the 12th-century. Despite financial problems caused by death duties and a decline in farm income a vast staff was maintained at Chatsworth, which included a butler, under butler, groom of the chambers, valet, three footmen, a housekeeper, the Duchess's maid, eleven housemaids, two sewing women, a cook, two kitchen maids, a vegetable maid, two or three scullery maids, a dairy maid, six laundry maids and the Duchess's secretary! In addition a further hundred or so people were employed to maintain the house, gardens and grouse moors. During the Second World War the contents of the house were packed away and the building was taken over by Penrhos College, a girls' public school. In 1949 the house was reopened to the public and ten years later the 11th Duke and his family returned to live there. Today Chatsworth House is the most visited stately home in the country. The house has over thirty rooms to explore and the gardens extend over 105 acres with giant water features, sculptures and magnificent views over the park. A farmyard is open to visitors to give them an insight into the working of the farms and woodland on the estate and the farm shop sells a wide range of local produce.

## Hardwick Hall

Hardwick Hall was built by Elizabeth, Countess of Shrewsbury, who is famously known as 'Bess of Hardwick'. She has been described as 'a builder, a buyer and seller of estates, a money lender, a farmer and a merchant of lead, coals and timber'. The same writer believed her to be 'a woman of masculine understanding and conduct, proud, furious, selfish and unfeeling'. It was these attributes which encouraged her to build one of the most splendid Elizabethan houses in the country. The death of her fourth husband, George Talbot, sixth Earl of Shrewsbury, in 1590 made Bess the second richest woman in the kingdom with estates, quarries, lead mines and farms throughout Derbyshire. Having just completed what is now known as Hardwick Old hall she began the planning and construction of a much larger and grander house only a few yards away. Work on this new Hardwick Hall began soon after the death of her husband and took around seven years to complete. It is believed that Bess employed Robert Smythson, as her architect. He had previously designed nearby Wollaton Hall in Nottinghamshire. The building accounts for Hardwick Hall provide a fairly detailed picture of the building work and some of the people involved. Bess was able to draw on her estates for stone and timber. For glass she established her own glassworks and appointed Sylvester Smith as her glazier. As well as manufacturing sufficient glass for the house he flooded the local market and established sales outlets and transport systems to London. We also known the names of the some of the senior craftsmen employed at Hardwick. A certain John Painter acted as overseer and general foreman. As a reward for his services he was paid two pounds a year and given a farm. Master craftsmen included John Roads, the master mason, Thomas Acres, the marble mason and Abraham Smith, the plasterer. A small army of masons, paviours and wallers, carpenters, joiners, sawyers, slaters and smiths, painters, plumbers and glaziers all laboured on the site and were paid wages ranging from fourpence to sixpence a day. When completed the house was lavishly furnished. In 1591 Bess travelled to London and returned with 13 second hand tapestries depicting the Story of Gideon from the Old Testament, for which she paid over £320. A detailed account of the contents of the house is contained in the inventory completed in 1601. Her own bedchamber contained a beautiful bed. The tester and posts were covered in scarlet with silver lace laid on it, and it had scarlet and silver curtains and a valance embroidered with gold thistles. Other furniture listed in this room included a chair of russet satin striped with silver, a table with a 'turkey' carpet laid on it, several stools and a number of embroidered cushions. Bess lived for ten years in the new hall and died there on 13 February 1608 at the age of 78. Her descendants, the Earls and Dukes of Devonshire chose to make Chatsworth their principal home and as a consequence Hardwick Hall remains virtually as built in 1591–7, with many of the original contents listed in the inventory of 1601. During the Second World War parts of the park were handed over to the army and the RAF and a training centre for airborne forces was established there. Following the death of the 10th Duke of Devonshire in 1950 the house, park and estate were accepted by the Treasury in part payment of death duties. They were presented to the National trust in 1959.

*Hardwick Hall – More glass than wall*

## Kedleston Hall

The Curzon family have owned the estate at Kedleston since the 13th-century and have lived in a succession of manor houses near to or on the site of the present hall for over several generations. Sir Nathianiel Curzon (later the first Lord Scarsdale) began the construction of the present Kedleston Hall in 1759. Initially the architects entrusted with the work were Matthew Brettingham and James Paine, who designed the north front in the fashionable Palladian style of the period. Robert Adam was engaged to landscape the park and design garden buildings but before long he was also put in charge of the house. His work can be seen in the design of the south front which he based on the Arch of Constantine in Rome. He was also responsible for the interior decoration including the furniture, even down to such detail as the design of the cast iron stoves and the fire irons. He designed the many fine staterooms including the library, great drawing room, dining room and state bedroom but his greatest achievement was almost certainly the great hall and saloon, which have been described as two of the greatest 18th-century interiors in England. Not everyone approved of Adam's design. Dr Samuel Johnson declared that 'it would do excellently for a town hall. The large room with the pillars would do for the judges to sit in at the assizes, the circular room for a Jury Chamber, and the room above for prisoners.' In his diary he wrote: 'The Bedchambers were small, low, dark and fitter for a prison than a house of splendour'. While the house was being built Lord Scarsdale moved the public highway and the village, which lay near the old house, outside the boundaries of the present park. The old formal gardens with their canals and ponds were transformed into an area of parkland with serpentine lakes. The new North Lodge, the bridge and cascade and the fishing lodge on the upper lake were all designed by Adam, while Samuel Wyatt was responsible for the stables and George Richardson for the Hexagonal Temple and the Orangery to the south-west of the house. Lord Scarsdale died in 1837 but his successors continued to reside at Kedleston. Few changes were made to the house or the estate but Alfred, the fourth Lord Scarsdale, installed a gas works and a steam-powered saw mill towards the end of the 19th-century. His eldest son, George Nathaniel Curzon had a glittering political career. He was Viceroy of India from 1899 until 1905 and the Indian Museum within the house contains many of the treasures which he collected during this period. He continued to climb the political ladder and held a number of cabinet posts including Lord Privy Seal, Leader of the House of Lords and Foreign Secretary. In the 1921 Birthday Honours he was created Marquis Curzon of Kedleston .On his death in 1925 the Viscountcy of Scarsdale passed to his nephew, Richard who died in 1977. By this time the house and estate were facing serious financial problems which were only solved when, in 1987 Lord Scarsdale and his trustees agreed to present the house and park and some of the contents to the National Trust. At the same time the National Memorial Fund provided the unprecedented sum of £13.5 million which enabled the majority of the contents of the house to be purchased, and an endowment established for future maintenance.

## Sudbury Hall

The first manor house at Sudbury was built in 1613 by Mary Vernon for her son Edward and his wife Margaret. Following the death of Dame Mary, the young Vernons made their home elsewhere and it was left to their son, George Vernon, to take up his position as squire of Sudbury. He inherited the property in 1659 and decided to build a more imposing mansion, possibly with help from the money he received from his mother and his new young wife, Margaret Olney. He lived at Sudbury for over forty years and for almost the whole of that time was engaged in building or decorating his house, laying out the garden or improving the village. He built his new house without the help of an architect although he would have been able to draw inspiration and ideas from books of architectural drawings and styles. The house which he built is largely Jacobean, although some elements owe more to the classical style of architecture. Experts have noted that the lower sections of the house are less advanced than the upper parts and have suggested that this is a direct result of Vernon's developing expertise and his employment of more highly skilled craftsmen. The interior of the house benefitted from the work of some of the best artists and craftsmen of the period and contains some magnificent plasterwork, carving by Grinling Gibbons and murals by Louis Laguerre. The great staircase was carved by Edward Pierce at a cost of £112 15s, 5d. and is regarded as one of the finest of its kind in the country. It is the long gallery, however, which is probably the finest feature of the house. It is unusual to find a long gallery in a Charles II house and architectural historians have puzzled over its existence. It nevertheless provided a light and spacious area which could be enjoyed by members of the family and their guests. Outside the house a formal garden was crated leading down to a series of ponds, developed from medieval fish ponds. Over the years few changes were made to Sudbury Hall although George's son Henry added a linking building from the Hall to the stable wing (on the site of the present East Wing). In the 18th-century the formal gardens and ponds were replaced by a more natural landscape and a lake. In the 19th-century some minor alterations were made to the interior of the house and in the 1880s a new East Wing was added. The house was occupied by a number of different tenants during parts of the 18th and 19th centuries and Queen Adelaide, the widow of William IV lived here for three years from 1840. The ninth Lord Vernon returned to the house in 1922 and employed the fashionable decorator Lenygon to redecorate the rooms. Following his death the house passed into the care of the National Trust and was opened to the public in 1972.

# Industrial Archaeology

Industrial Archaeology is the study and recording of industry including the remains of industry such as mills, mines, railways, factories and machines. Derbyshire has a rich industrial heritage dating back to Roman times when lead was mined here and a type of pottery known as Derbyshire Ware was manufactured at a number of sites within the county. By the 18th and 19th centuries, coal mining, textiles and engineering were all important and in the 20th and 21st centuries names such as Stanton and Staveley, Rolls-Royce and Qualcast became known throughout the world.

## Power

Water was used to power corn mills from at least the Saxon period and several mills are mentioned in the Domesday Book. Later water power was used in the textile industry in fulling mills and other processes. The Derby Silk Mill, regarded by many as England's first factory, used water power and in 1771 Arkwright's cotton mills at Cromford used water to power his spinning machines. Later in the 18th and 19th centuries Arkwright and others constructed a number of water powered cotton mill at places such as Belper, Matlock, Chesterfield and Wirksworth. A number of windmills also exist in Derbyshire. From the 14th to the 18th-century these were used to grind corn and were often sited on hills or high ridges. In the 20th-century power stations were constructed on the banks of the Trent and the Derwent at Drakelow, Willington, Spondon and Derby. In recent years a number of wind turbines have been constructed within the county. A number of water and windmills can still be seen throughout the county. Some of the best examples include:

Heage Windmill.

Cat and Fiddle Windmill at Kirk Hallam.

Caldwell's Mill at Rowsley.

Stainsby Mill at Hardwick.

## Brewing

Brewing in Derbyshire dates back to the medieval period. There is documentary evidence of large-scale brewing at Derbyshire's monastic houses and later in some of the large country houses such as Hardwick, Chatsworth and Calke. An important ingredient of beer is malt which is grain that has been encouraged to germinate under controlled conditions. This process was carried out in a malting, where the barley was germinated on the floor before being transferred to kilns for drying. A number of these maltings were established in both Derby, Chesterfield. The first commercial breweries were established in Derbyshire in the 18th-century. Chesterfield had three important breweries and Derby four, of which the most important and last surviving was Offiler's. By the end of the 19th-century many towns and villages in the county boasted at least one local brewery. These included Zachary Smith's Trent Brewery at Shardlow, Hill's of Cromford and John Hair & Son at Melbourne. Mergers and take-overs have seen a decline and virtual disappearance of brewing in Derbyshire. Relics of this once important industry can be found in maltings, brewery buildings and traditional public houses throughout the county. The following are good examples:

A number of malt houses in Derby.

The brew house at Calke Abbey.

The Dolphin Public House in Derby (The city's oldest pub).

Coaching Inns at places such as Ashbourne, Chesterfield, Derby and Wirksworth.

## Textiles

Derbyshire's involvement in the textile industry dates back to the Middle Ages when both Derby and Chesterfield were important centres of the wool trade. The country's first silk mill was constructed at Derby in 1721 and in 1771 Richard Arkwright and his partners opened the world's first water powered cotton mill at Cromford. In the years which followed similar water powered cotton mills were established throughout Derbyshire at places such as Belper, Derby, Chesterfield and Wirksworth. Derbyshire was also an important centre of the hosiery industry in the 18th and 19th centuries and was particularly significant in the Erewash Valley, at Belper and Crich. Lace was manufactured in a number of areas with Long Eaton being a particularly important centre. Important sites relating to the textile industry include the following;

Derby Silk Mill.

Arkwright's Cotton Mill at Cromford.

Masson Mill between Matlock Bath and Cromford .

The remains of textile communities with mills, workers housing, schools and churches at Cromford, Belper and Darley Abbey.

Lace factories at Long Eaton and Beeston.

Framework knitters cottages in a number of Derbyshire villages including Melbourne, Crich and Breadsall.

*Masson Mill near Cromford*

## Lead Mining

Lead was first mined in Derbyshire by the Romans. It continued to be mined and smelted in the Saxon period and the Domesday Book records seven lead works in Derbyshire. In the Middle Ages the construction of castles, churches and monasteries led to an increase in production. Despite this, for hundreds of years lead mining was conducted on a small scale. The mines were generally shallow workings which required little capital outlay beyond that required for tools, candles and simple haulage equipment. The ore that was obtained was then dressed at or near the site of the mine by simple hand sorting, crushing and washing in a local stream. The ore was smelted in boles. These were primitive smelting hearths, built on the tops of hills, where the blast was provided by strong winds. From the 16th-century these boles were replaced by water-powered bellows. The 18$^{th}$ and 19$^{th}$ centuries saw considerable improvements in mining technology. Steam power began to be used to pump water out of mines and above ground changes in smelting took place with the introduction of the cupula or reverbatory furnace. The financing and organisation of the industry also began to change. A number of enterprises were financed by wealthy landowners or joint stock companies. By the 20th-century the industry was in considerable decline and lead mining in the county was confined to a few large mines. The last of these, Magpie Mine, near Sheldon, was finally abandoned in 1958. The story of the lead mining industry is told at the Lead Mining Museum in Matlock Bath and the Wirksworth Centre. Other significant remains include:

Magpie Mine near Sheldon
Roman pigs of lead in a number of local museums.
The engine house of Meerbrook Sough Mine near Wirksworth.
The Moot Hall at Wirksworth.
Stone carving of a medieval lead miner in the church at Wirksworth.
The Stonedge cupula at Spitewater just off the Matlock–Chesterfield road.

## Coal Mining

Coal has been mined in Derbyshire for many hundreds of years and by the Middle Ages there is evidence of widespread but small scale mining in various parts of the county. By the 16th and 17th centuries the great landowners of the county were beginning to exploit the coal deposits beneath their lands and there are descriptions of coal being mined as deep as 240 feet beneath the surface. The dawn of the industrial revolution led to an increased demand for coal and a number of substantial coal-mining enterprises were established. These included the Butterley Company, the Stanton Ironworks Company and the Clay Cross Company. Derbyshire remained an important coal mining area throughout the nineteenth and twentieth centuries and at the time of nationalisation (1947) around 60,000 people were employed in over 100 collieries throughout the county. The 1970s and 1980s were marked by industrial unrest and decline and today there are no deep mines remaining in the county. The remains of this once great industry can, however be seen at many places throughout the county including the following:

Pleasley Colliery buildings.

The Woodside Colliery engine house and winding gear at Shipley.

The headstocks and winding gear at Western Pit on the site of the Midland Railway Trust at Butterley.

Colliery engine house at Stanley.

*Colliery buildings at Pleasley*

## Iron and Steel

The commercial manufacture of iron in Derbyshire dates back to at least the medieval period, and there is evidence of early iron working at places such as High Peak Forest, Duffield Frith, Horsley Wood and Brampton near Chesterfield. From the 16th-century a number of blast furnaces were operated by wealthy landowners such as the Earl of Shrewsbury, Sir Francis Willoughby and the Foljambes. John Hurt of Alderwasley built the first coke-fired furnace in Derbyshire in 1764. There was a massive increase in the production of iron during the first half of the 19th-century and by 1839 34,327 tons of iron was being produced in fourteen furnaces. Three companies dominated the iron industry in Derbyshire; Smith's of Chesterfield, the Butterley Company and the Stanton and Staveley Company. Between them they made a major contribution to the local and national economy, exporting their wares worldwide and providing employment for thousands of people. Today iron and steel are no-longer manufactured in Derbyshire but the following places remind us of this once important industry:

Blast furnaces at Morley Park, near Ripley.

The Cannon Mill at Chesterfield.

The gatehouse of the Butterley Company at Hammersmith near Ripley.

Displays relating to the Stanton Ironworks in Ilkeston Museum.

## Pottery and Porcelain

The manufacture of pottery dates back to prehistoric times and bronze age urns have been discovered in various parts of the county. The Romans also manufactured a type of pottery known as 'Derbyshire Ware' which was used to store and transport a wide range of foodstuffs. In medieval times there were potteries at Chesterfield and Derby and by the 16th-century there was a flourishing pottery industry at Ticknall. By the 19th-century a number of pottery manufacturers had been established in different parts of the county. At Brampton near Chesterfield as many as ten pottery works produced a wide range of earthenware goods. At Swadlincote, T. G. Green continued in operation until the early years of this century and their distinctive blue and white "Cornish ware" was found in homes throughout the country. The Denby Pottery works which was founded in early 19th-century still survives. Porcelain manufacture in the county is synonymous with Royal Crown Derby. The present factory was established in 1878 but the business traces its history to the original factory which was set up in Nottingham Road, Derby around the year 1750. Queen Victoria gave permission to include the title 'Royal' in the company's title in 1890. Sites relating to the pottery and porcelain industries include:

The Bottle Kiln at West Hallam.

Denby Pottery and Visitor Centre.

Bottle kilns at Woodville, Swadlincote and elsewhere in the county.

Royal Crown Derby Factory and Visitor Centre.

Sharpe's pottery buildings at Swadlincote.

Displays relating to pottery and porcelain manufacture in Derby Museum.

## Engineering

Derbyshire was home to a large number of engineering businesses from the 18th-century onwards. In Derby, the firm of Andrew Handyside produced a wide range of constructional ironwork for railways, collieries and agriculture. The company also exported iron bridges, roofs, engines and boilers to countries throughout the world. Leys Malleable Castings, founded in 1873 produced castings for the railway, agricultural and electrical industries. Other more specialist engineering companies included Qualcast, manufacturing lawn mowers, Fletcher and Stewart, manufacturing sugar refining equipment and International Combustion, producing steam generating equipment for a number of different applications. Elsewhere in the county important engineering companies included Bryan Donkin at Chesterfield, the Ferodo Works at Chapel-en-le-Frith and the Park Foundry at Belper. By far the most significant of Derbyshire's engineering concerns was the Butterley Company. It was responsible for the construction of the roof of St Pancras Station as well as structural ironwork for projects all over the world. Many of the old engineering works have been demolished but reminders of this on once important industry include:

Park Foundry building at Belper dating from 1899.

Butterley Company housing in Golden Valley (The earliest dating from the late 18th-century).

Displays relating to Stanton Iron Works in Ilkeston Museum.

Friargate Bridge in Derby (manufactured by Handyside).

Cast iron street furniture including manhole covers, pillar boxes and ornamental fountains in several towns and villages.

## Motor Car Manufacture

Derby was the home of Rolls-Royce cars for almost half a century. The company moved here from Manchester in 1908; attracted by the price of land, cheap electricity and the availability of skilled labour. A modern factory covering 1.5 acres was constructed on Nightingale Road. It was powered and lit by electricity and a system of tram or trolley cars as well as an overhead traveller was used to deliver parts and materials to where they were needed. The early success of the company has been attributed to three factors; sound manufacturing policies, well promoted sales and service arrangements and on the production and continuous improvement of one model. For many years this was the iconic Silver Ghost but this was later superseded by various versions of the Rolls Royce Phantom. Bentley was purchased by Rolls-Royce in 1931 and by 1934 a new 3.5 litre Bentley, based on a Rolls-Royce chassis, was being produced at Derby. The last Rolls-Royce car to be built at Derby was the 25/30 hp Wraith. This was launched in 1938 and a total of 492 were manufactured before production at Derby ceased at the outbreak of the Second World War. From 1945 the Derby factory concentrated on the manufacture of aero engines and the construction of cars was transferred to Crewe. Derbyshire ceased to be involved in motor manufacture until Toyota commenced production here in 1992. Following a successful campaign by Derbyshire County Council, the company built a new factory at Burnaston. The first car to be manufactured at Burnaston was the Carina E. Five years later this was replaced by the Avensis. At the time of writing various models of the Auris are manufactured here. For those interested in the story of motor car manufacture in Derbyshire the following may be of interest:

Rolls-Royce Nightingale Road Factory, Derby.

The Rolls-Royce Heritage Centre at Derby (Open occasionally to the general public).

A statue of Sir Henry Royce outside the Rolls-Royce factory in Derby.

The Toyota Works at Burnaston.

*The Rolls-Royce Factory, Nightingale Road, Derby*

## Aero Engineering

Derby is the home of one of the most famous and important companies engaged in the aero industry today. Rolls-Royce began production of aero engines during the First World War. Its Eagle engine powered a number of different aircraft including the Vickers Vimy which in 1919 completed the first non-stop transatlantic flight. The company's reputation for reliability combined with a willingness to innovate helped ensure its commercial success in the twenties and thirties. In the Second World War Rolls-Royce engines powered the Spitfires and Hurricanes which won the Battle of Britain as well as some of the aircraft of Bomber Command which carried the War into the heart of Germany. The company was also the first in Britain to become involved in the design and manufacture of jet engines. The first allied jet fighter (the Meteor) and later versions of the World's first jet airliner (the Comet) were both powered by Rolls-Royce engines. The success of the company continued in the post-war world and by the 1960s the aero engine division of the company employed around 35,000 people, mostly in Derby. A decade later the company was in deep financial trouble arising from the huge development costs of a new engine, the RB211. On 4 February 1971 Rolls-Royce shares were suspended on the stock exchange and receivers were appointed to take charge of the company. In order to safeguard important military contracts the government took the company in public ownership but it was returned to public ownership in 1987. The revolutionary RB211 proved to be the basis for the recovery of the company and its unique three shaft design led to the development of the highly successful Trent range of engines in the 1990s. The company celebrated its centenary in 2004 when it proudly proclaimed that its engines powered aircraft in 500 airlines and 160 armed forces. The company's heritage is all around and can be seen in the many present day airliners and military aircraft which are powered by Rolls-Royce engines. In the summer the distinctive sound of the merlin engine can still be heard as spitfires and hurricanes of the Second World War take part in air displays around the country.

## Roads

Turnpike roads began to be constructed in Derbyshire in the 18th-century. These were roads which were constructed or improved by a turnpike trust. In return they were allowed to charge a toll to all those who used the road. The tolls charged by each turnpike trust varied according to the type of vehicle or animal which were using them and were usually specified in the Act of Parliament which authorised them. The first road in Derbyshire to be improved under a turnpike act was part of the route between Manchester and Buxton. This was authorised by Parliament in 1725 and was followed in 1738 with the turnpiking of the Derbyshire section of the London-Manchester highway. Other turnpike acts followed in rapid succession and by 1820 Derbyshire was covered by a network of turnpike main roads as well as a number of shorter turnpikes that acted as feeders. Evidence of these turnpike roads can be seen in:

Toll Houses at several places including Ashbourne, Holbrook, Woodville and Derby.

Stone and cast iron mileposts at the sides of a number of roads within the county.

Coaching inns throughout the county including fine examples at Ashbourne, Buxton, Chesterfield, Derby and Wirksworth.

The Carriage Museum at Darley Dale which contains a number of horse drawn vehicles including a traditional stage coach.

## Canals

The canal network in Derbyshire began with the construction of the Trent and Mersey and Chesterfield canals, both surveyed by James Brindley in 1771. These were followed over the next twenty years by the Erewash, Peak Forest, Cromford, Nutbrook and Derbyshire canals. Passengers were also carried. In 1816 it was reported that a boat left Swarkestone every morning to carry market people to Derby for a fare of sixpence. For half a century the canals were the most important form of transport for heavy goods. In Derbyshire, as elsewhere, they carried raw materials and manufactured goods and foodstuffs more cheaply and reliably than ever before and provided ordinary working people with cheaper food and fuel. Railway competition led to decline and dereliction but in recent years many have been restored. The Chesterfield Canal Trust, for example, has achieved considerable success in restoring parts of the canal and trip boats now operate from Tapton Lock near the centre of Chesterfield. Much interesting canal architecture still exists. The inland canal port of Shardlow is now a conservation area which includes warehouses, canal-side taverns, lock keepers cottages, stables and bridges. Elsewhere particularly interesting buildings and structures include:

The Buxworth Canal basin (with wharves and warehouses, it was opened in 1797 as the point of interchange between the Peak Forest Canal and the Peak Forest Tramway).

Wigwell aqueduct on the Cromford canal.

Trent Lock at the junction of the Erewash Canal and the River Trent.

High Peak Wharf at Cromford (the transhipment point between the canal and the Cromford and High Peak railway).

## Railways

The first railways in Derbyshire were horse drawn tramways used to transport coal, iron and stone. A number were constructed along the lines of the Erewash and Chesterfield canals. Following the success of the Liverpool-Manchester Railway in 1830 'railway mania' swept the country and a number of companies constructed lines in Derbyshire. At Derby three companies (the Midland Counties Railway, the North Midland Railway and the Midland Counties Railway) agreed to share a single station. The first train arrived in the town on 30 May 1839 and only a few years later the three companies amalgamated to form the Midland Railway Company. Derby also developed as a manufacturing centre for locomotives and rolling stock. By the 1890s the area covered by the locomotive works alone employed almost 5,000 people. Derby remained an important railway manufacturing centre until the latter half of the 20th-century but the last new diesel locomotive to be constructed at Derby was completed in 1967. In the following year the Locomotive and Carriage and Wagon Works was renamed as British Rail Engineering and it was here that the innovative High Speed Trains were designed and built. Privatisation and increased foreign competition have led to a decline in the railway manufacturing in Derby. The railway network remains important today. In the Victorian era they transformed the lives of millions of people. Cheap travel enabled millions of ordinary people to take day trips and later holidays to the seaside. Later they allowed the emerging middle class to commute to work from the suburbs. As in the rest of the country, the railways brought change and benefits such as national newspapers, standard time and fresh food from the countryside. Mergers and nationalisation were followed by the closure of many branch lines and stations in the 1960s. Many of the buildings first constructed in the 19th-century are still visible and many are still in use. Some of the most interesting and significant buildings include:

Railway roundhouses at Derby and at Barrow Hill near Staveley.

Midland Railway Housing at Derby.

The Midland Hotel at Derby (the oldest surviving purpose built railway hotel in the country, and possibly the world).

The North Midland Railway building at Chesterfield (the only surviving building of Francis Thompson's original North Midland station of 1840)

In addition the county is home to a number of railway heritage centres and preserved railways. These include:

The Midland Railway Centre at Butterley near Ripley.

Peak Rail, which operates a steam and heritage diesel service between Matlock and Rowsley.

The Steeple Grange Light Railway near Wirksworth.

The Ecclesbourne Valley Railway which operates a heritage diesel railcar service between Wirksworth and Duffield with some steam hauled services on the short branch line between Wirksworth and Ravenstore.

# Directories, Diaries, Journals, Gazetteers and Reminiscences

## William Camden (1586)

### Derby

Darby... the chiefe towne of all this shire...A proper towne, it is, none of the least, not without a good trade and resort unto it. On the East side of it, the river Derwent, making a verie faire shew, runneth downe carrying a full and lofty streame under a beautifull stone bridge upon which our devout forefathers erected a faire Chappell which is now neglected and goeth to decay...Five churches there bee in it of which the greatest named All Hallowes, dedicated to the memorie of All-Saints, hath a tower steeple that for height and singular fine workmanship excelleth.

## Celia Feinnes (1695)

### Derby

Derby lies down in a bottom built all of brick or for the most part, in it are 5 churches built of stone... there is also a fine stone conduit in the Market Place which is very spacious well pitch'd, a good Market cross; this is a dear place for strangers notwithstanding the plentyfullness of all provisions my dinner cost me 5s and 8d., only 2 servant men with me and I had but a shoulder of mutton and bread and beer; here they make great quanteties of gloves, I did not observe or learn any other trade or manufacture, they had only shops of all sorts of things; they carry much of their carriages on sledges to secure their pitching in the street.

### Chesterfield

Coale pitts and quaraes of stone are all about even just in the town end, and in the town its all built of stone; the church stands in a place of eminency, the town looks well, the streets good the market very large; it was Saturday which is their market day and there was a great market like some little faire, a great deal of corne and all sorts of ware and fowles, there I bought for myself 2 very good fatt (pullings as thye call them) pullets for six pence both and I am sure they were as large and as good as would have cost 18 pence if not two shillings apiece in London, so said all my company; in this town is the best ale in the kingdom generally esteem'd.

## Daniel Defoe (1726)

### Derby

Derby ...is a town of gentry rather than trade; yet it is populous, well built, has five parishes. A large market place, a fine town house, and very handsome streets.... The trade in the town is chiefly in good malt and good ale; nor is the quantity of the latter unreasonably small, which as they say, they dispose of among themselves, though they spare some to their neighbours too.

### Chesterfield

Chesterfield is a handsome populous town, well built and well inhabited, notwithstanding it stands in the farthest part of this rock country. There is however, nothing remarkable in this town but a free school and a very good market, well stored with provision; for here is little or no manufacture.

### Wirksworth

Wirksworth is a large well-frequented market town, and market towns being very thin placed in this part of the country, they have the better trade, the people generally coming twelve or fifteen miles to the market, and sometimes more; though there is no very great trade to this town but what relates to the lead works, and to the subterranean wretches, who they call Peakrills, who work in the mines, and who live all round this town in every way. The inhabitants are a rude boorish kind of people, but they are a bold, daring and even desperate kind of fellows in their search into the bowels of the earth.

## Carl Phillip Moritz (1782)

### Derby

At midday I saw Derby in the valley in front of me. I was now a hundred and twenty-six miles from London. Derby is a small, unimposing town; it was market day and I had to make my way through a crowd of people, but here I suffered no rude inquisitive stares as at Burton.

### Matlock

The situation at Matlock itself surpassed all I had expected of it. On the right were several elegant houses for those taking treatment for their ailments at their baths. Smaller cottages hung on the rocks like nests. On the left ran the river in a deep ravine, almost hidden from sight under a high majestic arch of overhanging trees.

## John Byng, Viscount Torrington (1789 and 1790)

### Cromford

By two o'clock I was at the Black Dog at Cromford; around which is much levelling of ground, and increase of buildings for their new market, (for this place is now so populous as not to do without) which has already been once held, and will be again tomorrow. This house and village appear so clean, and so gay, as to quite revive me, after the dirt and dullness of Bakewell...Speaking as a tourist, these vales have lost all their beauties; the rural cot has given place to the lofty red mill, and the grand houses of the overseers; the stream perverted from its course by sluices, and aqueducts, will no longer ripple and cascade. Every rural sound is sunk in the clamours of the cotton works; and the simple peasant is changed into the impudent mechanic...I took a short walk to look at the weather, and at Sir Richard Arkwright's new house. The inside is now finishing; and it is really, within and without, an effort on inconvenient ill taste; built so high as to overlook every beauty, and to catch every wind; the approach is dangerous; the ceilings are of gee-gaw fret work; the small circular stair case, like some in the new built houses of Marylebone, is so dark and narrow, that people cannot pass each other.

### Cromford Mills

I saw the workers issue forth at 7 o'clock, a wonderful crowd of young people, made as familiar as eternal intercourse can make of them; a new set then goes in for the night, for the mills never leave off working... These cotton mills, seven stories high and filled with inhabitants remind me of a first rate man of war, and when they are lighted up, on a dark night, look most luminously beautiful.

### Derby

Derby looks well in approach, especially the steeple of All Saints Church; and the entering street is handsome...The town is crowded by the county militia assembled for their annual exercises...The silk mills quite bewildered me; such rattlings and twistings! Such heat and such stinks! That I was glad to get out: we should be full as happy, if silk mills had never been...There is a coffee house, a gloomy hole, upon the market place, where in we went to read the papers; and of the burning of the opera house, which must have been the work of intention! Our supper was slight and short.

### Buxton

Buxton is a most uncomfortable, dreary place; and The Grand Crescent might be better named The Devonshire Infirmary... Snug lodging-houses, with adjoining small stables were more necessary and comfortable, than useless, ill-contrived grandeurs: but the Duke, I supposed was made prey of by some architect.

### Bakewell

I found Bakewell to be a much better place than I expected, and the inn, the White Horse, a very good one. The landlady instantly brought before me a quarter of cold lamb, a cold duck, salad, tarts and jellies; and I was eager to enjoy them...Being satisfied I sought the clerk and found him at his day school, amidst his scholars; who appeared to be quite happy at a little respite, for he seemed to be a great tyrant..

## Joseph Farington (1808)

### Tideswell

Though Tideswell ranks amongst the market-towns of Derbyshire yet, with the exception of the church, it is but a humble looking place. The houses are low, ir-

regularly situated, and ill built and there is altogether an air of poverty and mean-
ness about it, with a want of cleanliness and comfort in its general appearance.

## Stephen Glover (1843)

### Derby

Derby is rapidly increasing in population and improvement. The principal streets
have been improved upon McAdam's plan, and the footpaths are paved with stone
or bricks. The houses are mostly built with red bricks, which are made in the vicinity of the town. The public buildings are generally built of durable stone procured
in the county... The chief branch of the manufacture is silk-sewings, doubles, vel-
vets, sarcenets, &c., lace, hosiery, small wares, porcelain, spar ornaments, marble
chimney pieces, watches, jewelry, colours, patent shot, white and red lead, patent lead piping, copper and tin plates, sheet iron, tobacco pipes, soap, wrought
iron boilers, tanks, boats, &c., steam engines, iron lathes, printing presses, &c.,
besides several extensive iron foundries, breweries, and establishments for dying
and bleaching.

## Richard Keene, A Six Days ramble over Derbyshire Hills and Dales in the year 1858

### Eyam

Supper in Mrs Fox's old-fashioned room, and a chat over our tobacco with her,
round the fire, was not the least pleasant sensation of the day. This cottage where
we were staying stands at a short distance to the west of the church, and next to
the house where the plague broke out in the memorable 1665; indeed it is under
the same roof, and was built at the same time. The walls are of immense thick-
ness and well built, the floors are of stone nicely sanded and the roof is covered
with the same material...Inside the walls are washed with a bright blue colour (a
favourite fashion of the peak) and behind our venerable hostess hands a row of
glittering household utensils; an antique clock ticks against the wall, surmounted
by a curious old jug made in the shape of as bear, a geat curiosity and as ancient
as the clock; a bright fireplace anfd a good fire; the door pen until late in the night,
whereat the jessamine peeps in and nods its star-like flowers; and the four travellers round the fire, kicking up their slippered feet, complete the picture. Old Mrs

Fox is telling us stories of bygone days and puffing at intervals on her long clay pipe, which she seems to thoroughly enjoy. The air grows chill, the door is closed, amd we sit till midnight listening tyo our ancient friend's details of ther plague, the gibbeton Wardlow Mires, amnd other interesting mattersd connected with the locality.

## Tideswell

Tideswell, a small market town with a large parish and a fine church, is a place of considerable antiquity, and takes its name from an ebbing and flowing well which once existed here. It boasts a free grammar school, founded in the reign of Queen Elizabeth; but the chief glory of Tideswell is its church which is of the decorated order of gothic architecture...After seeing the church, there is little else at Tideswell to interest the stranger, and I was not very favourably impressed with the general appearance of the town.

# Bemrose's Guide to Derbyshire (1869)

## Bakewell

Bakewell possesses all the characteristics of a comfortable town, being drained watered and lighted; having good hotels, respectable shops and museums, literary and charitable institutions, schools, banks and baths and those sure evidence of civilisation, a savings bank and a County Court.

## Derby

Derby, the county town of this interesting shire cannot be said to present many objects of attraction to the eye of the tourist; however, much of its mills, iron works and other valuable adjuncts, may endear it to men of business.

## Willington

The village of Willington is pleasantly situated on the north bank of the Trent, at a distance of about seven miles south west from Derby, and is a noted resort of anglers during the season. Opposite the station is an "honest ale-house" where the brethren of the angle are wont to congregate for gossip and refreshment.

### Wirksworth

Wirksworth has its Free Grammar School Parochial Library, Mechanics Institute, Temperance Hall, Savings Bank, Cricket ground and all the other social and religious institutions which denote an intelligent and thriving population.

## John Marius Wilson, Imperial Gazetteer of England and Wales (1870-72)

### Derby

A main street runs through the town from north to south; and is, in some parts, wide and open – in others narrow, winding, and, from the amount of traffic flowing through it, frequently dangerous to passengers...The town hall on the south side of the market place is a stone edifice, surmounted by a lofty clock-tower, and pierced with arches leading to the municipal hall and the new market...The city hall comprises a pilastered front of 1660 and new hall and court of 1829. Government offices in the Grecian style at a cost of nearly £6,000 were built in1869. The county jail was built in 1826 and has capacity for 337 male and 29 female prisoners. The assembly rooms have a pedimented front and are very commodious. The old theatre in Bold Lane was recently converted into a mission hall. A structure in Corn market and Victoria Street comprising the Athenaeum, the post office, and the Royal hotel, was erected in 1839 at a cost of upwards of £20,000; and presents two imposing fronts 185 and 134 feet long. The Mechanics' Institute in Wardwick , is a large building with a pedimented front. The town and county library, and the town and count y museum also occupy a large house in Wardwick. A large commodious corn exchange in connection with a large and elegant public hall was erected in 1860 and a convenient cattle market was constructed in 1861. Two excellent bridges cross the Derwent. A park of 6 acres was presented to the town by M Bass Esq. In 1867.

## Black's 1872 Tourist's Guide to Derbyshire

### Belper

Belper is a thriving and busy market town in the parish of Duffield, eight miles north of Derby. The market place is in the upper or old part of the town. Market day, Saturday, and there are several well attended and important fairs in the course of the year...In 1776 Mr Strutt erected the first cotton mill at Belper, and from this has sprung that important branch of trade which has so greatly increased the town, and has made it so busy a centre of industry.

### Chesterfield

Chesterfield, the second town in the county...is irregularly built, with narrow streets, a spacious market place and an interesting church.

## Dr Samuel Hyde, 1898

### Buxton

No English health resort surpasses Buxton in the salubrity of its situation; the beauty of its surrounding scenery; the extent, comfort and luxury of its baths; the music and other charms of its Pavilion Gardens; its opportunities for every form of indoor and outdoor recreation; its magnificent hotels and lodging houses; its cleanly roads and well-lighted streets; its ample supply of the purist water; its complete and efficient system of drainage and sewage disposal; its accessibility and splendid railway services from all parts of the kingdom. These and many other advantages, the origin and result of steady growth and development, have won for Buxton a foremost position amongst the health resorts of Europe.

## Rene Cutforth (in 'Order to View') 1969

### Swadlincote

Swadlincote is a little town in South Derbyshire. It is known locally as Swad and is a bit of a joke, being no beauty spot....I was born within a mile or two of Swad and lived there until I was 17... It was so ugly it made you laugh. The whole district was a loose assemblage of gigantic holes in the ground, some of them half a mile across, where clay was dug out for the various works which made drainpipes and teapots and crockery and jugs, bowls and chamber pots, and large hideous vases of poisonous green to put aspidistras in. Along the edges of the holes, dividing them one from another like threads in a spiders web, ran the dark grey spoil heaps, a tangle of derelict railway lines and the little black streets of houses, steeply up or down hill. No proper grass grew anywhere, but a sage green vegetation like little prehistoric Christmas trees covered the older tip heaps, and at some point on every skyline the twin wheels and black scaffolding of pit-head gear would mark the shaft of a coal mine.

# Derbyshire Personalities

## Richard Arkwright

Richard Arkwright was the inventor of the spinning frame and has been described as the father of the factory system and the first intellectual property entrepreneur. Born at Preston in 1732, the youngest of thirteen children, he was apprenticed to a barber. Later, as a travelling barber and wigmaker he came into contact with families engaged in spinning and weaving. Building on the ideas of others he succeeded in constructing a prototype roller-spinning machine which could be operated by an unskilled worker and was capable of being linked to an external source of power. He moved to Nottingham in April 1786 and entered into a partnership with two wealthy stocking manufacturers, Samuel Need and Jedediah Strutt. They financed the construction of a cotton mill at Nottingham which was driven by horse power. When this proved to be successful they decided to build a much larger water-powered cotton mill at Cromford in Derbyshire. This opened in 1771 and was a considerable commercial and technological success. In order to attract a workforce Arkwright transformed Cromford from an isolated hamlet into a thriving and well provided community with good quality houses and an extensive range of services. The first houses in North Street were constructed in 1777 and set the standard for future mill housing. Arkwright also built a school, a chapel and an inn (the Greyhound). Shops were built and in 1790 Arkwright secured the right to hold a Saturday market in the village. According to a contemporary account he gave two balls at the Greyhound to his workmen and their wives and families with a week's jubilee at the time of each ball. Arkwright also ensured that productivity remained high and his mill operatives worked two twelve-hour shifts, six days a week. Strict rules were applied to ensure that the workers remained on task and fines were imposed on any who failed in their duties. Following his success at Cromford, Arkwright went on to build more mills, either with others or independently. A second mill at Cromford was completed in 1777 followed in the next few years by others at Cressbrook, Rocester, Ashbourne, Bakewell and Wirksworth. Masson Mill was completed in 1784. All were driven by water and operated according to the same system, which he had perfected in his original mill at Cromford. His empire continued to grow and he began to amass a huge fortune. With wealth came enhanced social standing and in 1787 he was appointed High Sheriff of Derbyshire and shortly afterwards was knighted by King George III. He died on 3 August 1792, aged 60. He changed forever the way in which we work and the historian David Jeremy recently declared: 'The Arkwright system substituted capital for labour, machines for skill, factory for home and mill discipline for family work routines.'

## Olave, Lady Baden-Powell

Olave, Lady Baden-Powell, the first World Chief Guide was born at Stubbing Court, near Chesterfield in 1889. In At the age of 23 she married Sir Robert Baden-Powell, the hero of the Boer War and the founder of the Scout movement. She soon became enthusiastically involved in the Scout and Guide movement. In 1916 she was appointed County Commission for Sussex and two years later became Chief Guide. She made a significant contribution to the expansion of the Guide movement throughout the world and in 1930 she was appointed World Chief Guide, a post she held for the rest of her life. Following the death of her husband in 1941 she continued his work of expanding Scouting and Guiding across the globe. She travelled around the world five times and visited over a hundred countries. When she died in 1977, hundreds of tributes were paid from throughout the world.

## Michael Thomas Bass MP

Michael Thomas Bass MP was a member of the famous brewing family and Liberal MP for Derby from 1848 until 1883. After taking control of the company in 1827 he succeeded in increasing production and sales. Within a few years the brewery had grown to become the largest and best known in the country. In Parliament he supported free trade, low taxes and the improvement in living standards for the working class. In 1870 he supported the campaign by railwaymen for shorter working hours and in the following year he helped to establish the Associated Society of Railway Servants Union. A generous philanthropist to his adopted town, he provided Derby with a library, a museum, a School of Art, swimming baths and a recreation ground. He rejected the offer of a peerage and continued to serve in the House of Commons until shortly before his death in April 1884. His statue stands in Museum Square.

## Richard Bell MP

Richard Bell MP was one of the first two Labour Members of Parliament, and the first English one, to be elected after the formation of the formation of the Labour Representation Committee in 1900. The General Secretary of the Amalgamated Society of Railway Servants, he was elected for Derby alongside a Liberal in the 1900 General Election. His success was no doubt aided by the fact that Derby was an important railway town at this time. He was re-elected in 1906 but replaced by Jimmy Thomas in 1910. He retained his involvement in trade union affairs during his time as a Member of Parliament and in 1904 became the President of the TUC. After leaving Parliament he worked for the Employment Exchange Branch of the Board of Trade and later became Technical Officer to the Minister of Labour. He continued in local politics and served as a member of Southgate Urban District Council from 1922 until 1929. He died in 1930.

## William Bemrose

William Bemrose founded the famous Derby printing firm of that name in 1827. His first premises on the corner of Irongate and Sadlergate was attacked by rioters in 1831 after he was seen to be opposed to the Parliamentary Reform Bill. Ironically after the passing of the Reform Act he was awarded the contract to print the register of electors for the town. The coming of the railways provided a boost to the business. Bemrose printed the timetables, tickets and other stationery for the three railway companies operating out of Derby. When they were amalgamated into the Midland Railway Company in 1844, Bemrose won the combined contract for their printing. He was also one of the pioneers of travel guides and in 1847 published the Travellers Penny Guide. This success led to a move to larger premises and the acquisition of new steam powered machinery. He later pioneered lithography, colour printing and other techniques. When he died in 1880 he left behind a firm which was to grow into one of the most successful printing firms in the country.

## Catherine Booth

Catherine Booth, born Catherine Mumford at Ashbourne in 1829, was the co-founder of the Salvation Army. She married William Booth in 1855 and the two worked together to support the poor and underprivileged. In 1864 she and her husband founded the Christian Mission in London's East End. In 1878 it was renamed the Salvation Army. In the early days Catherine concentrated on raising money from wealthy supporters to fund their work with the poor. Among her achievements were the Food for Millions shops which provided cheap meals, which were for the needy. She also campaigned to improve the wages and working conditions of women, particularly in the 'sweated' industries. When she died of cancer in 1890 the Salvation Army was well established in towns and cities throughout the country.

## James Brindley

James Brindley the famous canal engineer was born 1716 in the tiny village of Wormhill near Tunstead in Derbyshire. After a successful career as a millwright he came to the attention of the Duke of Bridgewater who commissioned him to build a canal to transport coal from his mines at Worsley to Manchester. The canal was a huge engineering and commercial success. Brindley's reputation soon spread and he was soon employed to construct more canals throughput the kingdom. In 1771 he had begun work on the Chesterfield Canal but in the same year while surveying a new branch of the Trent and Mersey Canal he was caught in a storm and fell ill. He died on 27 September 1772.

*James Brindley*

## Paul Burrell

Paul Burrell, who became famous as the butler to Dianna, Princess of Wales, was born at Grassmoor, near Chesterfield in 1958. He entered Royal service as a footman at Buckingham Palace and later joined the household of Prince and Princess of Wales at Highgrove House. He served as butler to the Princess until her death in 1997. He was awarded the Royal Victoria medal in November 1997 for service to the Royal Family. Since the death of Princess Dianna he has been the subject of considerable controversy.

## Jedediah Buxton

Jedediah Buxton was a child prodigy and a mathematical genius. Born at Elmton, near Bolsover around 1707 he received only a limited education and could not read or write. His mathematical feats included calculating the area of the lordship at Elmton merely by striding over it. He was examined by the Royal Society in 1754. They were so impressed by his ability that they presented him with a generous gratuity. He predicted the date of his own death in 1772 and was buried in an unmarked grave in the churchyard at Elmton.

## Barbara Castle

Barbara Castle, the Labour MP and cabinet minister was born at Chesterfield in Derbyshire but soon moved with her parents to Yorkshire. She joined the Labour Party at an early age and after gaining a degree from Oxford University she worked as a journalist. She was elected as Member of Parliament for Blackburn in the Labour landslide of 1945 and held a number of ministerial posts in Harold Wilson's government in the 1960s. As Minister of Transport she introduced breathalyser test and as Minister of Employment later steered trade union reform through the House of Commons. In 1968 she became Secretary of State for Employment and was responsible for legislation which improved pensions and directed that child benefits should be paid directly to mothers. After losing her place in the cabinet she resigned from the House of Commons and served for ten years as a member of the European Parliament. She was created Baroness Castle of Blackburn in 1990 and continued to play an active role in politics until her death in May 2002.

## Thomas Cook

Thomas Cook the founder of the travel firm and the originator of package holidays was born at Melbourne in 1808. He organised his first excursion in 1841 when he arranged to take 504 temperance campaigners from Leicester to a rally in Loughborough. Despite some early setbacks he persevered and achieved considerable recognition by transporting thousands of people to the Great Exhibition of 1851. He later pioneered the concept of the package tour and the traveller's cheque. He became a rich man and used some of his wealth to build a row of cottages in Melbourne for poor and deserving persons. He died at Leicester in 1892.

## George Nathaniel Curzon

George Nathaniel Curzon was born at Kedleston Hall in 1859 and was educated at Eaton and Oxford. He became Member of Parliament for Oxford in 1886 and the following year began extensive travels throughout the East. His travels provided the material for three successful books but he soon began a meteoric career in politics. He became Under-Secretary for India in 1891 and for Foreign Affairs in 1895. In 1898, aged only 39 he became Viceroy for India. He introduced a number of social and political reforms but often found himself in conflict with his officials. He resigned his post in 1905 following a dispute with Lord Kitchener and returned to England. For the next few years he devoted himself to the study of art and archaeology and the question of university reform. He returned to politics as Lord Privy Seal in the coalition of 1915 and became a member of Lloyd George's War Cabinet in 1916. In 1919 he became Foreign Secretary, a post which he held until 1924. He was created a marquis in 1921. Curzon had ambitions to become Prime Minister but that ambition eluded him; probably because by this time it was generally believed that the head of government should be a member of the House of Commons. He died in 1925 and is buried in Kedleston Church.

## Erasmus Darwin

Erasmus Darwin was born near Newark in Nottinghamshire and lived for many years in Litchfield where he became a popular physician and a prominent member of the local community. He was a founder member of the Lunar Society and a friend of some of the greatest scientists, engineers and thinkers of the time. He was probably the most notable and visionary polymath of his age and wrote of such things as air travel, canal lifts, copying machines, evolutionary theory, steam carriages, submarines, water closets and female emancipation! He moved to Derby in 1781, following his second marriage to Elizabeth Pole. At his home in Full Street he sank an artesian well and constructed a manually operated ferry across the Derwent. He founded the Derby Philosophical Society and established a medical practice which charged patients only what they could afford to pay. He later opened a clinic and dispensary to treat and eradicate smallpox, which was funded by subscribers and staffed by local physicians and pharmacists in rotation. It was during his time at Derby that he published some of his most famous works including, Zoonomia, or the Laws of Organic Life, which began to explore some of the issues relating to the theory of evolution. He died in April 1802 at Breadsall Priory, near Derby.

## William Duesbury

William Duesbury was the founder of the company which eventually became Royal Crown Derby. In 1769, together with John Heath a local banker, he established a china factory at Nottingham Road in Derby. Under Duesbury's management the business prospered and its figures and tableware gained a national reputation. Products included beautifully decorated dinner, dessert, tea and coffee services, which were hand painted by talented artist. Figures produced at the factory included depictions of royalty and national heroes as well as well known actors and authors. In 1769 Duesbury was able to purchase the Chelsea China Factory and a few years later the

Bow Manufactury was also acquired and closed down. As a consequence, Duesbury was able to extend the range of his products and improve their quality. Originally Duesbury sold his wares through individual sales at fashionable venues but in 1773 premises in Bedford Street, Covent Garden were leased as a warehouse and showroom. This allowed members of the nobility and other wealthy customers to consult pattern books and place their orders. It also led to the patronage of King George III who gave the company permission to incorporate the royal crown into the markings on his porcelain and this became known as Royal Crown Derby. Duesbury died in 1786 but his successors have continued to produce some of the best china in the world. The factory at Osmaston Road, Derby still counts members of the royal family among its customers.

## John Flamsteed

John Flamsteed, the first Astronomer Royal, was born at Derby in August 1646. He was educated at Derby Grammar School but he suffered from a serious rheumatic condition which forced him to continue his studies at home. Here he constructed a quadrant to measure the sun's approximate distance from the Earth and accurately calculated the solar eclipses of 1666 and 1668. He spent some time at Cambridge University but it seems that he never took up permanent residence. He continued to make astronomical observations and in March 1675 Charles II appointed him the first Astronomer Royal. He devoted the rest of his life to observing and making meticulous records for a star catalogue which was published some years after his death. It contained details of 2,935 stars to much greater accuracy than in any previously published work. John Flamstead School at Denby is named after him and he also is commemorated in Flamsteed crater on the moon.

## John Lombe

John Lombe achieved fame as an industrial spy and the man responsible for building the first silk mill in this country. The half-brother of a wealthy silk merchant, he was despatched to Livorno to discover learn the secrets of the Italian silk manufacturers and introduce their machinery into this country. Working secretly at night he drew diagrams of the Italian machines and smuggled them back to this country in bales of silk. Back in Derby he worked with his half brother (Thomas Lombe) to replicate the machines and build this country's first silk mill. This is also regarded by many to be Britain's first factory

## Florence Nightingale

Florence Nightingale is regarded as the founder of modern nursing. Her family came from Lea Hall, near Matlock in Derbyshire. Despite their protests she trained to be a nurse at Kaiserworth and Paris and in 1853 became the superintendant of a hospital for invalid women in London. The following year, following the outbreak of the Crimean War she was placed in charge of a group of 38 women and sent to manage a military hospital at Scutari where she did a great deal to improve conditions. She became a popular heroine and on her return served on a Royal Commission which succeeded in improving army medical conditions. In 1860 with a fund of £45,000 raised by public subscription she was able to establish a school for nursing at St Thomas' Hospital, London. Her *Notes on Nursing* (1859) and *Notes on Hospitals* (1863) did much to improve standards in hospitals as well as raising the status of nursing. In 1907 she became the first woman to be awarded the Order of Merit but died three years later on 13 August 1910, aged ninety.

## Sir Maurice Oldfield

Sir Maurice Oldfield was a famous spymaster who was born at Over Haddon in 1915. He was educated at Bakewell Grammar School from where he won a scholarship to Manchester University. He served in the Intelligence Corps during the Second World War and rose to the rank of lieutenant colonel. He joined the Secret Intelligence Service in 1946 and was soon recognised as a high-flyer. He held a number of posts in different parts of the world before becoming deputy head of MI6 in 1965. He was appointed as C (Head of MI6) ten years later. He received a number of honours during his career and was knighted following his retirement in 1974. He returned to the intelligence services in 1979 when he became co-ordinator of security and intelligence in Northern Ireland. He was forced to resign after only a year because of ill health. He died in March 1981 and was buried in the family plot at Over Haddon.

## Joseph Paxton

Joseph Paxton became Head Gardener at Chatsworth House in 1826. The Duke of Devonshire was impressed by his work and his ideas and gradually added to his responsibilities. Under Paxton's care Chatsworth became the most famous garden in England. He transformed the Chatsworth landscape by altering the flow of streams, creating lakes and transplanting dozens of mature trees. With the help of Derby architect, John Robertson, he relocated and rebuilt the neighbouring village of Edensor. He established a rockery and an arboretum and built over twenty glasshouses to house the Dukes collection of exotic plants. Two of his most spectacular projects, however, were the construction of the Emperor Fountain and the building of the Great Conservatory, which at the time was the largest glass building in the world. He went on to use the experience gained in this project to submit designs for the building of the Crystal Palace to house the Great Exhibition of 1851. In recognition of this Paxton was awarded a knighthood. He continued to contribute to horticultural publications and was involved in the design of a number of houses and gardens. In 1854 he was elected as a Member of Parliament, a post he filled until his death in June 1865. His obituary in the Times stated that Paxton 'rose from the ranks to be the greatest gardener of his time, the founder of a new style of architecture, and a man of genius, who devoted it to objects in the highest and noblest service possible'.

## Samuel Plimsol

Samuel Plimsol was elected as a Liberal MP for Derby in 1868. He campaigned passionately and tirelessly to improve safety conditions for merchant seamen. Ships were frequently over-loaded and sometimes over-insured and these 'coffin ships' as they were known, were responsible for the deaths of many sailors. As a result of his campaigning the government was eventually forced to pass a Merchant Shipping Act which gave stringent powers to the Board of Trade to inspect merchant vessels. The mark that indicated the safe limit to indicated the safe limit to which a ship might be loaded became known as the 'Plimsol Line'. After retiring from Parliament he served for a number of years as honorary president of the National Sailors and Firemen's Union. He died in 1898 and is commemorated in a monument on the Victoria Embankment, London.

## Charles Rolls

Charles Rolls was the co-founder of the Rolls-Royce Company which manufactured motor cars and later aero engines. Born in 1877 he had an adventurous spirit and a flair for engineering. He won a number of driving trials and set a world land speed record at Phoenix Park, Dublin in 1900. In 1904 he was introduced to Henry Royce, who owned an engineering company in Manchester. Under a contract signed in the same year it was agreed that C S Rolls and Co would sell all the cars made by Royce Ltd. These early cars won a reputation for reliability and luxury and their success led to the formation of Rolls-Royce Ltd in 1906. In 1908 the company moved to new premises in Derby. Despite his company responsibilities Rolls continued to take part in a number of exciting and dangerous activities. In 1910 he became the first aviator to fly non-stop across the Channel and back. Later the same year he was killed when his aeroplane crashed during an airshow near Bournemouth. His was the first recorded aviation death in Britain.

## Henry Royce

Henry Royce was the co-founder of the Rolls-Royce Company. He established an electrical and mechanical engineering company in Manchester in 1844 and made his first car in 1904. He was introduced to the Hon Charles Rolls in the same year and in 1906 the Roll-Royce Company was founded. In 1908 the company moved to new premises at Derby but only two year later Rolls died in a flying accident. Royce was very much the mechanical genius behind the success of the company and his cars won a reputation for total reliability. At the outset of the First World War he reluctantly agreed to manufacture under license a number of Renault V8 aero engines. Believing that his company was capable of producing a much better engine, he set about designing the first Rolls-Royce engine, christened the Eagle. This was used to power a number of British aircraft including the FE 2 d fighter and the Vickers Vimy bomber. After the war Royce concentrated on aero engine design and in the 1930s his R engines were later modified to become the famous Merlin which powered the Spitfires and Hurricanes of the Battle of Britain. Henry Royce died on 22 April 1933.

## George Sorocold

George Sorocold was one of this country's earliest hydraulic engineers. Born in Derby in 1668, he was responsible for the town's first water supply which utilised a water wheel to pump supplies through four miles of elm pipes. He was responsible for similar schemes in other parts of the country. Other work included the improvement of drainage systems for mines, the design of atmospheric engines and projects to improve river navigations. His most impressive project was the design and construction of the Derby Silk Mill for John and Thomas Lombe. By the time of his death, around 1738, he was widely regarded as one of the country's finest engineers.

## George Stephenson

George Stephenson the famous railway engineer lived at Chesterfield for much of his life. Born in Northumberland in 1781 his achievements included the building of the Stockton and Darlington Railway and the much more significant Liverpool–Manchester Railway in 1830, for which he designed the Rocket locomotive. He came to Derbyshire to supervise the building of the North Midland Railway and discovered rich seems of coal and iron deposits while digging the Clay Cross Tunnel. He formed a company to exploit these finds later and moved to Tapton House near Chesterfield. His company built houses for the tunnel navvies and later, as they sank colliery workings, for the miners and their families. Stephenson was a benevolent employer and his company also provided schools, shops, chapels and a Mechanics Institute for his workforce. He died in 1848 and is buried in Trinity Church, Chesterfield.

*Statue of George Stevenson outside Chesterfield Railway Station*

## Jedediah Strutt

Jedediah Strutt was a textile manufacturer and the owner of cotton mills at Belper and elsewhere in Derbyshire. In 1758 he secured a patent for a machine to manufacture ribbed stockings. The 'Derby Rib' was a huge success and earned a fortune for Strutt which he was able to use to develop a substantial hosiery business and provide the financial support for Arkwright's water-powered spinning mill at Cromford. The two men later went their own ways and Strutt went on to develop mill communities at Belper and Milford. Strutt and his sons built houses, schools and chapels for their workers and established farms to provide cheap food and milk. Other benefits included a sick club, a dancing room, an orchestra and a choir. The Strutts forbade corporal punishment and instead relied on a system of fines or forfeits to maintain good order and productivity in their mills. Jedediah Strutt died in 1797 and is buried in the Unitarian Chapel he had built in Belper.

## Percy Toplis

Percy Toplis achieved fame when his life was dramatised in the TV series *The Monocled Mutineer*. Born at Chesterfield in 1896, he soon slipped into a life of petty crime. He joined the army in 1915 and claimed to have played a leading art in the British Army mutiny at Etaples. After the war he returned to a life of crime. He frequently posed as an army officer and was involved in forgery, fraud, black-marketeering and eventually murder. He was killed in a police ambush in Cumberland on 6 June 1920.

## Jimmy Thomas MP

Jimmy Thomas MP was Member of Parliament for Derby from 1910 until 1936. An official of the Amalgamated Society of Railway Servants, he succeeded Richard Bell as the Labour MP for Derby in 1910. Despite being elected to Parliament he continued to play a leading role in the trade union movement. He led the successful national railway strike of 1919 and in the following year became President of the TUC. He was highly regarded by his constituents and in 1929 was made an Honorary Freeman of Derby. His Parliamentary career ended in disgrace in 1936 when, as a cabinet minister, he was found guilty of passing budget secrets to a friend and another MP. He was obliged to resign his seat and leave public life. He died in London in January 1949.

## Sir Barnes Neville Wallis

Sir Barnes Neville Wallis was born at Ripley in 1887. He was famously responsible for designing the bouncing bomb which was used in the Dam Busters raid on Germany in 1943. He was also responsible for the design of the Wellington Bomber using the innovative geodetic style of construction. He later developed a number of deep penetration 'earthquake' bombs which were used to attack German strategic targets such as submarine pens and V2 rocket launch sites. After the war he worked for the British Aircraft Corporation on the design of hypersonic aircraft and swing wing technology. He was knighted in 1968 but continued to be involved in a variety of projects until his death in 1979. A pub in Ripley is named in his honour.

## Vivienne Westwood

Vivienne Westwood was born at Glossop in 1941. She was educated at Glossop Grammar School and later worked as a primary school teacher. Her life changed when she met Malcolm McClaren, the manager of the Sex Pistols. They set up a shop in London and become known as the leading creators of punk fashion. Following her split with McClaren she continued to design clothes but began to move from street fashion towards haute couture. She was named Designer of the year in 1990 and 1991 and in 2004 the Victoria and Albert Museum held a retrospective of her work. An OBE was followed by a DBE in the 2006 New Year's Honours.

# John Whitehurst

John Whitehurst was a famous clockmaker and scientist. Born in Congleton in 1713, he set up in business at Derby around 1736. He constructed a turret clock for the town's new guildhall and in recognition the corporation enrolled him as a burgess which gave him freedom to trade in the town. He soon won a reputation both for his ingenuity and the quality and accuracy of his work. He was a founder member of the Lunar Society and counted Matthew Boulton and Benjamin Franklin among his friends. He also had a keen interest in geology and in 1778 published An Enquiry into the Original State and Formation of the Earth; Deduced from Facts about the Laws of Nature. Following his appointment as Stamper of the Money Weights at the Royal Mint he moved to London where he died in 1788.

# Quote, Unquote

**Barnes Wallis (Inventor of the 'bouncing bomb')**

'There is a natural opposition among men to anything they have not thought of themselves.'

**Brian Clough (Manager of Derby County FC)**

'I wouldn't say that I was the best manager in the world. But I was in the top one.'

'I like my women to be feminine, not sliding into tackles and covered in mud.'

'The River Trent is lovely, I know this because I have walked on it for 18 years.'

'They say Rome wasn't built in a day, but I wasn't on that particular job.'

'Don't send me flowers when I'm dead. If you like me, send them while I'm alive.'

**Tony Benn, MP for Chesterfield**

'All war represents a failure of democracy.'

'If you file your waste-paper basket for fifty years, you have a public library.'

'A faith is something you die for, a doctrine is something you kill for. There is all the difference in the world.'

'The House of Lords is the British Outer Mongolia for retired politicians.'

'It is wholly wrong to blame Marx for what was done in his name, as it is to blame Jesus for what was done in his.'

**William George Spencer Cavendish, 6th Duke of Devonshire (speaking at the time of the 1832 Reform Act)**

'The members of the aristocracy have sometimes been considered in an unfavourable light by the people. For much of this they are indebted to the manner in which the present constitution, Parliament has enabled them to interfere and dictate in their representation...Let them stand on their merit, and I have no fear that the people of England will be unjust to the aristocracy of England, united by mutual kind feelings and good office and not by close boroughs and mock representation.'

**Sir Henry Royce (One of the founders of Rolls-Royce)**

'Strive for perfection in everything that we do. Take the best that exists and make it better. When it does not exist, design it.'

'Accept nothing nearly right or good enough.'

'Whatever is rightly done – however humble – is noble.'

'I have only one regret, that I have not worked hard enough.'

**Dame Ellen MacArthur (World renowned yachtswoman)**

'People often ask me if I miss the sea. Sure I do – but when I'm at sea I always miss the fields and farms so I think I take Derbyshire a little bit less for granted than I might otherwise do.'

'You don't fear for your life in the middle of a storm, you can't really afford to.'

'Never in my life before have I experienced such beauty and fear at the same time. Ten icebergs so far today...'

**Florence Nightingale (The nursing pioneers who lived at Lea in Derbyshire)**
'It may seem a strange principle to enunciate as the very first requirement in a Hospital that it should do the sick no harm.'

'The first possibility of rural cleanliness lies in water supply.'

'The only English patients I have ever known refuse tea, have been in typhus cases; and the first sign of their getting better was their craving again for tea.'

'I attribute my success to this – I never gave or took any excuse.'

'Drink and dress seem to be great barriers against civilisation in these parts.'

'The people do not even understand their own interests: they will live in wretched quarters, perhaps even seven in a family and a lodger in two miserable bedrooms – happy too if grown-up sons and daughters are in the same bedroom and even (up into teens) in the same bed... What wonder if immorality is rampant.'

**Erasmus Darwin, the scientist, poet and philosopher who founded the Derby Philosophical Association**

'A fool is a man who never tried an experiment in his life.'

'It is often hazardous to marry an heiress as she may not infrequently be the last of a diseased family.'

'(Retirement) is a dangerous experiment and generally ends in either drunkenness or hypochondria.'

**Joseph Paxton, Gardner at Chatsworth House and designer of the Crystal Palace**

'I left London by the Comet coach for Chesterfield, and arrived at Chatsworth at half-past four in the morning of 9 May. As no person was to be seen at that early hour, I got over the old greenhouse gate by the old covered way, explored the pleasure grounds, and looked around the outside of the house. I then went down to the kitchen garden, scaled the outside wall, and saw to the whole of the place, set the men to work there at six o'clock; then returned to Chatsworth and got Thomas Weldon to play me the waterworks, and afterwards went to breakfast with poor, dear Mrs Gregory and her niece; the latter fell in love with me and I with her, and thus completed my first morning's work at Chatsworth before nine o' clock.'

'No occupation is more worthy of an intelligent mind, than the study of nature and natural objects and whether we labour to investigate the structure and function of the human system, whether we direct our attention to the classification and habits of the animal kingdom, or prosecute our researches in the more pleasing and varied field of vegetable life, we shall constantly find some new object to attract our attention, some fresh beauties to excite our imagination and some previously undiscovered source of gratification and delight.'

'Botany – the science of the vegetable kingdom, is one of the most attractive, most useful and most extensive departments of human knowledge. It is, above every other, the science of beauty.'

**Jeremiah Brandreth, the leader of the Pentrich Revolution composed the following verse to encourage his followers**

Every man his skill must try,
He must turn out and not deny;
No bloody soldier must he dread,
He must turn out and fight for bread;
The time has come you plainly see,
The government opposed must be.

**Charles Markham, (Managing Director of the Staveley Coal & Iron Company )**

'No boy should be allowed to go to work that cannot read and write – and if he can read and write, I think that the rest of the education should be done in great measure by himself ... with the facilities of a cheap press, and the use of libraries about the country, if he has any emulation in him he will rise to the surface in the present day.'

## Vivienne Westwood, Fashion Designer

'I am attracted to people who make this effort in knowing what suits them – they are individual and stylish.'

'My son has followed fashion since he was a punk. He and I agree that fashion is about sex.'

'Feminists wish women to seem like men. They are not men.'

'Fashion is very important. It is life enhancing and like everything that gives pleasure, it is worth doing well.'

'It is not possible for a man to be elegant without a touch of femininity.'

## Edwina Currie, Member of Parliament

'The strongest piece of advice I would give any young woman is: Don't screw around and don't smoke.'

'Governments should not start running morality campaigns. Governments are no better than the people who elect them.'

'Business should stand or fall on their own two feet.'

'One wants to mutter deeply that apart from having two good legs I also have two good degrees and it is just possible that I do know what I am talking about.'

## Thomas Hobbs (Philosopher and tutor to William Cavendish)

'Reading is a pernicious habit, it destroys all originality of sentiment.'

'It is not wisdom but Authority that makes a law.'

'All generous minds have a horror of what are commonly called 'Facts'. They are the brute beasts of the intellectual domain.'

'Such is the nature of men that howsoever they may acknowledge many others to be more witty or more eloquent, or more learned, yet they will hardly believe there be many so wise as themselves.'

'Curiosity is the lust of the mind.'

'Leisure is the mother of philosophy'.

### George Stephenson, Railway Engineer

'The rage for railroads is so great that many will be laid in parts where they will not pay.'

'I should say that no locomotive ought to exceed 40 miles per hour.'

'The principal upon which a safety lamp might be constructed I stated to several persons long before Sir Humphrey Davy came into this part of the country.' (Stephenson invented a miners safety lamp similar to the better known Davy Lamp.)

### Catherine Booth, Co-founder of the Salvation Army

'If we are to better the future we must disturb the present.'

'I don't believe in any religion apart from doing the will of God.'

'We are made for larger ends than Earth can encompass. Oh, let us be true to our destiny.'

### Timothy Dalton, the actor who played James Bond in a number of films

'You can't relate to a superhero or a superman, but you can relate with a real man who in times of crisis draws forth some extraordinary quality from within himself and triumphs, but only after a struggle. Real courage is what faces you and knowing how you face it.'

**George Nathanial Curzon**

'The Government of India is a mighty and miraculous machine for doing nothing.'

'I hesitate to say what the function of the modern journalist may be but I imagine that they do not exclude the intelligent anticipation of the facts even before they occur.'

'Gentlemen do not take soup at luncheon.'

**Benny Rothman, one of the leaders of the Kinder Tresspass**

'We ramblers, after a hard week's work, and life in smoky towns and cities, go out rambling on weekend for relaxation, for a breath of fresh air and for a little sunshine. And we find, when we go out that the finest rambling country is closed to us. Because of certain individuals who shoot for about ten days per annum we are forced to walk on muddy crowded paths, and denied the pleasure of enjoying of the utmost the countryside.'

**Sir George Crewe, Squire of Calke Abbey, 1815-32**

'London is to me a hateful place, unless I had a comfortable quiet house of my own, where I could be surrounded with my usual occupations.'

'It (the waltz) is indeed a mode of dancing which cannot be practiced without a violation of modesty, or at least a profanation of female delicacy which is highly revolting to every well-regulated mind. The close contact in which the persons of the parties must necessarily come is such which a modest woman cannot allow.'

# Notable Towns

## Alfreton

Alfreton is a small town within the Amber Valley district with a population of around 8,000. The district council maintains an office in the town where local residents can pay their council tax and obtain advice and information on a range of council services. Formerly a mining town, most of the population now find employment in light industry, warehousing, retail and service industries. The Thornton's Chocolate factory is located just outside the town on the site of the former Swanwick Colliery. It was officially opened by the Queen on 15 March 1985. The town is a popular with local shoppers and retains a market hall with around thirty stalls selling a wide range of goods including fresh fruit and vegetables. A number of national chain stores have branches in the town including Boots, W H Smith and Argos. There are also a number of charity shops and independent traders. A large Tesco store on the edge of the town attracts shoppers from the surrounding area. The town centre has number of pubs and restaurants as well as fast food outlets. The parish church of St Martin is mainly a 19th-century structure but parts date from the 13th-century The town has some fine 18th-century buildings including Alfreton Hall (now a wedding venue and conference centre) and the George Hotel. Also of interest is the town's historical lock-up. Built around 1820 it contains two individual cells, one for men and the other for women. Alfreton has good transport links. The A38 skirts the town and Junction 28 of the M1 is only a few miles away. Alfreton Railway Station provides regular services to London, Liverpool, Leeds and Nottingham. The town has excellent recreational and leisure facilities including a library, leisure centre, swimming pool and golf course as well as a number of parks and play areas. The local football club, Alfreton Town FC play in the Conference National division of the Football League. Secondary Education is provided by Alfreton Grange Arts College (previously known as Mortimer Wilson School) and there is also an Adult Community Education Centre in the town.

## Ashbourne

Ashbourne is a historic Georgian market town on the southern edge of the Peak District. With a population of around 10,000, it attracts large numbers of holiday-makers and day trippers from the surrounding areas and further afield. Dating from Saxon times, Ashbourne is mentioned in the Domesday Book as Esseburn when a church and a priest were recorded. The town contains a number of historic buildings including the 13th-century parish church, a Tudor grammar school, and elegant Georgian town houses, almshouses and coaching inns. Ashbourne was first granted a market charter in 1257 and the cobbled market place still hosts a traditional outdoor market every Thursday and Saturday throughout the year. There are a number of independent retailers within the town. These include deli-catessens, gift shops, antique shops, butchers and fishmongers, art galleries and a gunsmith. The town is also served by a number of supermarkets. Ashbourne has a number of restaurants and tea rooms and in 2005 became a Fairtrade Town committed to increasing the range of fairtrade products available in the town. The town is also well known for its gingerbread. According to local legend French prisoners held in the town during the Napoleonic Wars gave the recipe to a local baker. Ashbourne is nationally known for its annual two-day Royal Shrovetide Football Match which is held on Shrove Tuesday and Ash Wednesday each year. The game is played by two teams, the Up'pards and the Down'ards over two eight hour periods. There a few rules and the game has been described as moving brawl which continues through the roads of the town, across fields and even along the bed of the local river. Not surprisingly many shops close for the day and board up their windows!

## Bakewell

Bakewell is a small market town in the Derbyshire Dales and is the only town located within the Peak District National Park. It's population is only about 4,000 but it attracts large numbers of domestic and international visitors during the summer months. The town stands on the River Wye which is spanned by a 13th-century five-arched bridge A market was established here in 1254 and a street market is still held on a Monday. The old market hall, dating from the late 17th-century is now an information centre for the Peak District National Park, a major employer in the town. The town also contains a number of other interesting and historic buildings. The Old House, originally a 16th-century yeoman house, was restored by the Bakewell Local History Society and now houses a museum of early domestic life. The parish church of All Saints was founded in 920 though most of the building dates from the 13th-century. A large and elegant Coaching Inn, the Rutland Arms still attracts visitors to the town and it was here that the famous Bakewell Pudding originated. Agriculture remains the town's most important activity and the Cattle Market is one of the largest in the county. The Bakewell Agricultural Show, one of the largest agricultural shows in the country, is held on the first Wednesday and Thursday in August at the Bakewell Showground. It regularly attracts around 65,000 visitors. The town is perhaps best known for the Bakewell Pudding. It is still sold in the town and a number of shops lay claim to the original recipe. The town has a small hospital, a library, a leisure centre and a secondary school but for other services and entertainment people travel to Chesterfield, Derby or Sheffield. Bus companies operate regular services to all these places.

## Belper

Belper is a small town in the Derwent Valley. It is administratively part of Amber Valley District Council and has a population of around 20,000. It is believed that the name 'Belper' is a corruption of Beaurepaire, meaning beautiful retreat. A local hunting lodge of this name is mentioned in charters dated 1139 and 1272. St John's Chapel, originally consecrated as the Chapel of St Thomas in 1250 still stands and is believed to be the oldest building in the town. Nail making was an important 'cottage industry' in the town for many years but in the 18th and 19th centuries the Strutts constructed a number of textile mills in the town. They also built houses for their workers as well as a school, a church and a chapel. The town was also an important centre of the hosiery industry and large numbers of framework knitters worked in and around the town. The coming of the railway in 1840 brought further prosperity and allowed local people to commute to Derby. The textile and hosiery industry remained the principal source of employment until the latter years of the 20th-century although iron founding and engineering companies were also established in the town. The main shopping area is centred around King Street and provides the usual mix of independent traders, chain stores, banks, cafes and charity shops! The recently refurbished Ritz Cinema is also situated here. The town also has three supermarkets. Belper still has its own railway station on the Midland Main Line which provides a regular service to Derby and Matlock. The town is also served by regular bus services to Derby and surrounding towns and villages as well as longer routes to London and Manchester. The major operator is Trent Barton, which operates from a garage in the centre of the town. Secondary education is provided by Belper School and Sixth Form Centre which has about 1,400 pupils on roll. It is situated adjacent to a well equipped leisure centre and swimming pool. Belper Town football Club, known as the Nailers, have a home ground at Christchurch Meadow and currently play in the Northern Premier League. A local newspaper, *The Belper News*, is published weekly.

## Buxton

Buxton lies in the north-west of the county, only three miles from the county border with Cheshire. The town's importance as a spa dates back to the Romans who named the town Aquae Armentiae. For centuries it continued to be visited by people hoping to benefit from the curative powers of the warm springs. The town largely grew in importance in the late 17th-century when it was developed by the Dukes of Devonshire, with a second resurgence with the coming of the railways. Its hey-day as a spa is reflected in a number of significant buildings including the Old Hall Hotel, the Crescent, the Royal Devonshire Hospital Building, the Pump Room and the Opera House. Today Buxton is an important tourist and cultural centre with a population in excess of 20,000. The annual, Buxton Festival features performances by some of the best orchestra and ballet companies in the country. The Gilbert and Sullivan Festival attracts entries from both Britain and abroad. The week long Four-Four Time Music Festival is held in February and features a variety of rock, pop, folk, blues jazz and world music. Buxton Museum and Art Gallery contains an interesting collection of exhibits including archaeological finds and 19th and 20th-century paintings. There are a number of sports clubs based in the town catering for football, cricket, rugby and hockey. In addition the Buxton also has two golf courses. The town has a wide variety of shops. The pedestrian-friendly Spring Gardens offers a combination of familiar high street names and local specialist retailers whilst the Cavendish Arcade is a unique and vibrant mix of crafts, boutiques, books and chocolate! Officially the highest market town in Britain, markets are held here on Tuesday and Saturday. There is also a monthly farmers market in the Pavilion Gardens and an annual Continental Market which attracts traders from across Europe. Whilst tourism makes an important contribution to the local economy; retail, quarrying and higher education also provide employment. The Devonshire Campus of the University of Derby is housed in the Devonshire Royal Hospital building and provides courses in areas such as hospitality, sport and outdoor recreation, public services and events management. The local railway station is managed and served by Northern Rail and provides services to Manchester Picadilly and beyond. A weekly tabloid newspaper, *The Buxton Advertiser*, circulates in and around the town. Buxton is twinned with Oignies in France and Bad Nauheim in Germany.

## Chapel-en-le-Frith

Chapel-en-le-Frith is located in the north of the county. Known as the 'Capital of the Peaks' it lies just off the A6 between Buxton and Stockport. During the Middle Ages it was an important administrative and market centre within the Royal Forest of the Peak. By the 18th-century trade in livestock and wool had become so significant that as many as eleven fairs were being held annually in addition to the weekly markets. This trade declined during the 19th-century as a consequence of the increasing use of railways for the movement of cattle. Today the town's old cobbled market place contains a number of interesting features including a set of stocks, a horse trough constructed to celebrate Queen Victoria's Diamond Jubilee and a recently restored war memorial. Most of the shops are clustered around the market place and along the busy main street. In addition to the usual chain stores there are a number of independent traders. The town also has two supermarkets. The town's largest and most widely known employer is Ferodo Ltd which makes friction materials for the motor industry. The company was founded in 1897 by Herbert Frood, a local man who had noticed the problems faced by local carters on the steep hills in the area. He patented a brake block made from woven cloth impregnated with resin, and from this developed a whole range of friction materials that are used by the motor industry today. The town has a population of around 33,000 and is well provided with a range of services and amenities including a library, post office, health centre, leisure centre and secondary school. Chapel-en-le-Frith has a wide range of thriving community organisations including football and cricket clubs, a morris dancing side, a WI, choirs and a town band. The town still retains a railway station which is located about a mile from the centre of the town. This provides frequent services to Buxton and Manchester. A regular bus service links the town with Buxton, Stockport and Manchester Airport.

## Chesterfield

Chesterfield is the second largest settlement in Derbyshire with a population of over 100,000 people. It was for many years a substantial market town but by the 19th-century it had grown into an important industrial town with iron works, pottery, coal mining and heavy engineering all providing employment. Chesterfield is today a confident and thriving town with a wide range of educational, sporting, cultural and entertainment facilities. The Pomegranate Theatre stages a wide range of amateur and professional productions and a number of famous actors began their career here. The Winding Wheel is the town's principal live music venue, whilst a multi-screen cinema shows all the latest films. Chesterfield has a number of parks and open spaces including *Queens Park*. This was opened in 1887 to commemorate the Golden Jubilee of Queen Victoria but has recently been restored. Facilities include a cafe, boating lake and miniature railway. The Queen's Park Leisure Centre, opened in 1987 has an indoor swimming pool, a fitness centre and a number of indoor courts which can be used for a variety of activities. For those who prefer to enjoy sport as a spectator Chesterfiled Town Football Club play at a modern stadium on the edge of the town. Chesterfield still has its own railway station. This was extensively modernised in 2005 and a statue of the railway pioneer George Stephenson was placed outside the main entrance in the same year. There are regular services to a number of destinations including Sheffield, Derby and London. Local bus services are provided by a number of different companies including Stagecoach, Trent Barton, TM travel, and Hulley's whilst National Express operates services to and through Chesterfield to a wide variety of destinations nationwide. Because of its location Chesterfield lies within the catchment area of Radio Sheffield. The local newspaper is the *Derbyshire Times* which serves a wide area including Chesterfield, Alfreton, Matlock, Bolsover, Shirebrook and Clay Cross. Chesterfield College was created in 1984 following the merger of Chesterfield College of Technology with the College of Art and Design. In 1993 it became the first Associate College of Sheffield University and now offers foundation degrees in a number of subjects including construction, electrical and electronic engineering and early years education. The town also boasts an award winning public library and a museum and art gallery.

*A view of Chesterfield*

## Clay Cross

Clay Cross has a population of around 9,000 residents and is located a few miles south of Chesterfield. Until 1974 it had a separate urban district council. Today it is part of North East Derbyshire. Coal mining was once the major source of employment in the town but in recent years new businesses have been attracted to Coney Green Business Park and Danesmoor Industrial Estate. The town centre is well served by a number of independent shops and is currently undergoing a £22 million redevelopment programme which has so far included a new bus station, a supermarket and a relief road. Other developments have included the building of the new Sharley Park Community Primary School. Despite its small size the town also boasts a library, a leisure centre and a community hospital. A small market is also held in the town every Saturday from 9.00 am until 1.00 pm. Clay Cross has excellent transport links to Chesterfield and Derby via the A61 and with Sheffield and Nottingham via the M1. The railway station closed in 1967 but there have been suggestions that a new station should be built here at some point in the future. The town has its own parish council which is responsible for a social centre and the cemetery, as well as providing support for a number of local voluntary organisations. It has also produced an audio tour which guides people round some of the local places of interest including 19th-century colliery housing, the Board School and St Bartholemew's Church. An annual gala provides fun for all the family with a variety of stalls, brass bands, demonstrations by local organisations, refreshments and a fun fair!

## Derby

Derby is the only city in the whole county and has a population of around 234,000. The Romans established a fort here and a civilian settlement. The Saxons and Vikings lived here and by the middle Ages it was a flourishing town, important for ironworking and the woollen industry. By the Georgian era a number of county families kept elegant town houses in the town. Pickford's house and other dwellings in Friargate are good examples of these. The town grew rapidly in the 19th-century with the arrival of the railways and the establishment of a number of engineering firms. By the 20th-century the major employers were Rolls-Royce, the Locomotivive and Carriage and Wagon Works, Qualcast, Leys Malleable Castings and British Celanese. Today only Rolls-Royce remains. Many people are employed in health, local government and the service sector of the economy but new industries such as information technology, financial services and food production have been attracted here in recent years. The town grew rapidly during the 20th-century and its boundaries were extended in 1901 and 1928. A further enlargement in 1968 took in most of the surrounding suburban areas. In 1977 as part of the Queen's Jubilee celebrations Derby became a city. *The Derby Telegraph* is the city's daily newspaper and BBC Radio Derby attracts thousands of listeners from Derby and the surrounding areas. The city attracts shoppers from the surrounding towns and villages. The Westfield Centre, incorporating the former Eagle Centre is the city's main indoor shopping mall. It opened in 2007 and contains a food court, multi-screen cinema and a theatre. Over 200 stores are gathered here. The Eagle Centre Market is adjacent though in recent years it has suffered a decline in trade. The town also has a separate market hall which opened in 1866. Elsewhere in the city the Cathedral Quarter (Derby's first Business Improvement District) provides a different shopping experience with a variety of independent traders, pubs and restaurants. The city is well provided with facilities for further and higher education. Derby College has a number of campuses in the city and provides a wide range of technical and vocational courses as well as A level studies. The University of Derby, created in 1992 provides degree courses in a wide range of subjects including the arts, business, science and technology. Nottingham University is also involved in medical training. In 2003 it opened a graduate entry medical school at Derby Royal Hospital. Its schools of nursing and midwifery, previously based at the London Road Community Hospital, were relocated here in 2012. Derby is very much a multi-cultural city with around 15% of its population belonging to a range of ethnic backgrounds. Professional sport is well represented in the city. Derbyshire County Cricket Club play most of their matches here and Derby County Football Club play their home matches at the Pride Park Stadium. The city has a large number of parks and open spaces. The first public Park in Britain, the Arboretum, was opened in 1840 and has recently been renovated. Markeaton Park is the most visited open space in the city and contains a children's play area, boating lake and miniature railway. Allestree Park and Darley Park also provide a wide range of opportunities for relaxation and leisure. Derby has excellent transport links. The railway station, just outside the centre of the city, provides regular services to London, Leicester, Sheffield, Chesterfield and other major cities. A new bus station in the centre of the city was opened in 2010.

## Dronfield

Dronfield is a small town in North East Derbyshire with a population of around 23,000. It is situated midway between Sheffield to the north and Chesterfield to the south. The Peak District National Park lies only three miles to the west. The town contains many old and interesting buildings in the High Street and Church Street area. One of the most unusual is the Peel Monument which was built in 1854. It stands as a tribute to Sir Robert Peel and celebrates his repeal of the Corn Laws in 1846. Other significant buildings include the 12th-century parish church of St John the Baptist and Dronfield Manor. Dronfield's growth in the 18th and 19th centuries was based on coal mining although the town also benefitted from trade with the lead mining and grit-stone industries in the Peak District. Today the town serves as a dormitory community for Chesterfield and Sheffield but the Calleywhite Lane Industrial estate on the edge of the town provides premises for a wide range of manufacturing, technological and distribution companies. Dronfield Civic Centre hosts the majority of the town's shops including one of the supermarkets. It also houses the library, town hall and health centre. Market day is on Thursday when a variety of stalls are erected in the surrounding area. The more recently opened Forge Shopping Centre also provides a wide range of shops and services. As its name suggests the building in which it is housed was originally a forge and its history is told in the storyboards on display in the Church Street entrance. Dronfield Sports and Leisure Centre is also located in the centre of the town. It contains two pools, a fitness suite and a sports hall. Facilities are also available for a number of activities including badminton, squash, table tennis and indoor bowls. In terms of outdoor sport the town also has a number of amateur clubs for those interested in playing football, rugby or cricket. The town's football ground is now home to the world's oldest football team, Sheffield F.C. Dronfield Railway Station provides a frequent service to Sheffield, Chesterfield and Alfreton and regular bus services link the town to other nearby towns and villages. Dronfield is twinned with Sindelfingen in Germany.

## Glossop

Glossop is a small market town in the north of the county with a population of around 33,000. It is surrounded on three sides by the Peak District National Park and is known 'The Gateway to the Peak'. The area was occupied by the Romans and there are the remains of a Roman fort near by. This was named Ardotalia by the Romans but is now known generally as Melandra. A settlement was established here by the Saxons and by the Middle Ages the economy was based on sheep pasture and the production of wool by local farmers. A number of cotton mills were constructed in the area during the 18th-century and some of these have been converted to residential and retail use in recent years. Today Glossop attracts large numbers of visitors because of its proximity to the Peak District and tourism makes an important contribution to the local economy. These visitors also allow the town to sustain a wide variety of shops, restaurants and food outlets. Glossop has thriving indoor and outdoor markets selling a wide variety of goods. The Victorian Market Hall is open every Thursday, Friday and Saturday, whilst the outdoor market is open every Friday and Saturday. The town has a library and a leisure centre with a wide range of facilities including a fitness suite, sports hall, squash courts, sun dome and studio. There are a number of parks and open spaces in the town. Manor Park, close to the town centre, has formal gardens, woodlands, a playground, tennis courts, two bowling greens, crazy golf, putting, a miniature railway, cafe, open spaces, a lake and a river. A Bonfire and Firework Extravaganza is held here each year. The town is served by a weekly newspaper, the *Glossop Chronicle* and a local commercial radio station, High Peak Radio provides some local news and features.

## Heanor

Heanor is a small town in the Amber Valley district. It was mentioned in the Domesday Book when it had a population of around 70. The town grew considerably in the eighteenth and nineteenth centuries when coal mining and textiles provided employment for large numbers of people. Today the town has a population of around 23,000 most of whom are employed in the retail, food and service sectors. The Matthew Walker factory which produces large numbers of Christmas puddings is located on the Heanor Gate Industrial Park on the edge of the town. Heanor has its own library and a secondary school (Heanor Gate Science College) but the nearest railway station is at Langley Mill, two miles away. The local weekly newspaper is the *Ripley and Heanor News*. There is a large Tesco supermarket on the edge of the town but other shopping facilities are somewhat limited. There are regular bus services to Derby and Ilkeston.

## Ilkeston

Ilkeston was described by Pevsner as 'A town singularly devoid of visual attractions'. It dates from Saxon times and is mentioned in the Domesday book as Tilchestune. It grew in size and importance during the 18th and 19th centuries due to the development of the hosiery, mining and iron industries. The town was linked to canal network in the 18th-century with the building of the Erewash canal and in the following century the town became part of the railway system. The station closed several years ago but the town still has regular bus services to Derby, Nottingham, Chesterfield and other local towns and villages. The main providers are Trent Barton, Notts and Derby, Midland General and Doyle's. Today many people are employed in the service sector and others commute to Derby and Nottingham to find work. The town does not have a particularly wide range of shops. The Marks and Spencer store closed some considerable time ago and in recent years the number of empty premises and charity shops has increased. There is a small retail park on the edge of the town which includes a Marks and Spencer food store, a branch of Argos and a number of other chain stores. An open air market is held in the centre of the town on Thursdays and Saturdays. Ilkeston is well provided with leisure facilities including a cinema, bowling alley, swimming pool and leisure centre. The town's small museum has won a number of awards and attracts a large number of visitors. Ilkeston Football Club is known as 'The Robins' and play in the Northern Premier League. In summer Victoria Park plays host to a number of bands. Ilkeston also hosts what it claims to be the largest street fair in the country. The population of the town is around 38,000 and is able to support a hospital, library, job centre and a number of secondary schools. Derby College has a campus in Ilkeston. Its facilities include an industry standard hair and beauty salon, a purpose built technology centre and specialist construction classrooms. Erewash Borough Council has offices in the town and meetings of the Borough Council alternate between here and Long Eaton. The people of Ilkeston have their own distinctive dialect which was described some years ago in a book entitled *Ey Up Mi Duck!* A local newspaper, *The Ilkeston Advertiser*, is published weekly.

## Long Eaton

Long Eaton is part of Erewash Borough and has a population of around 45,000. It lies in the south-east of the county close to the border with Nottinghamshire. Hosiery and lace were important industries in the town and a great deal of the famous 'Nottingham Lace' was actually produced here. Many local people also worked in local coal mines and at the Stanton and Staveley Iron Works. Long Eaton has good shopping facilities. Two major supermarkets are located close to the town centre and a number of major high street chains including Boots, W H Smith, Argos and Clarke's are represented in the town. An economic decline has led to the closure of a number of stores and some are now derelict or house charity shops. A market is held here three times a week on Wednesday, Friday and Saturday. An annual street fair, the Chestnut Fair is held in the Waverley Street area in mid-November each year. Some of the offices of Erewash Borough Council are located in the town and the Council meets here alternately with Ilkeston. The town has a number of leisure facilities including parks a sports centre and a swimming pool. The Duchess Theatre plays host to a number of amateur dramatic and musical societies and the cinema shows all the latest films. The town has its own railway station which provides regular passenger services to London, Birmingham, Derby, Chesterfield and Sheffield. A number of bus companies provide services to Derby, Nottingham, Ilkeston and a number of other local destinations.

*Ilkeston Market place showing the library and the war memorial*

## Matlock

Matlock is the county town of Derbyshire despite having a population of only a little over 10,000. The town dates from Saxon times but remained a rather isolated settlement until the coming of the Midland Railway in 1849. Matlock Bath was already developing as a Spa but in 1853 George Smedley built the huge Matlock

Hydro on Matlock Bank. At one time there were around twenty hydrotherapy centres in the town, mostly on Matlock Bank. These attracted large numbers of visitors until well into the 20th-century. Smedley's Hydro closed in 1955 and re-opened the following year as the headquarters of Derbyshire County Council. The council is a major employer in town and many other people are employed in the tourist industry. The town has seen a number of changes in recent years. A bypass takes much of the traffic away from the town centre and in 2007 a large super-market was opened on the edge of the town. The town has only a limited number of high street traders and many people travel to neighbouring towns to do their shopping. A new bus station next to the railway station was built to create an inte-grated transport terminal. The former spa resort of Matlock Bath to the south of town is still a popular tourist destination with river gardens and a cable car. The Matlock Bath Illuminations are held here in September and October each year.

## Ripley

Ripley is a small town in the Amber Valley District and has a population of around 21,000 people. For many years Ripley was an industrial town. Coal mining was important and many people worked at the Butterley Engineering Works. Today many people commute to Derby to find work whilst others are employed locally in the retail and service sectors. A diverse range of businesses now occupy units on the Codnor Gate and Pease Hill industrial estates. The Headquarters of Derbyshire Constabulary is also located at Butterley Hall on the edge of the town. Markets are held here on Fridays and Saturdays each week and the streets adjacent to the Market Place contain a number of independent shops as well as chain stores such as Boots, Farm Foods, Bon Marche and Peacock's. A large Sainsbury's supermarket on the edge of the town sells a wide range of groceries and other items as well. Ripley also has a hospital, library and leisure centre. A local newspaper, *The Ripley and Heanor News*, is published weekly.

## Swadlincote

Swadlincote has a population of around 30,000 and is Derbyshire's most southerly town. It is close to the borders of both Staffordshire and Leicestershire. Ashby and Burton are both about five miles from the town. For many years Swadlincote was an important industrial town. Mining and the pottery industry were important employers. The centre of the town has been pedestrianised and a small market is held here. In recent years two large supermarkets; Morrisons and Sainsbury's have opened here. There are also a small number of independent retailers, national chain stores and charity shops in the town. Swadlincote has a library, a leisure centre and a number of parks. Swadlincote Ski Centre was opened a number of years ago on the site of an old colliery spoil heap. Today it provides facilities for skiing, tobogganing and snow-boarding. The establishment of the National Forest has led to a considerable amount of land reclamation and tree planting in the areas. The Pingle School provides secondary education from 11 to 18 although pupils from two other schools in the area go there for their sixth form education. There a number of parks in the area but few other recreational facilities and most people travel to Derby or Burton for their entertainment.

# Notable Buildings

Derbyshire has a wealth of interesting and historic buildings as well as a number of startling and innovative contemporary structures.

**Chesterfield Market Hall** was built in 1857 'for the shelter and safeguard of market people'. It was described by Pevsner as, 'the crudest show of High Victorian provincial prosperity'. At the time of writing the building was undergoing a major refurbishment and was expected to reopen in September 2013.

**The Crescent** at Buxton was built in the 1780s by the fifth Duke of Devonshire. Designed by Robert Carr at a cost of £120,000, it comprised a house for the Duke, three hotels, shops, a lending library and a post office as well as a large Assembly Room.

**Derby Roundhouse** is the oldest surviving railway roundhouse in the world. It was built by Robert Stephenson in 1839 for the North Midland Railway and having lain derelict for a number of years, was recently restored to become the main campus of Derby College.

**The Devonshire Royal Hospital** in Buxton was built in 1790 as stabling for horses. In 1857 an area over the stabling block was given over as a hospital. The magnificent slate dome was added in 1880 and at that time was the largest unsupported dome in the world with a span of 154 feet. The building is now part of Derby University.

**Friargate Bridge** in Derby was built by Andrew Handyside & Co in 1878 to carry the Great Northern Railway Line into Derby. It comprises two parallel cast iron segmental arch bridges set close together. The bridge is decorated with fine pierced ironwork incorporating the Derby 'Buck in the Park' emblem.

**Heage Windmill** was built in 1797 and restored in 2002. It is a Grade II listed building and the only working, stone towered, multi-sailed windmill in England.

**The Moot Hall** at Wirksworth was built in 1841 to replace an earlier building in the Market Place. It was here that the Barmoot Courts for the King's field in the Wirksworth wapentake were held to regulate the lead industry and settle disputes. The court meets here twice a year and a special dish for measuring lead ore is still held here.

**The nailers' shop** in Joseph Street, Belper is a rare survival of the many such workshops which existed in the town in the 18th and 19th centuries. Over 600 people were employed in the nail making industry in the locality in the 1840s.

**Riber Castle** was built in the mock-medieval style by John Smedley, the industrialist and owner of the Hydro at Matlock, between 1862 and 1868. Over the years the building has had a variety of uses. From the 1960s until September 2000 it housed a wildlife park. Following its closure the building was allowed to fall into disrepair but it has recently been converted into luxury apartments.

**The Blue Peter** public house at Alvaston, Derby is one of three pubs built in the 1930s by Offiler's Brewery in the art deco style (also described as streamline modern) The others were the Blue Boy and the Blue Pool.

**Shipley Model Farm** was built in 1860–61 to the designs of W. Eden Nesfield. Originally part of the Shipley Hall estate it was conceived as an ornamental structure with a mock medieval tower and a dairy with stained glass depicting the four seasons. The building is in private ownership but is visible from the Shipley Country Park which is open to the public.

**Somersal Herbert Hall** has been described as the finest timber-framed house in Derbyshire. It was built for John and Ellen Fitzherbert in the mid-16th-century.

**Prior Overton's Tower** at Repton was built in 1437 and is the oldest brick building in Derbyshire. Originally part of Repton Priory it now belongs to Repton School.

**Pickford's House** in Friargate, Derby is a typical Georgian town house that was built by the architect Joseph Pickford around 1769. It served as both his office and a family home. Today it is a museum of Georgian life and costume.

**Swarkestone Pavilion** dates from 1630–32. It was built as a 'bowle alley house' and a grandstand in the Jacobean style. The builder was a mason, Richard Shapperd but its design has been attributed to John Smythson, the famous architect. The building was used for the front cover of the Rolling Stones album, Beggars Banquet.

**Sudbury gasworks** was built by Lord Vernon in 1874 to supply Sudbury Hall. It is a unusual building with Dutch gables, diamond shaped chimney stacks and diaper patterned brickwork.

**Bretby Hall** was built for the fifth Earl of Chesterfield by Sir Geoffrey Wyatville in 1812–13. One of the later owners of the estate was Lord Carnarvon, the Egyptologist, who sold the property to finance the famous expedition to find the tomb of Tutankhamen. In 1926 the Hall was purchased by Derbyshire County Council and was operated as an orthopaedic hospital until the 1990s. It was then sold to a property developer who converted the building into luxury apartments.

**Stephenson Memorial Hall** in Chesterfield was built in 1879 as a tribute to the famous railway pioneer. It is now home to Chesterfield Museum and Art Gallery and the Pomegranate Theatre (the first civic theatre in Britain).

**The station waiting room** at Cromford was built around 1860 in the French chateau-style.

Derby College's **Joseph Wright Centre** is a impressive modern building constructed in 2005 at a cost of £12 million. Inspired by scientific and technological art forms this stunning building is part of Derby College and provides IT suites, modern science laboratories, art and drama studios and a spectacular central atrium.

**The Clock Garage** at Woodville is an unusual Art-Deco style building which was constructed when motoring was beginning to become more popular and more accessible to the middle classes. It is now used by a Kwik-Fit Tyre & Exhaust Centre.

**The Strand Arcade** in Derby was completed in 1881 and is said to be based on the Burlington Arcade in London. It was designed by Giles and Brookhouse as a commercial venture for the wealthy railway contractor, Sir Abraham Woodiwiss, and for over a century was a popular shopping venue. Today a number of shops in the arcade stand empty as the retail focus of the city has changed since the opening of the Westfield Centre.

**The former Boots the Chemists** shop on the corner of St Peter Street and East Street in Derby is one of the city's most distinctive buildings. Designed by Albert Bromley, this highly decorative Arts and Crafts-style building is adorned with statues of local worthies; Florence Nightingale, John Lombe, William Hutton and Jedediah Strutt. The building is now partly occupied by a coffee shop.

**The Assembly Rooms** in the Market Place Derby were completed in 1977 to replace the previous 17th-century Assembly Rooms which were destroyed by fire in 1963. This modern brick, concrete and glass structure is the city's principal entertainment venue and has two main halls; the Great Hall with a seating capacity of 1,200 and the smaller Darwin Suite. As well as plays, pantomimes and concerts the Assembly Rooms also hosts a number of displays and exhibitions including an annual beer festival and a Christmas Craft Fair.

**The Silk Mill Inn** at Derby has an interesting mural covering the whole of a side wall. Created in 1986 by the Derby Community Arts Project, it depicts the events of the 'Silk Mill Lockout' of 1833–4 which was one of the key events in the development of the trade union movement in this country.

**The Round Building** at Hathersage is a circular cutlery factory. It was designed by Sir Michael Hopkins for David Mellor in 1990 and has become one of the iconic works of modern British architecture. The site was previously the village gas works and the factory was built on the foundations of the original gas cylinder. Built in local gritstone with a spectacular lead roof this highly functional building has won a number of architectural and countryside awards including the BBC Design Prize. The factory is open to visitors and on weekdays they are able to see David Mellor cutlery being made.

**The Scala cinema** in Ilkeston is one of the earliest purpose built cinemas in the country. Built in the Art deco style it was opened in 1913 and can seat up to 400 people.

*The Scala Cinema at Ilkeston*

**The Sherwood Foresters War Memorial** at Crich was built in 1923. Designed in the form of a lighthouse, its flashing beacon has a range of 38 miles. Constructed originally as a monument to those who gave their lives in the First World War, it was rededicated in 1952 to include those who had died in the Second World War. Another memorial was erected on the site in 2008 to commemorate those who have died on active serviced since 1945 in Palestine, Korea, Northern Ireland and Afghanistan. The monument is open to the public and the viewing platform offers spectacular views across Derbyshire.

**The Toyota Factory** at Burnaston commenced production in December 1992. When building the factory great care was taken to minimise its impact on the environment. Low level buildings were chosen to blend into the surroundings and over 250,000 trees and shrubs were planted on landscaped mounds. Sound insulation was included to minimise noise pollution and other safeguards were built in to prevent the transmission of dust and other pollutants.

**Derby Theatre** was one of the last municipal theatres to be built in the UK. Situated within the Eagle Centre complex it was opened on 20 September 1975 by the Duke of Devonshire. The theatre was operated under the name of the Derby Playhouse from its opening until 2008 when it closed following financial failure and a period in administration. After a period of uncertainty it was for a time operated by Derby City Council. Today the theatre is part of Derby University. It stages a wide range of professional and amateur productions as well as providing opportunities for its students to gain experience in theatre studies.

**Norbury Manor House** dates from the 13th-century and provides a good example of the type of dwelling which would have been the home of a Lord or a prosperous merchant. The two storey building had storage space on the ground floor with living quarters in a communal hall above.

**Winster Market House** was built in the late 17th or early 18th-century and in 1906 became the first property to be acquired by the National Trust in Derbyshire. The upper part of the Market Hall is brick built but was probably originally timber framed. The arches were originally open and used by miners and street traders, whilst dairy produce was sold on the upper storey. The building is open to the public and contains information boards and a scale model of Winster village.

**John Smedley's Hydro** is a former hydrotherapy complex in Matlock. It was built by John Smedley in 1853 and was the largest establishment of its type in the town. Following its closure as a hydro the building was purchased by Derbyshire County Council in 1955 to become its administrative headquarters.

**The Midland Hotel** in Derby (now Hallmark Hotel) was the first purpose built railway hotel to be constructed outside London. It was designed by Francis Thompson and opened 1841 for the 'accommodation of the gentry and nobility'. Queen Victoria stayed here on a number of occasions in the 1840s.

**North Street,** Cromford, was built in 1771 to house workers at Arkwright's Mill. It is one of the earliest examples of workers housing in the county.

**Ireton Farm**, Kedleston, was the first model farm in Derbyshire. It was built in 1813 as a home farm to supply Kedleston Hall.

**Council housing** built in the Allenton and Osmaston Park Road area in the 1920s pioneered the use of cast-iron frames to speed construction.

**The Hearse House Visitor Centre** at Chapel-en-le-Frith was built in 1818 to house the parish hearse, a simple vehicle which was available for hire at a small fee to anyone who could provide a horse. The building was restored by the Chapel-en-le-Frith Amenity Society and opened as a visitor centre by the Duchess of Devonshire in 1992.

**The Jacobean House** on the corner of the Wardwick and Becket Street is a 17th-century town house in brick with stone dressings and mullioned windows. It was originally much larger but three bays were demolished to make way for Becket Street.

**The Quad** building in Derby is a centre for art and film which opened in 2008. This controversial steel and glass building contains two cinemas, two gallery spaces, a digital studio, participation spaces, digital editing suite, artists' studio and the British Film Institute Mediatheque.

*The Quad Building*

# Twin Towns

## Amber Valley Borough Council

Amber Valley Borough Council is twinned with Blackstone Valley, Rhode Island in the USA and has partnership agreements with Laholm in Sweden, and Glogow in Poland.

**Blackstone Valley** is a region of Rhode Island and Massachusetts and is known as the Birthplace of America's Industrial Revolution. The area is popular with tourists and a number of old mills have been converted to museums dedicated to the history of labour and immigration. The Blackstone Valley comprises a total of 21 communities in Rhode Island and Massachusetts. The Rhode Island side includes the towns of Burriville, Central Falls, Cumberland, Gloucester, Lincoln, North Smithfield, Pawtuckett, Smithfield and Woonsocket while the Massachusetts communities include Blackstone, Douglas, Grafton, Hopedale, Mendon, Milbury, Northbridge, Sutton, Upton, Uxbridge and Worcester.

**Laholm** is a small town in Sweden with a population of just under 6,000 people. The town has a number of attractive modern buildings but retains a number of streets which date back to medieval times. Employment in the area includes light industry, forestry and agriculture. The area has good transport links in all directions and is close to two airports.

**Glogow** is one of the oldest towns in Poland. It has a population of around 74,000 inhabitants and is situated on the banks of the River Odra in the province of Lower Silesia. The town suffered massive devastation during the Second World War but many of its historic buildings have now been restored. A copper foundry was established here in the 1960s and it remains the largest industrial enterprise in the town..

## Belper

Belper has a friendship link with Pawtucket in the USA. This arose because Samuel Slater, who established the first water-powered cotton mill in America, came from Belper where he had been apprenticed at Strutt's Mill in the town. Pawtucket in Providence County, Rhode Island has a population of over 71,000 people. The city still relies heavily on manufacturing for employment and goods produced here include textiles, jewellery and metals. Hasbro, one of the world's largest manufacturers of toys and games has its headquarters in Pawtuckett.

## Bonsall

Bonsall has a link with Chernobyl in Russia. The Chernoblyl Children's Lifeline-Bonsall Link was formed in December 2002 for the purpose of bringing a group of children and an adult leader/translator from Belarus to the Bonsall, Matlock and Wirksworth area each summer for a month's respite care. The link raises funds to pay for the children's travel and medical insurance costs and organises and funds a programme of recreational and educational visits for the group while in the UK. Their four week stay helps them to repair their immune systems and offers a respite from the relentless bombardment of radiation ingested and inhaled which still afflicts large areas of Belarus following the 1986 Chernobyl Nuclear Disaster.

## Buxton

Buxton is twinned with Bad Nauheim in Germany and Oignies in France.

**Bad Nauheim** is a spa town in the Wetteraukreis district of Hesse in Germany. With a population of over 30,000 people the town is noted for its salt springs which are used to treat heart and nerve diseases. The town is also well known for the manufacture of saxophones!

**Oignies** is a commune in the Pas-de-Calais department in the Nord-Pas-de-Calais region of France and has had links with Buxton since 1940. The town has a population of around 10,000 inhabitants and was previously a coal mining area. Today most people are employed in light industry.

## Chesterfield

Chesterfield is twinned with Tsumeb in Namibia, Troyes in France, Darmstadt in Germany and Yangquan, Shanxi in China.

**Tsumeb** is a mining town in the Oshikito region of Namibia and has a population of around 15,000 people. In addition to mining there are over 100 commercial farms around Tsumeb. The main crops grown are maize, sorghum and sunflowers although irrigation projects have enabled citrus fruits to be grown with considerable success. The link with Chesterfield was formalised in 1993 following the visit of a miners delegation from Namibia in the mid-1980s

**Troyes** is a town of about 61,000 people in the Champagne-Ardenne region of France. Situated on the River Seine it has good road and rail links to the rest of France. It is an attractive town with many narrow streets of restored half timbered houses as well as an impressive gothic cathedral. The Lacoste fashion clothing company has its production headquarters in the town and it is also home to the prize-winning chocolate maker, Pascal Caffet.

**Darmstadt** is a city of about 144,000 inhabitants in the state of Hesse, Germany. It is home to a number of technological companies and research institutions and has been promoting itself as a "city of science" since1997. Industries include chemistry, pharmacy, biotechnology and telecommunications and it has important links with the European Space Agency. Darmstadt has good road and rail links and a modern tram system has recently been developed in the city.

**Yangquan** is a city in the Shanxi province of China. It has a population of over 1.3 million and is an important mining centre. Other industries include metallurgy, chemicals, machinery and construction equipment. Nearby tourists spots include Niangzi Xiao Pass and Pingding Guanshan Forest Park.

## Darley Dale

Darley Dale is twinned with Onzain in France. Onzain is a commune in the Loiret-Cher department of central France. It has a population of around 3,500 people. The surrounding area is popular with holiday-makers with lakes, campsites and a wide range of outdoor activities available for visitors.

## Derby City Council

Derby City Council has been twinned with Osnabrook in Germany since 1976. With a population of over 160,000 it is the third largest settlement in Lower Saxony. It has a number of historic buildings including St Peter's Cathedral. Like Derby, Osnabruk is an industrial city with the manufacture of copper, vehicle construction and engineering all important to the local economy. It also has a number of parks and a wide range of cultural facilities. The city is also home to two universities; the university of Osnabruk and the Applied Science University. Osnabrook has good road and rail links with the rest of Germany and shares the Munster Osnabruk International Airport with the nearby city of Munster. An unusual aspect of the twinning is an exchange of envoys each year although because of economic restrictions this has recently been placed at risk.

## Derby County Council

Derbyshire County Council is twinned with Toyota City, Alchi Japan and Yangpu, Shanghai, China. It also has links with Mamelodi in South Africa.

**Yangpu** is one of 18 districts in Shanghai, China and has a population of around 1.3 million. It is predominantly a residential district but it also contains the offices of major financial institutions and trading houses. Important government buildings are located here as well as major museums and other cultural centres. The Yangpu District is also home to two of China's most distinguished universities; Fudan University and Tongji University.

**Malmodi** is situated on the north eastern outskirts of Pretoria, South Africa and is a former black township of around one million inhabitants. A friendship link between Malmodi and Derbyshire County Council was formed in 2005.

**Toyota City** on the main Japanese island of Honshu was previously known as Koromo. The town was an important centre of silk production until the 1930s. Following the decline of the silk industry the Toyota Automatic Loom Company began to manufacture cars here and in 1937 the Toyota Motor Company was established in the town. Production started steadily particularly in the years following the Second World War and the city changed its name to Toyota in 1959. Today Toyota City has a population of over 400,000 people and is home to a number of universities and technical colleges, as well as a sports stadium and art gallery. The city is also twinned with Detroit in the USA.

## Dronfield

Dronfield is twinned with Sindelfingen near Stuttgard in Germany. It has a population of around 60,000, many of whom are employed in the automobile industry. The town contains a number of interesting and historic buildings including the Old City Hall (Rathaus) ,the 12th-century St Martin's Church and a number of half-timbered houses. In the market place there is a friendship fountain which commemorates the town's links with its partner towns. Sindelfingen has an annual international street fair which features ethnic food and performances from its partner towns as well as from various local ethnic groups. The town has good transport links via the A8 and A81 motorways. The nearest airport is at Stuttgard.

## Glossop

Glossop is twinned with Bad Vibel a spa town in Hessen, Germany. It has a population of around 31,000. New shopping and business centres have been established in recent years but the town still retains a number of old buildings including the town hall and a moated castle. A district livestock show is held in the town each year.

## Ilkeston

Ilkeston is twinned with Chalons-en-Champagne (formerly called Chalons-sur-Marne) in France. The town is the capital of both the department of Marne and the Champagne-Ardenne region of France and has a population of around 50,000. Chalons has a strong industrial tradition and today people are employed in a wide range of industries including research, technology and automotive engineering. The old town has a number of historic buildings including a 12th-century cathedral and cloister, town hall and town gate. During the summer months a tourist train runs through the area.

## Long Eaton

Long Eaton is twinned with Langen in Germany and Ramorantin in France.

**Langen** is a town of around 36,000 in Hess, Germany. It is the headquarters of the Deutsche Flugsicherung, the company which provides Germany's air traffic control and is also home to the Paul-Erlich-Institut, a federal serum and vaccine manufacturing business. The old town contains a number of timber framed houses and the Old Town Hall which is now a museum. The former hunting palace of Schloss Wolfsgarten is on the outskirts of the town. Langen has good road and rail links and Frankfurt Airport is only about 10km away.

**Ramorantin-Lanthenay** is a small town in the Loir-et-Cher department of France with a population of around 19,000. Until 2003 the town was home to the Matra automobile company but the local population now work in a more diverse range of businesses. A major food festival is held in the town each year on the last weekend of October.

## Matlock

Matlock is twinned with Eaubonne, Val-D'oise, a commune in the northern suburbs of Paris, France. It has population of around 19,000 many of whom commute or find employment in the service industries. The commune is proud of its heritage and a number of historic buildings have been preserved. These include the 18th-century Chateau de la Chesnaie, Castle Lombard and St Mary's Church. The town has two railway stations which provide fast and regular services to the centre of Paris which is just 16km away.

## New Mills

New Mills is twinned with Alsfeld a town in the centre of Hesse in Germany. With a population of around 18,000 its economy centres on the woodworking and textile industries. The historic town centre, the Altstadt, contains a large number of timber framed buildings dating from the 14th-century and the Regional Museum is housed in two restored 17th-century houses.

## Ripley Twinning Association

Ripley Twinning Association is twinned with Chateau Renault in France. Previously the town had an official twinning arrangement with Lons but this has now lapsed.

**Chateau-Renault** is a commune in the Indre-et-Loire department of France and is located about 28km from Tours, the department capital. It is a small town with a population of only about 5,000 residents. In the 19th-century the town was famous for the leather produced here and there is now a leather and tanning museum in the town. Today people are employed in a wide range of small scale industries including sheet metal manufacturing, floor covering, cardboard, electrical components and precision mechanical engineering. Weekly markets are held here on Tuesdays and Saturdays.

**Lons-le-Saunier** is a picturesque spa town in the heart of the Jura department of France. It has a rich historical and cultural heritage with numerous statues and fountains around the town. The streets which radiate from the square are lined with 17th-century houses. It was the Romans who first exploited the thermal spa here, renowned for its high salt content. Not surprisingly they called the town 'Ledo Salinarium' or 'Town of Salt'. Founded in 1898 the thermal spa is still in use today and offers a range of spa treatments and fitness packages.

## Tansley Village

Tansley Village has an informal twinning arrangement with the small town of Babadag in Tulcea County, Romania. The two countries have occasional exchange visits and more frequent postal and email contacts through an organisation called TABALINK (Tansley Babadag Association). Babadag is located on a small lake and has a population of around 8,000 people. The Romanian Army operates a military training facility on the edge of the town. US forces have recently started to train at Babadag as part of Romania's integration into NATO. A wind farm was constructed here in 2011.

## Whaley Bridge

Whaley Bridge is twinned with Tymbark a small village in southern Poland with a population of about 2,400 people. It is located about 47km south-east of the regional capital, Krakow. The main employer is a company which produces fruit preserves, drinks and juices.

## Winster

Winster is twinned with Monterubbiano, a small hill town in the Province of Fermo in the March region of Italy. It has a population of about 2,500 and is located about 8km from the Adriatic coast. The surrounding area is one of farmland and orchards. For many years most people were employed on the land although in the last thirty years light industry has become more important. In recent years tourism has also begun to contribute to the local economy. The town has a number of historic buildings including several churches, monastic cloister gardens, the Park of San Roco, the Palazzio Communale, the Secret Palace and castle walls. There is also an archaeological museum in the town whose exhibits illustrate the history of the area from the stone-age until the middle ages.

# Wirksworth

Wirksworth is twinned with Die in the Drome Valley of France and with Frankenau in Germany.

**Die** is a small town in the Rhone-Alps region of France. It has a population of less than 5,000 and is a popular tourist centre. Visitors come here throughout the year to enjoy hiking, skiing and other outdoor pursuits. The surrounding area is warm, dry and sunny and is important for wine production Local wines included Clairette de Die, a popular sparkling wine and Crement de Die which is a blend of sparkling wine and liquer. The town has a number of medieval buildings which also attract tourists.

**Frankenau** is a small town in the Waldeck-Frankenberg district in Hesse, Germany. It has a population of around 3,000 and is located on the edge of the Kellerwald Nature Park. It is a popular holiday centre and visitors come here to enjoy hiking, cross country skiing and hunting. The town has a number of interesting features including the Notre-Dame Cathedral, the Roman Ramparts and a monumental gate dating from the 3$^{rd}$ century.

# The Arts and Entertainment

## Writers and Poets

**William Howitt** was one of the 19th-century's most popular and prolific poets and writers. He married Mary Botham in 1818 and the two collaborated over a long and successful literary career. Collaborative works included *The Forest Minstrel and other poems* and *The Literature and Romance of Europe*. With his wife, he travelled widely in Europe and Australia and wrote countless volumes on a wide range of topics including politics, natural history and rural life. His most popular work was probably *A Book of Seasons* which included William's own sketches and descriptions of each month of the year. In a lengthy collaboration with the publisher Cassell he produced, *Cassell's Illustrated History of England* and with his wife, *Ruined Castles and Abbeys of Britain*. He wrote a number of travel books which received a great deal of popular acclaim. Schools in Heanor are named after William and Mary Howitt.

**D. H. Lawrence** was born in Eastwood, just over the border in Nottinghamshire but he lived and worked at Mountain Cottage in Middleton-by-Wirksworth for a brief period. It was here that he wrote *Wintry Peacock*, a short romantic story. He used the Erewash Valley as the setting for a number of novels and Derbyshire has been used as the location for a number of the film and TV adaptations of his books.

**Samuel Richardson** was born at Mackworth in 1689 and is regarded by many as the 'father of the modern novel'. He started life as a printer in London and was later commissioned to write a collection of letters to instruct the lower classes in the art of letter-writing. His first novel, *Pamela*, published in 1740 was praised for its realism and helped to gain respectability for this new literary form. His later novels; *Clarissa* and *Sir Charles Grandison* were avidly read and admired by Jane Austin among others; and perhaps inspired later novelists.

**Anna Seward**, the 18th-century poet, famed as the Swan of Lichfield was born at Eyam in December 1747. She moved to Lichfield at the age of ten when he father became a canon of the cathedral there. Rejecting the conventional role of a wife and mother, she devoted herself to writing poetry. She was a prolific writer and produced hundreds of poems, including elergies and sonnets during her lifetime. Her best known works include *Ode to Content, Portrait of Miss Levett, Receipt for a Sweet Jar* and the poetical novel *Louisa*. Such was her fame that Sir Walter Scott published three volumes of her poetry posthumously in 1810.

**Alison Uttley**, the creator of *Little Grey Rabbit* and *Sam Pig* was born Alice Jane Taylor at Castle Top Farm near Cromford in December 1884. She was educated at Lady Manners School, Bakewell before going on to study at Manchester University where she became only the second woman to obtain a degree in Physics. She married James Uttley in 1911 but, following his suicide in 1930, she began writing seriously to provide financial support for herself and her son. Her works included tales of *Little Grey Rabbit, Hare, Squirrel* and later *Sam Pig*. All were hugely successful and she later went on to write for older children and adults. *The Country Child*, published in 1931 is a fictionalised account of her childhood in Derbyshire, whilst *A Traveller in Time* features Dethick, and tells the story of a child transported back in time to be involved in the Babington Plot to free Mary Queen of Scots from Wingfield Manor. Allison Uttley was awarded an Honorary Doctor of Letters degree by Manchester University in 1970. She died six years later.

## Actors, Comedians and Presenters

**Sir Alan Bates** was an outstanding actor who enjoyed a film and stage career spanning six decades. Born at Derby in 1934, he attended the Herbert Strutt Grammar School in Belper and was awarded a scholarship to RADA. After a stage debut with the Midland Theatre Company in Coventry he moved to the Royal Court Theatre in London. A starring role as Jimmy Porter in John Osborne's *Look back in Anger* led to other major roles in both the West End and on Broadway. He enjoyed a film career which spanned three decades that included leading roles in *Whistle Down the Wind, Women in Love, Prayer for the Dying* and *Gosford Park*. He also appeared in a number of television plays including adaptations of *Hard*

*Times* and *The Mayor of Casterbridge*. He was awarded the CBE in 1995 and was knighted in 2003, shortly before his death.

**James Bolam** was born in Sunderland but brought up and educated in Derby. He attended Bemrose School where he became involved in drama productions. After leaving school he joined Derby Shakespeare Company and appeared at Derby Playhouse, After National Service he trained at the Central School of Speech and Drama in London. After a successful stage career he found fame in the TV comedy series, *The likely Lads* and its sequel *Whatever happened to the Likely Lads*. His next major TV role was as Jack Ford in the period drama, *When the Boat Comes In*. Since then he has appeared regularly on the small screen in a variety of productions. Some of his best known appearances have included leading roles in '*The Beiderbeck Trilogy, Born and Bread* and *New Tricks*. He received an MBE in the 2009 Birthday Honours.

**Timothy Dalton** spent his childhood in Milford and Belper and was educated at the Herbert Strutt Grammar School at Belper. He became involved in local amateur dramatics, appearing in *Arms and the Man* and taking the title role in *Billy Liar*. A successful stage TV and cinema actor, he is best known for his role as James Bond in *The Living Daylights* and *License to Kill.*

**David Dixon** is best known for his role as Ford Prefect in the television version of *A Hitch Hikers Guide to the Galaxy*. Born at Derby in 1947, his family later moved to Nottingham. He trained at the Guildhall School of Music and Drama and achieved early success as David Ashton in the TV series *A Family at War*. He continues to be a fairly familiar face on television in a variety of more minor roles.

**Judith Hann** became well known for her work on BBC television's *Tomorrows World* series. Joining the programme as a reporter she went on to become its first female and longest serving presenter. Born at Derby in 1942 she worked as a journalist before pursuing a television career. Since *Tomorrows World* she has appeared on a number of science and medical programmes and written several books on a variety of topics.

**John Hurt** was born at Chesterfield in 1940. After winning a scholarship to RADA he pursued a successful stage, television and film career. Film roles have included appearances in *Alien, Elephant Man, Scandal* and *Harry Potter*. In 2002 John Hurt was awarded an honorary degree by the University of Derby, and, in 2004 the CBE.

**Michael Knowles** was born at Derby in 1937 and was educated at Bemrose School where he first showed his talent for drama. His television career started in 1969 with the role of Captain Cutts in *Dad's Army* but he is best known for his portrayal of Captain Ashworth in the series *It Ain't half Hot Mum*. He also played Terry Meldrum in the BBC comedy drama, *You Rang M'Lord?* Michael Knowles is also a successful radio and television scriptwriter.

**Robert Lindsey** has been described as one of the most versatile and successful actors on stage and screen. Born at Ilkeston in 1949, he attended Gladstone Boys' School where he first became involved in drama. He was awarded a scholarship to RADA and soon became a familiar face on television. In 1975 he won a leading role in the comedy series *Get Some In!* and two years later took the title role in *Citizen Smith*. Other television roles followed but in the 1980s he returned to the theatre, appearing in a number of leading West End productions. He is best known for his role as Ben Harpur in the popular BBC sitcom *My Family* (2000–2011) but he has also starred in the detective drama series *Jericho* and played a supporting role as Captain Pellew in the *Hornblower* series. In 2010 he starred in the title role of Derby Live's production of *Onassis* before its transfer to the West End.

**Kevin Lloyd** was born at Derby in 1949 and after training to be an actor enjoyed a successful and varied stage career. He appeared in a number of minor television roles before winning the part of Harry Blackburn in the second series of *Auf Wiedersehen Pet*. He is best known for his portrayal of 'Tosh' Lines in *The Bill*. He made more than 400 appearances over almost ten years but personal problems led to the termination of his contract. He died in 1998.

**Arthur Lowe** was born at Hayfield in 1915. He began his acting career in repertory theatre at Hulme Hippodrome and later began to earn small roles in film and television. In 1960 he achieved fame as Leonard Swindley in *Coronation Street* but he is best remembered for his role as Captain Mainwaring in *Dad's Army*, a series which ran for eighty episodes over nine series. He continued to appear in a number of television, film and stage roles but increasing ill health led to his death in 1982. He is commemorated by a blue plaque at his birthplace in Hayfield.

**Jeremy Kemp** was born Jeremy Walker at Chesterfield in 1935. He studied acting at the Central School of Speech and Drama and had a successful film and television career spanning almost fifty years. He appeared in a number of well known films including *The Blue Max, Operation Crossbow* and *A Bridge Too Far*. His TV credits include *Colditz, Space 1999* and *Murder She Wrote*.

**Joan Rice** was a film starlet in the 1950s. Born at Derby in 1930, she was given a contract by the Rank Corporation and achieved stardom playing Maid Marian in the 1952 version of *Robin Hood and His Merrie Men*. Other film roles included *A Day to remember, The Steel Key* and *His Majesty O'Keef* where she co-starred with Burt Lancaster. She built a career in repertory theatre in the 1960s but returned to the big screen in 1970 to play a small role as the grave robber's wife in *The Horror of Frankenstein*. In later life she devoted herself to business interests outside show business. She died in 1997.

**William Roache** is best known for his role as Ken Barlow in the long running TV soap opera, *Coronation Street*. He is the longest serving cast member and the only remaining member of the original cast, having appeared since the first episode on 9 December 1960. He was born at Ilkeston in 1932 and after National Service decided to pursue a career in the theatre. After working in repertory theatre he began to seek work in television. He played minor roles in a number of Granada Television productions before successfully auditioning for the role of the Ken Barlow, a young student. He received a lifetime achievement award at the British Soap Awards in 2000 and became an MBE in the 2001.

**Steven Blakely** was born at Chesterfield in 1982. He began his acting career as a member of Derby Playhouse Community and Youth Theatre before going on to work professionally at Derby Playhouse. He has a number of stage and TV appearances to his credit but is best known for his role as PC Geoff Younger in the TV series, *Heartbeat*.

**Jane Rossington** starred as Jill Richardson in *Crossroads*, the long-running TV soap opera of the sixties and seventies. Born at Derby in 1943, she later moved with her family to Sutton Coldfield. Her early career included work in television and radio and included roles in *The Archers* and television's first hospital drama series; *Emergency Ward Ten*. Her role in *Crossroads* lasted for twenty-four years and she was the only cast member to remain with the series throughout its entire run.

**Tracey Shaw** is another Derbyshire actress to have played a major role in *Coronation Street* where she played the role of Maxine for over eight years. Born at Belper in 1973 she attended St Benedict's School, Derby before studying for a degree in Theatre Studies at the Arden School of Theatre at Manchester.

**Gwen Tayor** has become a popular and familiar face on television Born in 1939. She was brought up in Cromford and Crich. Her family moved to Derby where she attended Parkfield Cedars Girls Grammar School. A successful TV career has included leading roles in series such as *Duty Free*, *Heartbeat* and *Coronation Street*.

## Artists and illustrators

**Michael Barnfather** is one of this country's leading landscape artists. Born at Ilkeston in 1934 the family later moved to Belper. He studied at Derby School of Art before joining Rolls-Royce as a technical artist. After achieving some success and recognition as an amateur artist he began to paint full-time in 1964. Many of his paintings capture the hills, woodlands and farms of Derbyshire. A book of his paintings entitled *Michael Barnfather's Derbyshire* was published in 2002.

**William Billingsley** was a famous painter of flowers on china. He was apprenticed to William Duesbury at the Derby China Works in 1774 and in 1790 became the chief flower painter there. He left Derby to set up the Pinxton China Works in partnership with John Coke. The partnership broke up after only a few years but Billingsley continued to decorate Pinxton and other porcelain at his Mansfield Decorating Establishment. Several examples of Billingsley's work can be seen in the Derby Museum and Art Gallery.

**Zachariah Boreman** was one of the prolific and best of the china painters employed at the Derby China Works in the latter years of the 18th-century. His early work was imaginary landscapes, sometimes in monochrome but from 1780 he began to produce topographical landscapes of Derbyshire views. His work decorated many of the dinner services which were produced by the company at this time.

**Laura Knight** was born at Long Eaton in 1877 and went on to study at the Nottingham School of Art. She first exhibited at the Royal Academy in 1903. At the 1928 Summer Olympics in Amsterdam, she won the Silver medal in painting and a year later was made a Dame Commander of the Order of the British Empire. In 1936 she became the first woman to be elected to the Royal Academy. She became well known for her paintings of circus performers and ballet dancers but during the Second World War she received various commissions via the War Artists Advisory Committee. These included *In for Repair, Balloon Site, Ruby Loftus* and *Take Off*. In 1945 she was one of a number of artists commissioned to document the Nuremburg War Trials. She found this a daunting ordeal but it resulted in *The Dock, Nuremburg* which was completed in 1946. With the War over she returned to London where she resumed her paintings of ballet, the circus and gypsies. She continued painting until almost the end of her life in 1970. Her work can be found in galleries throughout the country. The Castle Art Gallery at Nottingham has a particularly fine collection.

**Pollyanna Pickering** is a well known wildlife artist who currently lives and works at Oaker, near Matlock. Born in Yorkshire, she trained at Rotherham School of Art and the Central School of Art in London. She has lived in Derbyshire since the 1960s and specialises in wildlife painting, mainly in gouache. She travels widely to study and paint endangered species in their natural habitats. Pickering is one of the most published artists in the UK. In addition to her books and limited edition prints her work features on greetings cards, calendars and giftware. Original works have been exhibited in a number of leading galleries including the Royal Academy. In 1998 she held the inanugural exhibition in the then new wildlife gallery at the Derby Museum and Art Gallery. She holds the post of honorary patron of the Wildlife Arts Society International and in 2008 was awarded an honorary degree from the University of Derby in recognition of her work.

**Louise Raynor** was born at Matlock Bath on 21 June 1832. She studied painting from the age of fifteen, at first with her father (also a noted artist) and later with artist friends of the family including George Cattermole, David Roberts and Frank Stone. She began painting in oils but from 1860 her favoured medium was watercolour. She exhibited widely for over half a century through organisations such as the Royal Academy, the Society of British Artists and the British Institution. Typically her paintings depict street scenes in places such as London, York, Derby, Chester, Oxford and Cambridge. Derby Museum and Art Gallery holds a number of her works including the famous painting of Irongate c.1865. Her work is also held by other galleries including the Victoria and Albert Museum and the National Gallery. She was commercially successful in her own lifetime and her watercolours became so popular that orders were placed as far as twelve months in advance.

**Joseph Wright** is Derby's most famous painter and is known as 'Wright of Derby'. Born in Irongate, Derby in 1734, he attended Derby Grammar school before moving to London to study under Thomas Hudson, a fashionable portrait artist of the period. He worked in Liverpool as a successful portrait painter before travelling to Rome to study the art and architecture of antiquity. Returning to Derby in 1775 he continued his work as a portrait painter but also began to produce work that made use of the contrast of light and dark. His fascination with science and industry led him to produce a number of paintings illustrating scientific themes including *The Orrery* and *Experiment on a Bird in an Air Pump*. Wright had connections with Erasmus Darwin and other members of the Lunar Society and his paintings include portraits of scientists and industrialists such as Richard Arkwright, Jedediah Strutt and John Whitehurst. Joseph Wright died on 29 August 1797 at his home in Queen Street, Derby, His paintings hang in many of the major art galleries of the world but the largest collection is in Derby Art Gallery!

# Sport in Derbyshire

## Snooker

**Fred Davis** was a professional billiards and snooker player and has the distinction of being one of only two players ever to win the world title in both. Born at Chesterfield in 1913, he was originally a billiards player and won the United Kingdom Professional Billiards Championship in 1951. The decline in popularity of this sport forced Fred to begin competing in snooker tournaments. He was even more successful in snooker and won the World Championship on three occasions (1948, 1949 and 1951). He competed at this level for several decades and played regularly in the BBC Pot Black series. He was awarded the OBE in 1977 and won the World Billiards Championship in 1980. He continued to play both billiards and snooker for many years and only retired in 1993 at the age of 79. He died five years later.

## Cricket

The first recorded game of cricket in Derbyshire took place in September 1757 when Sheffield Cricket Club played a match against Wirksworth at Brampton Moore near Chesterfield. Chesterfield Cricket Club was founded some years later and played its matches at various locations in the town including the recreation ground at Saltergate. In February 1894, however, the club obtained the use of the new cricket ground on Queen's Park. The club played its first game there on 5 May of the same year and two years later won its first Derbyshire League title. In 1899 an impressive new pavilion (still in use today) was built at a total cost of £499 18s 6d. Although it achieved some success in the first half of the 20th-century the 'golden years' of the club were between 1947 and 1957 when the first XI won the Derbyshire League title six times in ten seasons. Following this period of success the club joined the Bassetlaw League, where it played for the next 41 years. In 1999 the club joined the Derbyshire Premier League in which it continues to play.

*Derby Racecourse from a 19th-century engraving*

**Derbyshire County Cricket Club** was founded on 4 November 1870. The first President was the Earl of Chesterfield who had played both for and against all England. The following year the club joined the (then unofficial) County Championship and on 26 and 27 May played its initial first class match against Lancashire at Old Trafford Cricket Ground. The club has enjoyed mixed fortunes throughout its history although it won the County Championship in 1936 and became Division Two Champions in 2012. The club's home ground is at Derby though in the past it has also played regularly at Ilkeston, Buxton and Chesterfield, where occasional matches are still played. Its limited overs team is called the Derbyshire Falcons. Kit colours are white for County Championship matches and blue for one day and 20/20 competitions.

**W G Grace** the legendary cricketer played at Derby Cricket Ground on Nottingham Road for three days in August 1874.

**Freddie Truman** the famous Yorkshire and England cricketer played for Derbyshire County Cricket Club for one season in 1972. By this time he was reaching the end of his career and played only in one-day matches.

**Quorndon** won the All England Village Cricket competition at Lords in 1983.

## Boxing

**Jack Bodell** was a British Heavyweight boxing champion. He was born at Newhall near Swadlincote in 1940 and after leaving school he started work as a miner and began boxing. He won the National Coal Board and the British Amateur Boxing Association's light-heavyweight championships three years in succession and turned professional in 1962. Over the next few years he built a successful career and was defeated only six times in his first forty contests. By the late 1960s he was being matched against some of the top boxers in the country. He was defeated by Henry Cooper but won fights against both Brian London and Billy Walker. The highlight of his career came in September 1971 when he met Joe Bugner for the British, European and Commonwealth titles, a fight which he won after fifteen gruelling rounds. This success was, however short lived and after a succession of defeats he retired from boxing. A local pub briefly renamed one of its bars 'The Bodell Bar".

## Football

**Pride Park football stadium** was opened in 1997 as the home ground of Derby County Football Club and replaced the iconic Baseball Ground which the team had used since 1895. With space for 33,597 spectators Pride Park has the sixteenth largest capacity of any English football stadium. The design closely resembles the Riverside Stadium at Middlesborough and was designed by the same team of architects (The Miller Partnership) The stadium was officially opened by the Queen on 18 July 1997 in front of 30,000 spectators. Plans have recently been announced for the development of land outside the stadium to include a multi-use sports arena, cafes, restaurants and convenience stores and 2,000 square metres of office space.

**Gordon Banks**, England's World Cup winning goalkeeper played for Chesterfield FC between 1955 and 1959.

**The Baseball Ground** was the home venue for Derby County Football Club from 1895 to 1997. It was originally built by Sir Francis Ley who attempted to introduce baseball into the UK. When this failed to grow in popularity the venue was used by Derby county Football Club. The club's reserve and youth teams continued to play here until 2003 when it was demolished.

**Steve Bloomer** is probably Derby County's most famous player of all time. Brought up in Derby he first achieved success in Junior football and at the age of fourteen joined Derby Swifts who played on Chester Green. He signed professional forms in 1892 and scored twice in his debut for the Rams against Stoke in September 1892. Apart from a four year stint at Middlesbrough from 1906 until 1910, he played for Derby County until his retirement in 1914. During that time he played 525 League and Cup games for Derby, scoring a total of 332 goals. He scored eighteen hat tricks and still holds the record for the most goals (six) in a match. His first England cap came in 1895 and he played for his country on 23 occasions, serving once as captain in 1902 in a game against Scotland. Following his retirement he took a coaching job in Berlin but the outbreak of the First World War resulted in his internment. After the war he returned to England and worked for his former team as a coach. He went on to coach Real Irun and helped them to win the Spanish Cup. He suffered from ill health in his later years and died on 16 April 1938. A memorial of Steve Bloomer hangs in the fish market in Derby.

**Chesterfield Football Club** was founded in 1867 when the Chesterfield Cricket Club advertised for members to play during the winter months. This club collapsed in 1881 but two other clubs (both known as Chesterfield Town FC) played in the football league between 1884 and 1917. The present Chesterfield FC was formed as Chesterfield Municipal Football Club in 1919. Chesterfield have spent most of their history in the lower divisions of the Football League. The team enjoyed mixed fortunes for many years but were promoted to Division Three in 1985. Further success came in 1995 when they won the Division Three Play-off final at Wembley and were promoted to the Second Division. Two years later they reached the semi-final of the FA Cup. The club continued to do well and on 7 May 2011 beat Gillingham to secure the League Two title. In 2010 the club moved to a new £13 million stadium at Whittington Moor.

**Brian Clough OBE** is regarded by many commentators as one of the most successful English football managers of all time. Born in Middlesborough in 1935 he joined his local club at the age of 16. He made his first-team debut in September 1955 and over the next six seasons he scored 197 goals in 213 league appearances. It was also during this period that he earned two England caps, against Wales and Sweden, both in 1959. He transferred to Sunderland in 1961 where he continued to score goals at a prolific rate. A football accident at the age of 30 brought an end to his playing career but in 1965 he took up a post at Hartlepool to become the youngest manager in the Football League. Two years later he moved to Derby County which he led to the League Championship in 1972 and the European Cup semi-finals a year later. He resigned from Derby County in 1973 and after brief periods with Brighton and Leeds he became manager of Nottingham Forest. Once again he showed his magic touch. Under Clough's management the club went on to win promotion into the First Division followed by, four League Cups and two European Cups. In 1993 after 16 years in the top flight, Nottingham Forest were relegated from the Premier Division and Brian Clough announced his retirement as manager. He was awarded an OBE in the 1991 Queen's Birthday Honours for services to Association Football. He died on 20 September 2004 of stomach cancer. In August 2005 a stretch of the A52 linking Derby and Nottingham was renamed Brian Clough Way. In 2010 a statue of Brian Clough and his assistant Peter Taylor was unveiled outside the Pride Park Stadium in Derby.

**Derby County Football Club** was founded in 1884 and in 1888 became one of the founder members of the Football League. The club was originally formed as an off-shoot of Derbyshire County Cricket Club and played its matches at the cricket club's Racecourse Ground. In 1895 the Club moved to a new stadium (the Baseball Ground) and adopted its now traditional colours of black and white. The club performed well in the following decades and were FA Cup runners-up in 1898, 1899 and 1903. The 1920s and 1930s also saw considerable success for the club but their greatest achievement came in 1948 when they won the FA Cup for the first and only time in their history. In recent years the club's most successful period came under the management of Brian Clough and his assistant Peter Taylor. Under their leadership Derby County won promotion to the Premier League in 1969 and went on to their first ever Football League Championship in 1972. In the following season the club reached the semi-finals of the European Cup. Following disagreements with the Board of Directors Clough and Taylor left Derby County in 1973. Despite their departure the club's league success was repeated in the 1974-5 season when they won the title under the leadership of Dave MacKay. There followed a period of relative decline and the club was relegated to the Second Division in 1980 and the Third Division in 1984. Revival came under the leadership of Arthur Cox who steered the club back to the top flight of English football in 1987. The next few years were a roller-coaster of disappointment and success and in 1997 the club moved into a new 30,000 seat stadium at Pride Park. In 2006 the club won promotion to the Premier league only to be relegated at the end of the following season. In 2009 Nigel Clough (the son of Brian) was appointed manager and under his leadership the club has made steady but unspectacular progress.

Derbyshire has several successful non-league football clubs. These include Alfreton Town F C (the Reds), Belper Town F C (the Nailers), Buxton F C (the Bucks), Ilkeston F C (the Robins) and Matlock Town F C (the Gladiators) The city of Derby has three non-league clubs: Mickleover Sports, Graham Street Prims and Borrowash Victoria.

## Horse racing

Horse racing at Derby dates back to at least the 18th-century. Races took place on Sinfin Moor until 1803. When the moor was enclosed a new racecourse was laid out on the Siddals. Local landowners complained however, and in 1845 the races moved again; this time to the Nottingham Road area which is still known as The Racecourse. Horse racing at Derby flourished for over ninety years and some of the top jockeys in the country rode here. The last race was held in August 1939 shortly before the outbreak of the Second World War.

**Chatsworth International Horse Trials** are held in May each year. The three day event includes dressage, show jumping and cross-country events as well as Pony club mounted games, ferret racing and birds of prey displays.

## Gliding

**The Derbyshire and Lancashire Gliding Club** was founded in 1934 and is based at Camphill between Great Hucklow and Abney. The World Gliding Championships were held here in 1954. The club has a number of single and dual-seat gliders as well as a full size simulator with a full set of flying controls.

## Fishing

**Fly and Coarse fishing** are both popular in Derbyshire. The rivers of the Peak District are world famous for fly fishing but coarse fishing also takes place on the lower reaches of the Derwent and Trent as a well as numerous lakes gravel pits and canals throughout the county.

**Derby Railway Angling Club** was founded in 1895 for employees of the then Midland Railway; although today membership is open to all. The club claims to offer anglers one of the most diverse and comprehensive angling opportunities in the Midlands. The club's stated objective is 'to encourage the healthy art of angling and to acquire, develop and protect water for angling purposes'.

## Cycling

**Thomas Gascoyne** was a professional cyclist. Born at Whittington, near Chesterfield in 1876, he began his cycling career in 1893 and was soon competing internationally on both bicycles and tandems. At one point in his career he held world records for both 25 mile and flying start quarter mile races. He emigrated to Australia at some time in the early 20th-century and after living for a number of years in comparative obscurity returned to competition cycling. He joined the Australian Army at the start of the First World War and was killed in the Battle of Passchendale on 4 October 1917.

## Mountaineering

**Alison Hargreaves** was a famous mountaineer and the first woman to climb Mount Everest solo and without additional oxygen. Born at Mickleover, a suburb of Derby, in 1962, she began climbing in her teens and made her first trip to the Himalayan mountain range in 1986. She climbed the north face of the Eiger whilst pregnant but took a break from her mountaineering career to raise her two children. In 1993 the family moved to the Alps where Hargreaves became the first person to climb in one season the classic six North faces of the Alps. In 1995 she announced her intention to climb unaided, in one season, the three highest mountains of the world; Mount Everest, K2 and Kangchenjuga. She reached the summit of Everest on 13 May 1995. Only three months later she reached the summit of K2 but died on the descent when she was swept off the mountain during a violent storm. Her body was never recovered.

**Sir Jack Longland**, Director of Education for Derbyshire for almost thirty years, was one of the most distinguished mountaineers and climbers of his generation. As a student he joined Cambridge University Mountaineering Club in 1925 and in 1933 was a member of the British Everest Expedition which succeeded in reaching the North Col at 27,000 feet. He continued to combine climbing with his professional career and gained an international reputation as an alpinist and mountaineer. As Director of Education he founded the mountain training centre at Lea Green, North of Buxton. He retired in 1970 and having been knighted, served as Vice-Chairman of the Sports Council from 1970 to 1974. From 1974 to 1976 he served as President of the Alpine Club. He died in 1993.

## Sailing

**Dame Ellen MacArthur** is a world renowned yachtswoman who achieved international fame when she came second in the gruelling Vendee Globe round the world race. Born at Whatstandwell in 1976 she started saving her pocket money to buy her first boat at the age of nine. Other boats followed and at the age of eighteen she sailed single-handed round Britain. Following success in the Route du Rhum transatlantic race in 1998 she was named Yatchsman of the Year. In 2001-2 she took part in the Vendee Globe round-the-world event, finishing second and becoming the youngest woman to sail single-handedly round the globe. She was awarded the MBE and won the Helen Rollason award for courage and achievement in the face of adversity. In February 2005 she broke the record for a solo circumnavigation of the globe and was created DBE on her return. In 2003 she established a charitable trust to take young people sailing in order to help them regain their confidence on their way to recovery from cancer, leukemia and other serious illnesses. Following her retirement in 2005 she created the Ellen MacArthur Foundation to work with education and business to 'accelerate the transition to a circular economy'.

# Golf

**Melissa Reid**, the professional golfer, was born in Derby in 1987. She plays on the Ladies European Tour and was a member of the victorious European team in the 2011 Solheim Cup.

# Wildlife and the Countryside

Derbyshire County Council, in collaboration with the Countryside Agency has identified ten National Landscape Character Areas within the county. These are:

**Dark Peak** – An upland landscape of high moors and settled areas.

**White Peak** – A gently rolling upland limestone plateau punctuated by steep sided dales, scattered villages and isolated farmsteads within a pastoral setting

**Derbyshire Peak Fringe and Lower Derwent** – An undulating well-wooded, pastoral landscape on rising ground between the Derbyshire Coalfield and the Peak District.

**Nottinghamshire, Derbyshire and Yorkshire Coalfield** – Densely settled and industrial lowland characterised by mining settlements, mixed farming and woodland.

**Southern Magnesian Limestone** – A gently rolling agricultural plateau punctuated by large woodlands, nucleated villages and incised river valleys.

**Needwood and South Derbyshire Claylands** – A settled, pastoral landscape on gently rolling lowlands.

**Trent Valley Washlands** – An agricultural landscape set within broad, open river valleys with many urban features.

**Melbourne Parklands** – An undulating mixed farming landscape within country houses, landscaped parks and estate plantations.

**Leicestershire and South Derbyshire Coalfield** – A gently undulating landscape of shallow valleys and ridges dominated by mining and urban features.

**Mease/Sence Lowlands** – A gently rolling agricultural landscape with scattered villages and occasional country houses, bird-watching facilities and cycle hire.

Derbyshire County Council manages five country parks: Elvaston Castle Country Park, Grassmoor Country Park, Poulter Country Park, Shipley Country Park and Pleasley Country Park.

Around 80% of the land in Derbyshire is devoted to farming.

The agriculture of lowland Derbyshire is a mixture of pastoral and arable farming.

Market gardening is a common feature of the area around Melbourne and Swarkestone.

The Newton Wonder apple was first grown at Kings Newton, near Melbourne.

The Derbyshire Gritstone is one of the oldest British sheep breeds. It was bred to be adaptable to the difficult and rigorous environment of the wild rugged country of the Peak District.

The Derbyshire Redcap is a rare breed of chicken which originated in Derbyshire. The name 'Redcap' derives from the breed's unusually large Rose-type comb. They were popular on British farms until the middle of the 20th-century, particularly around the southern Pennines.

Rosliston Forestry Centre was developed as a collaborative venture between South Derbyshire District Council, the Forestry Commission and the National Forestry Company. Covering an area of 154 acres the centre includes woodland trails, bird-watching facilities and an amazing climbing frame in the form of a sparrowhawk.

In 1994 the UK Biodiversity Action Plan (BAP) set out priority habitats and species that required protection. Local BAPs have since been produced to meet targets for habitat and species protection specific to local areas In Derbyshire there are three Biodiversity Action Plans: Peak District BAP, Lowland Derbyshire BAP and National Forest BAP.

Amphibian and Reptile species recorded in the Lowland Derbyshire BAP include the great crested newt, the common toad, the common lizard and the grass snake. The same plan also identifies over twenty bird species.

The first school wildlife area in Derbyshire was created at Oakwood Junior School at Alvaston in 1978.

Some hedgerows in Derbyshire are over a thousand years old and contain several species of wildwood tree as well as some of the more recently introduced species including sycamore and horse chestnut.

There are over 80 Sites of Special Scientific Interest (SSSIs) in Derbyshire. These include some of the county's most spectacular and beautiful habitats.

A total of 88 plant species were recorded as part a pond survey undertaken in Derby during 2004–5. These included a number of rare or scarce species such as hairlike pondweed, pink water speedwell and horned pondweed. In the same survey the most recorded amphibian was the common frog although common toads, great crested newts and smooth newts were also noted.

Jacob's Ladder was chosen as the county flower of Derbyshire in 2002.

A number of orchid species are found in Derbyshire, particularly in the Peak District. Species include the Common Spotted, Fly, Bee, Early Purple, Fragrant, Frog, Marsh and Pyramidical orchids.

Fly Orchid is a rare plant in Britain and is found at only a very few sites in Derbyshire. It is a plant of limestone soil and can be found in grassland areas of the White Peak.

Elvaston Castle Country Park covers an area of around 200 acres of open parkland, woodland and more formal historical gardens. When opened in 1970 it was one of the first country parks in England.

A yew in Darley Dale churchyard is estimated to be 2,000 years old and may be the oldest yew tree in England.

The Old Man of Calke is an ancient oak tree in Calke Park. It has a circumference of around ten metres and may be as much as 1,000 years old. It is Derbyshire's largest known tree.

The remains of the Betty Kenny Yew in Shining Cliff Woods near Crich is said to be the inspiration for the lullaby, Rock-a-by-Baby. Betty Kenny and her husband worked as charcoal burners towards the end of the 18th-century, raising eight children, who were rocked to sleep in a hollowed out branch. Unfortunately the tree was badly damaged by fire in the 1930s and is now in a poor state.

Over 450 species of mosses and liverworts have been recorded in Derbyshire. Rare or unusual species include the Sausage-beard moss, the Flamingo moss and the Derbyshire Feather-moss.

The Harlequin Ladybird has begun to invade Derbyshire in recent years. These were originally introduced as a pest control agent to France and Belgium and pose a great threat to our native ladybirds and other insects.

Derbyshire Bee Keepers Association was founded in 1881. Its first president was the Duke of Devonshire and the annual subscription was five shillings for gentlemen and two shillings and sixpence for cottagers.

A recent report states that about 450 species of macro (large) moths and 679 species of micro (small) moths have been recorded in Derbyshire. These include relatively rare or unusual species such as the grey dagger, the white-spotted pinion and the small emerald.

The Horse Chestnut Leaf Miner was first reported in Derbyshire in 2005. This species of micro moth feeds on horse chestnut trees.

Derbyshire Ornithological Society was formed in 1954. Its aims are to promote the recording, study and conservation of birds and their habitats within the county. The Society publishes the Derbyshire Bird Report each year.

In 2012 thousands of people took part in the Great Garden Birdwatch in Derbyshire. The top twenty species identified were:

1. House Sparrow
2. Blackbird
3. Blue Tit
4. Starling
5. Woodpigeon
6. Goldfinch
7. Chaffinch
8. Collared Dove
9. Great Tit
10. Robin
11. Dunnock
12. Long Tailed Tit
13. Magpie
14. Greenfinch
15. Coal Tit
16. Jackdaw
17. Feral pigeon
18. Carrion Crow
19. Wren
20. Bullfinch

In the RSPB Big School Birdwatch held in 2012 the following were identified as the most common species in Derbyshire school playing fields:

1. Blackbird
2. Blue Tit
3. Woodpigeon
4. House sparrow
5. Carrion crow
6. Robin
7. Black headed gull
8. Magpie
9. Chaffinch
10. Collared Dove
11. Great Tit
12. Jackdaw
13. Starling
14. Feral Pigeon
15. Long tailed tit
16. Rook
17. Common Gull
18. Wren
19. Goldfinch
20. Song thrush

Over 190 species of birds have been recorded at Ogston Reservoir near Clay Cross. In winter the reservoir attracts a large wildfowl population which compete with thousands of roosting gulls for the attention of local birdwatchers.

The heron may be seen almost anywhere in Derbyshire, visiting waters of all kinds provided they hold fish.

All three species of woodpecker are found in Derbyshire. The green woodpecker is the largest. It is green-grey in colour with a bright green rump and red on the top of its head. The great spotted woodpecker is about the size of a blackbird with a distinctive black and white plumage. The lesser spotted woodpecker is the smallest of the three woodpeckers resident in Britain and probably the rarest in Derbyshire.

The great crested grebe is well established as a breeding species in lowland Derbyshire.

Several species of tit breed in the UK and all are fairly common in Derbyshire. They are the great tit, blue tit, coal tit, marsh tit, willow tit and long-tailed tit.

Several finches are to be found in Derbyshire including the Chaffinch, Brambling, Greenfinch, Goldfinch, Hawfinch, Redpoll, Bullfinch and Linnet.

The goldcrest is the smallest bird to be found in Derbyshire. It prefers to nest in coniferous woodland and as this is more commonly found in the Peak District, the goldcrest is more numerous here than in the south and east of the county.

The kestrel is the most common bird of prey in the Derbyshire Peak District. Although it will take a variety of prey it specialises in feeding on small mammals such as vole.

The teal is the smallest duck in Britain and hence also in Derbyshire. It is found predominantly in the Peak District particularly on the Chatsworth and the Derwent reservoirs.

The mallard is the most common duck in Derbyshire and is found throughout the county.

Five species of owl: barn owl, tawny owl, little owl, long eared owl and short eared owl are all found in Derbyshire.

Large numbers of pheasants are reared and liberated on many of Derbyshire's sporting estates each year to be shot in late autumn and winter.

The disused gravel pits at such places as Elvaston, Swarkestone, Willington, Egginton and Hilton contain a variety of wetland habitats. These attract a range of birds including Canada geese, Black-headed Gulls, Common terns, Water Rails and Willow Warblers.

Swallows, sand martins and house martins are all common summer visitors to Derbyshire. They tend to depend on buildings for breeding sites.

The cuckoo is a fairly common summer visitor to Derbyshire and has been observed throughout the county. Most arrive in late April and early May. Adults leave in July although juveniles have been observed as late as September or even early October.

Peregrine falcons have nested in the tower of Derby Cathedral since 2006 when an artificial nesting platform was created for them. In recent years a webcam has allowed thousands of people to watch them on the internet.

On 4 June 1927 Dr H. H. Hollick, Miss Kathleen Hollick and E. A. Sadler saw two Griffon Vultures over Ashbourne while watching for the return of homing pigeons.

During the early summer of 1997 a pair of hen harriers nested in the Goyt valley; the first breeding success in the Peak District for nineteen years. They did not return the following year and remain very rare not only in Derbyshire, but throughout the country.

Black grouse have recently been reintroduced into the Peak District in a collaborative project involving Severn Trent Water Authority, the National Trust and the Peak Park National Park Authority.

The wren, one of Britain's smallest birds is found throughout Derbyshire.

There are fifteen species of bat in Britain, of which eleven have been identified in Derbyshire.

The Common Pippestrelle is the most common species of bat found in Derbyshire.

Brand's Bat is rare in Derbyshire although it has recently been observed in the south of the county.

The Brown Long-Eared Bat has been observed in many parts of Derbyshire. It feeds in woodland areas and frequently roosts in buildings. It frequently hibernates in caves, mines and other underground sites.

Daubenton's Bat is found along the rivers and canals of Derbyshire.

Leister's Bat is a rare species nationally but is known to exist in parts of the Peak District.

Four species of reptile have been recorded in Derbyshire: slow worm, common lizard, grass snake and adder. Derbyshire's reptiles generally emerge from hibernation around April, but can be seen earlier, depending on the weather. Mating occurs April to May with young being born around August.

The grass snake is Britain's largest snake and can reach well over 120cm in length. In common with other snakes it can dislocate its jaw in order to swallow bulky items of prey such as frogs, young birds and even small rodents. It has been observed in many parts of Derbyshire but particularly on the eastern side of the county.

The adder, Britain's only venomous snake, is rare in Derbyshire but has been observed at one or two sites in the Peak District. It is smaller than the grass snake, usually up to 50cm long. Adders are generally grey or brown in colour with a zig-zag pattern along the back.

The common lizard is found in many parts of Derbyshire but particularly in the northern part of the county and the Peak District. They prefer sunny banks in a wide variety of dry habitats where they often bask on warm surfaces such as stones and roadside edges.

Derbyshire has five native species of amphibian: common frog, common toad, smooth newt, palmate newt and great crested newt.

The common frog is Derbyshire's most numerous amphibian. Its numbers have declined in recent years but it is still found throughout the county.

Otters were extinct in the county for many years during the latter part of the 20th-century. Although still uncommon in Derbyshire otters have been now been recorded on many of the rivers within the county and there are signs that a small but growing population is once again breeding on Derbyshire's waterways. They have even been seen in the River Derwent in the heart of Derby city centre. Otters make their home in the river bank in special dens known as holts. They eat mostly fish, especially eel but will also take frogs and waterside birds. Otters are a good indicator of clean water, free of pollutants.

Rabbits were introduced into Derbyshire by the Normans. They are found throughout Derbyshire.

Brown hares are found throughout most of Derbyshire. They like open habitats, and around 67% of all sightings within the county are on farmland. There has been a decline in population in recent years partly as a consequence of changes in farming practices.

The grey squirrel was introduced into the UK from North America. The first recorded sighting in Derbyshire was at Melbourne by Sir Vauncey Harper Crewe in 1906. They are now found throughout the county.

The dormouse was recently reintroduced into Derbyshire as part of a national programme. Dormice are protected under the Wildlife and Countryside Act which makes it illegal to disturb, harm or handle them without a license,

The harvest mouse has traditionally been associated with arable fields but recent surveys in Derbyshire have indicated that it is just as likely to be found in wetland habitats such as reedbeds and in rough grassland. Populations have been found at several sites in the east and south of the county. Changes in agricultural practices have led to a loss of habitat in some areas but this has been balanced by habitat creation schemes, particularly on old mining sites.

Mountain hares are found in the Derbyshire Peak District, which is the only population outside Scotland.

The polecat was on the verge of extinction in this country for much of the 20th-century and it was not recorded in Derbyshire until the 1990s. They are solitary, nocturnal animals and so are rarely seen. The polecat is best known for its ability to produce a powerfully unpleasant smell as a defence against predation. The majority of the polecat's diet is made up of rabbits, rats and amphibians, although they will eat anything from a hare to an earthworm!

Hedgehogs are found in gardens, parks, hedgerows, woodland and farmland in many parts of Derbyshire but are more commonly found in urban and suburban areas than in open countryside.

All three native species of deer are found in Derbyshire. Fallow deer are the most numerous and widespread.

Fallow Deer are found in a number of areas in Derbyshire, mainly in woodland habitats. There are currently three wild herds in the county; in South Derbyshire, the mid Derwent Valley and Morley. Park herds also exist at Calke Park, Chatsworth and the Chestnut Centre near Chapel-en-le-Frith. Private herds are maintained at Stanton Park and a site near Holloway.

Red Deer became extinct in Derbyshire at some point during the 18th-century and the wild herds which inhabit areas in the Goyt Valley, south of Whaley Bridge and at Big Moor above Barlow are derived from escapes from deer parks. Park herds can be seen at Chatsworth Park and Calke Park while smaller private herds are maintained at Alderwasley Park and other estates.

Roe Deer are rare in Derbyshire but have begun to re-colonise the county as they expand their range nationally from north to south. They are now fairly well established in the north east of the county although they have occasionally been recorded elsewhere in Derbyshire.

Muntjac deer have spread into Derbyshire in recent years and are now well established in the south of the county around Calke and Ticknall. They have also been seen at Carvers Rocks and Spring Wood nature reserves. Muntjac are a non-native species which originate in China. Their numbers have been steadily increasing since they were released from Woburn Park in 1925.

Foxes are common and widespread throughout Derbyshire including urban areas in and around Derby and Chesterfield.

Wolves became extinct in Derbyshire towards the end of the 15th-century though they seem to have survived longest in the Royal forest of the Peak. In 1586 William Camden wrote 'There is no danger of wolves now in these places though infested by them heretofore'.

# Nature Reserves in Derbyshire

Derbyshire Wildlife Trust manages over 40 nature reserves in the county covering over 1,600 acres. These range from flooded gravel pits in the south to moorland and upland areas in the north. Fourteen of these are Sites of Special Scientific Interest.

The **Avenue Washlands Reserve** at Chesterfield was created in 2005 on part of the decommissioned Avenue Coking Works. This wetland reserve is important for newts and water voles and birds such as lapwing, tufted duck and little grebe breed winter here and bittern have also been observed. The habitat also attracts a wide range of butterflies, dragonflies and other invertebrates.

**Barton Pool** near Long Eaton is a small wetland reserve which lies alongside a busy railway line. The areas of fen here support a number of plant species including greater pond sedge, greater yellowcress, reedmace and soft rush. The wetland habitat is important for a number of invertebrates and the trees along the boundary of the reserve provide a refuge for a range of birds.

**Broadhurst Edge Wood** at New Mills is a woodland reserve of approximately six hectares. The oak and birch trees here provide a welcoming habitat for a wide range of birds including kestrel, tawny owl, whinchat and redpoll. A total of 64 bird species have been recorded and 41 of these have bred here. A small pond near to the entrance of the reserve has been colonised by frogs and palmate newts as well as a number of invertebrate species. Birds and mammals are attracted to this site and brown hare, pygmy shrew, hedgehog and bank vole have all been observed.

**Brockholes Wood Reserve** in the North of Derbyshire is a site of special scientific interest and is one of the few remaining areas of upland oak woodland, with moorland. Small pockets of sessile oak woodland survive here alongside hairy birch and rowan. The berries provide food for mistle thrushes, blackbirds and fieldfare in autumn, whilst many other species enjoy the woodland cover. Elsewhere in the reserve a range of moorland plants thrive. These include bilberry, wavy hair grass and purple moor grass

**Carr Vale** on the outskirts of Bolsover is an important wetland reserve which is popular with birdwatchers. A mixture of open water, marsh, wet and dry grass and scrub and trees attract large numbers of wildfowl species in the winter months. Other winter visitors include flocks of finches and bunting which feed along the field boundaries. In spring and autumn migrating birds feed and roost here whilst in early summer the marsh and scrub here attract a range of breeding birds including reed and sedge warblers, whitethroat, yellowhammer and moorhen.

**Carvers Rocks** lies on the southern tip of Foremark Reservoir. It is owned by Severn Trent Water and is managed by Derbyshire Wildlife Trust. It is designated as a Site of Special Scientific Interest for its geology and plants. Its habitats include marsh, alder woodland and sphagnum moss. It is also contains one of the last patches of lowland heathland in Derbyshire.

**Chee Dale Nature Reserve** is a steep-sided gorge with grassland and ash woodland. It is designated as a Site of Special Scientific Interest and its ash woodland, limestone grassland and dramatic 200ft deep gorge are all internationally important. Several footpaths pass through the reserve including the Monsal Trail.

**Cramside Wood** between Cressbrook and Litton Mill is an area of ancient ash woodland above the River Wye. The ash and yew trees here provide shelter for a variety of woodland flowers in spring and summer including lily of the valley and sanicle.

**Cromford Canal Nature Reserve** is part of a former working waterway which is rich in wildlife. Plant life includes bank side species such as water mint and meadowsweet as well as a variety of meadow and woodland plants on the towpath. A number of different water birds are regularly observed here including ducks and moorhens. The wooded area along the canal also provides a home for birds such as blackbirds, robins and wrens. The canal is also one of the last remaining strongholds in the county of the water vole.

**Deep Dale** and **Topley Pike** is an area of grassland and an excellent example of a typical Peak District dry limestone dale. Bloody cranesbill and clustered bellflower are found on the steep upper slopes, whilst the screes provide an excellent habitat for the delicate limestone fern. The area attracts a number of invertebrates including the rare cistus forester moth.

**Derwentside Nature Reserve** lies next to the Cromford Canal, alongside the A6, about 1.5 miles from Cromford. This area of rough meadow and woodland is well known for its wild daffodils but other plants such as honeysuckle, wild garlic, guilder rose and yellow archangel are also found here. The plants attract a variety of insects which provide food for butterflies such as small tortoiseshell, comma, peacock and red admiral.

**Drakelow Nature Reserve** is an area of wetland comprising old gravel pits and riverside in the floodplain of the River Trent. Large numbers of wildfowl can be seen here during the winter months and in summer cormorants and a range of smaller species have been recorded. During the summer months the site is also rich in butterflies and dragonflies.

**Duckmanton Railway Cutting** was the first reserve acquired by Derbyshire Wildlife Trust specifically for its geology. A geological trail has been created here comprising seven trenches, each about two metres wide cut into the walls of the cutting. These allow visitors to observe a wide range of fossils from a number of different geological periods. In addition to the coal measures and a marine band, volcanic ash indicates that millions of years ago the area was periodically affected by volcanic eruptions. In addition to the geological importance of the site the area also attracts a range of birds and butterflies. Blue, green and willow tits have been observed here as well as great spotted woodpecker and yellow warbler. Butterflies recorded here include the speckled and the small tortoiseshell.

**Erewash Meadows** is a wetland reserve close to the Nottinghamshire border. The River Erewash flows through the reserve and at its downstream end forms a delta before flowing under Stoney Lane and the A610 Eastwood bye-pass. Resident species include water rail, reed bunting and lapwing.

**Gang Mine** is a grassland nature reserve which was established in an ancient lead mining area. A number of lead-tolerant plant species are found here including spring sandwort and alpine pennycress. Both are known locally as leadwort.

**Golden Brook Storage Lagoon** is a wetland reserve at Breaston. It was created to protect Long Eaton from flooding and for most of the year forms an area of shallow water which is home to a wide range of wetland and other plants. Birds such as snipe, reed bunting and water rail have all been observed here.

**Hadfield Quarry Nature Reserve** lies about a mile south of the village of Hope. The waters on the valley floor provide a home for the plamate newt and the reserve also supports a range of plants, beetles, butterflies and dragonflies.

**Hartington Meadows** covers an area of about 7.5 hectares. The grassland here is managed as part of a working farm and is cut for hay in mid-July. This encourages the growth of wild flowers which provide a riot of colour during the summer. The rough grassland is also a breeding site for a number of ground nesting birds.

**Hillbridge and Park Wood** in the Goyt Valley is a woodland nature reserve. Covering an area of 10 hectares the upland oakwood on this reserve is one of the largest in the area. In spring the woodland floor is covered in bluebells. The eastern boundary of the reserve is formed by the River Goyt and kingfishers and dippers have been recorded here. The reserve is also an important site for lichen and mosses.

**Hilton Gravel Pits** covers an area of 29 hectares. The former gravel pits now provide a combination of lakes, ponds and woodland which attracts dragonflies and damselflies. Fifteen species have been recorded here including the emperor and ruddy darter dragonflies and the emerald and red-eyed damselflies. The area also attracts many species of wildfowl including coot, great crested grebe and tufted duck. Kingfishers have also been observed and amphibians such as frogs, toads and great crested and common newts all breed here. The woodland habitat within the reserve encourages the growth of fungi including fly agaric and shaggy inkcap.

**Hollinhead** and **Markland Grips** near Clowne covers an area of around 20 hectares and contains areas of both woodland and grassland. Several tree species are found here including yew, growing on the sides of the valley and hazel coppice on the tops. Woodland flowers abound here including wood anemone, bluebell and dogs mercury. Colonies of bee orchid are to be found in the hazel coppice.

**Holly Wood** near Edlaston is a small woodland reserve. Sycamore are gradually being replaced with oak and other native broad-leaved species. A variety of birds breed here including blackcap, garden warbler and nuthatch. In the northern end of the reserve wetland plants such as marsh marigold and opposite leaved golden saxifrage flourish. The reserve is also home to foxes and badgers.

**Hopton Quarry** comprises three quarries covering a area of 8 hectares. It provides a good example of how wildlife can re-colonise worked-out limestone quarries. A variety of limestone plants grow here including a number of different orchids including the fly orchid, frog orchid and fragrant orchid.

**Ladybower Wood**, overlooking Ladybower Reservoir is an area of oak woodland with a few rowan and silver birch trees. The damp conditions here attract over 70 species of lichen. In spring and summer woodland birds such as pied flycatcher, redstart and wood warbler are found here. On the edge of the woodland, heather moorland provides a home for red grouse. Mountain hare have also occasionally been recorded here.

**Lock Lane Ash Tip** between Sawley and Trent Lock covers an area of 3.8 hectares. Once used as a tip for ash from the railways the site now provides a valuable habitat for a variety of wildlife. More than 200 species of moth as well as 16 types of butterfly have been recorded here and common lizards have been observed sunning themselves on the ash.

**Long Clough Nature Reserve** on the southern outskirts of Glossop covers an area of about 16 hectares. The reserve contains a variety of habitats including an area of oak woodland and a large sloping area of unimproved grassland which contains over 150 species of flowers, sedges and mosses. This grassland also contains a number of wet areas where flowers such as marsh marigold, marsh violet and heath spotted and common spotted orchid now flourish. A variety of birds including woodcock, tawny owl and willow warbler have been recorded here.

**Mapperley Wood** is a small woodland reserve on the southern edge of Shipley Country Park near Ilkeston. It comprises a narrow strip of woodland with a stream running through it. The reserve contains some of the county's most vunerable habitats including mature oak woodland, wetland and a small areas of acid grassland. A variety of birds are attracted here including woodland species such as great spotted woodpecker and nuthatch. In winter small numbers of waterfowl visit the ponds on the reserve.

**Millers Dale Quarry** in the Wye Valley is a disused limestone quarry which has been colonised by a number of unusual plants and animals. Orchids are found on the quarry floor and many other flowers flourish here. In Summer these include cowslips, harebells and wild strawberries.

**North Wingfield Nature Reserve** is a narrow strip of grassland with the River Rother running through it. The mixture of grassland and wetland here provides a refuge for a variety of plants and animals. The water vole, whose numbers have declined in many areas, has been observed here.

**Oakerthorpe Nature Reserve** is a small wetland area surrounded by woodland. Amphibians such as frogs, toads and common newts inhabit the ponds here and dragonflies and damselflies can be seen flying across its surface. The water vole which has declined sharply in recent years is also found here. Woodland flowers such as wood avens, bluebell and yellow archangel flourish here and a variety of wetland plants can be seen in the marshland areas.

**Overdale Nature Reserve** to the south of the Hope Valley is an area of upland pasture which contains a number of habitats. A variety of bird species have been recorded here including meadow pipit, skylark, whinchat, wheatear and curlew.

**Priestcliffe Lees Nature Reserve** is an area of steep limestone hillside above the River Wye and the Monsal Trail. Part of the area was previously used for lead mining and yellow mountain pansy and leadwort flourish here. Elsewhere in the reserve limestone flowers attract a variety of butterflies including the dark green fritillary. The ash woodland contains wych elm, bird cherry, blackcap and purging buckthorn. In summer birds such as redstart, blackcap and willow warbler visit the reserve.

**Risley Glebe Nature Reserve** covers just half a hectare but contains several different habitats and provides shelter for over 150 different plant species. In the summer butterflies such as the meadow brown and red admiral are seen here.

A brook flows through the reserve and the marshland area provides a home for frogs, freshwater shrimps and pond skaters. Dragonflies and damselflies are found here and kingfishers have been observed flying over the area. In the small woodland areas willow warblers, blackbirds and woodpeckers have all been recorded.

**Rose End Meadows Nature Reserve** near Cromford comprises sixteen small fields untouched by artificial fertilisers or herbicides. As a result the area resembles a limestone meadow of a century ago. In summer the area is covered by a wide variety of flowers including buttercups, cowslips, cow parsley and wood anemone. The profusion of flowers attract large numbers of insects and butterflies and a wide range of birds can be observed here throughout the year.

**Rowsley Sidings** has been described as a small mosaic of wet grassland, fen meadow and wet alder woodland. Covering a area of just one hectare this former railway siding is home to around 50 species of cranefly, including the Tipula maxima, the largest species found in Britain.

**Spring Wood Nature Reserve** on the eastern side of Staunton Harold Reservoir near Melbourne, has a mixture of trees including birch, oak, ash and alder. These provide nesting sites for a number of species of birds including great spotted woodpecker, nuthatch and tree creeper. Several species of fungi have been identified here including birch bracket and stinkhorn.

**Watford Lodge** is a small wetland reserve which provides a habitat for frogs, toads and palmate newts. Situated alongside the River Sett, visitors can enjoy the sight of kingfishers, wagtails and sandpipers. In the Lodge itself heron, mallard and moorhen have all been regularly observed.

**Willington Gravel Pits** is a wetland nature reserve which was created on a former sand and gravel quarry in the Trent Valley. The reserve is rich in bird life; attracting wildfowl, waders and grassland birds at different times of the year. Otters have been observed here and the area also attracts several species of dragonfly and damselfly

**Woodside Nature Reserve** at Shipley is located on the site of the former Woodside Colliery. It was purchased by the Derbyshire Wildlife Trust in 2011 and is the largest nature reserve in the county outside the Peak District National Park. The reserve contains a number of different habitats which attract a wide range of birds, butterflies and insects. Among the less common mammals which have been recorded on the site are brown hares and water voles.

**Wyver Lane** near Belper is an important wetland area in the Derwent Valley. It has a number of resident species including Canada geese, tufted duck and little grebe. They are joined throughout the year by other species including curlews, sandpipers, gulls and waterfowl. The reserve is one of the few remaining areas of wet grassland in the mid-Derwent Valley and is the only site with a large enough area of undisturbed grassland for wigeon to overwinter.

**There are number of national nature reserves in Derbyshire including the Derbyshire Dales, Dovedale and Kinder Scout.**

**The Derbyshire Dales National Nature Reserve** is managed by English Nature and consists of five separate limestone valleys in the Peak District National Park: Lathkill, Cressbrook, Monks, Long and Hay Dale. These represent a good example of all the major wildlife habitats of the White Peak. Flower-rich grasslands make up over half the area of the reserve and limestone plants such as common rock rose and salad burnett are abundant. Rarities include Jacob's ladder, spring cinquefoil and Nottingham catchfly. In Spring early purple orchids and cowslips flourish here. Insects are equally diverse and south-facing and west-facing slopes are home to less common species such as the northern brown argus butterfly and the cistus forester moth.

**Dovedale** was named as a National Nature Reserve in 2006. It is widely regarded as one of the country's finest wildlife sites with diverse plant life and interesting rock formations. Wren, kingfisher, heron and dipper have all been recorded here and the area is also home to a number of rare or unusual plant species including Solomon's seal, lily of the valley and Paris quadrifolia. Startling rock formations here include Pickering Tor, Reynard's Cave, Ilam Rock, Lionshead Rock and Dove Holes. Dovedale is owned by the National Trust and attracts thousands of visitors each year.

**Kinder Scout** is a National Nature Reserve covering an area of 700 hectares. This moorland plateau is one of the most famous upland sites in the country and comprises a number of different habitats including blanket bog and sub-alpine dwarf shrub heath. The area supports several upland breeding birds including birds of prey and waders, curlew and ring ouzel. Kinder is the most southerly location of the cloudberry and wildlife here include the mountain hare, which were reintroduced into the areas from Scotland in the 1830s.

# Rivers and Waterways

## Canals

**The Trent and Mersey Canal**, which passes through Derbyshire for some 14 miles of its length, was one of the first major canals to be constructed in this country. The Act of Parliament authorising the Canal received the Royal Assent on 14 May 1766. James Brindley was appointed as surveyor general and armies of navvies worked for eleven years to complete this huge project. From its opening in May 1777 the Trent and Mersey canal was a considerable commercial success. Goods such as coal, iron ore, stone, flint, clay, lime, pottery, salt, corn, cheese and timber were all transported along the canal. In addition from the ports came as such commodities as beer, wine, tobacco, sugar and cotton. This commercial success resulted in considerable financial gain for the shareholders. At one point £100 shares were selling at £840 and between 1820 and 1831 the annual dividend reached a phenomenal 75%! The canal continued to be successful until well into the 20th-century. Today hardly any freight is carried on the canal but it remains an important link between the many canals which are used by pleasure boaters. Marinas have been developed at a number of places including Shardlow, Stenson and Willington. The canal is also popular with fishermen, ramblers and bird-watchers.

**The Chesterfield Canal** was constructed between 1771 and 1777 and ran from Chesterfield to Northwood, past Shireoaks and Worksop to East Retford and thence to the River Trent at West Stockwith. It was promoted by a number of interests including the Cavendish family who owned a furnace and a forge at Staveley, the London Lead Company who wanted a more convenient shipping place than Bawtry for the products of their smelt mill at Ashover and several important landowners who wished to exploit their coal resources. James Brindley was appointed as the engineer but he died in 1772 and the project was completed by James Varley. The canal was not an immediate commercial success but the construction of horse-drawn tramways to collieries at Inkersall, Spinkhill, Norbriggs and Glasshouse Common led to an increase in traffic on the canal. The first dividend was not paid to shareholders until 1789. The traffic in that year comprised 42,379 tons of coal,

7,569 tons of stone, 4,366 tons of corn, 3,955 tons of lime, 3,862 tons of lead and 1,544 tons of iron together with much smaller quantities of pottery, ale and other sundry items. Tonnage reached its peak in 1848 when a total of 201,544 tons of goods were carried. By this time, however, the canal had already been taken over by the Manchester, Sheffield and Lincolnshire Railway and within ten years the amount carried had fallen to only 110,761 tons. In 1871 the Norwood Tunnel began to be affected by mining subsidence and although £21,000 was spent on repairs over the next 35 years the Royal Commission of 1906 reported that there were only 40 boats working on the canal and none beyond the tunnel on the Chesterfield side. In 1908 part of the tunnel finally collapsed bringing an end to almost all traffic above Shireoaks. The last commercial traffic was from the brickyards at Walkeringham to West Stockwith although this finally ceased in 1955. Within a few years the canal had become derelict and largely impassable. Fortunately this decline was halted and reversed. Today the canal is navigable from West Stockwith to Worksop

**The inland canal** port of Shardlow is one of only two such ports in the country. Shardlow was chosen by James Brindley to be the transhipment point where goods were transferred from the narrow boats which operated on the Trent and Mersey Canal to the larger barges which navigated the River Trent. As this transhipment was not usually from boat to boat, warehouses had to be built to store the goods until they were needed for the onward journey. In the area between the canal and the turnpike road (now the main road to Derby) a large number of impressive brick-built warehouses were constructed. Basins and inlets were excavated to provide access to these warehouses and wharfs were built to accommodate the hundreds of boats which unloaded their cargoes. As originally these barges were drawn by horses stabling was also provided for around 100 animals. Trade was so brisk that three firms trading in bulk goods maintained agents at Shardlow: Corte & Co, paper dealers of Leicester; Shipton & Co, timber merchants of Wolverhampton; and Daniel & Company, iron merchants of London. The port of Shardlow dealt with a wide variety of goods including, iron, coal, limestone, gypsum, salt, lead. pottery, cheese, ale, timber, malt and barley, and boats returned to Shardlow with cotton from Manchester which was transported to the Trent and sent on to Nottingham. So busy did Shardlow become that it became known locally as 'Little Liverpool' or 'a rural Rotterdam'. The coming of the canal to Shardlow brought industries in its wake including malting, brewing, boat building, rope making and corn milling.

Partly as a consequence of this the population increased from around 300 in 1789 to 1,306 in 1841. This 'golden age' was, however, short lived for with the coming of the railways Shardlow began to decline in importance and prosperity. Over the years the area fell into decline and many of the buildings became derelict. This decline was halted and reversed in 1975 when the Shardlow Wharf Conservation Area was created. Many of the buildings which served the canal have been restored to their former glory or converted to other uses and today the village stands as probably the best example of an 18th-century inland port surviving in this country.

**The Erewash canal** was built to carry coal from the collieries in the Erewash Valley to the Trent from whence it could be transported to Loughborough, Leicester and elsewhere. John Varley, who at one time had been apprenticed to James Brindley and was Clerk of Works on the Chesterfield Canal, was appointed Engineer at a salary of £220 per annum. The canal took about two years to complete and was officially opened on 10 December 1779 when a 'grand regatta' was held to celebrate the occasion. The building of the canal stimulated the sinking of more coal pits in the area and within a few years a network of tramways had been constructed to bring coal to the many wharves along the line of the canal. The opening of the Derby and Nutbrook canals resulted in an increase in traffic and by 1808 a total of 270,000 tons of coal was carried on the canal. Other cargoes included limestone, lead, iron, millstones, chalk and marble. This growth in trade brought increased prosperity for the shareholders. Dividends increased dramatically and by 1830 the original £100 shares had a market value of £1,300. Within a few years railway competition led to a long period of decline and neglect. Traffic had virtually ceased by the end of the Second World War and nationalisation in 1947 did nothing to revive the fortunes of the Erewash Canal. Closure came in 1968 when the Transport Act of that year defined it as a 'remainder waterway'. To prevent it becoming derelict the Erewash Canal Preservation and Development Association was formed. The canal was eventually restored to cruising standard and the restoration of the Great Northern Basin was completed in 1973. In May 2008 a boat rally was held here with over 100 boats attending.

**The Nutbrook canal** was built as an independent branch of the Erewash Canal for the purpose of serving the West Hallam and Shipley collieries. It carried little but coal, iron and limestone and was only 4.5 miles long. The Nutbrook Canal was promoted by Edward Miller-Mundy, the owner of collieries at Shipley and Sir Henry Hunloke of Wingerworth near Chesterfield, the owner of the estate and collieries at West Hallam. Benjamin Outram was appointed as the engineer and the canal was completed in 1796. Traffic in coal from the Shipley and West Hallam collieries built up rapidly and within about ten years about fifty thousand tons was being carried annually. Like other canals in the area the Nutbrook canal was affected by railway competition. The building of branch lines from the Erewash Valley Railway to the Nutbrook and Shipley collieries resulted in a decline in traffic and the canal also suffered from mining subsidence. Traffic eventually ceased in 1895 although the lower part of the canal was used as late as 1947 by the Stanton Ironworks Company. Since that time much of the line has been obliterated and it is now virtually impossible to trace the route that it took.

**The Cromford Canal** was promoted by Sir Richard Arkwright who wanted to link his mills at Cromford with the terminal basin of the Erewash Canal at Langley Mill. He was joined in the enterprise by a group of business associates who represented interests in lead, limestone, coal, iron and cotton. The advantages of a canal connecting Cromford to the Trent and with the major ports of Liverpool and Hull meant that the finance for the canal was raised in a matter of weeks. There were some problems with construction and the canal was not finally opened until August 1794 at a cost of nearly twice the original estimate of £42,697. Once opened, however, the canal contributed a great deal to the economic and commercial development of the area. It extended the markets available to both local manufacturers and coal and mineral owners in the area. It led to a reduction in the price of coal and other necessities to the people of mid-Derbyshire and was a financial success bringing handsome rewards to its shareholders. Coal, limestone and ironstone were important cargoes and a number of tramways were built to connect collieries, limestone quarries and ironstone workings to the many wharfs along the canal. Apart from coal and coke, which consistently provided over 75 per cent of its trade the canal was also used for transporting a wide variety of raw materials and manufactured goods. It served Arkwright's cotton mills by transporting both raw cotton and textile yarn; chert was conveyed from Bakewell to the Potteries and building stone from local quarries was carried throughout the country. The Butterley Company made substantial use of the canal. Two shafts were sunk into the Butterley Tunnel from the Ironworks yard and goods were transferred to and from the barges below by whimsies. For many years the canal carried limestone from Crich to act as a flux in the Butterley furnaces and the wide range of goods manufactured by the company were carried by waterways throughout the Kingdom. This success lasted for a number of years and the opening of the Cromford and High Peak Railway in 1831 linking Cromford with the Peak Forest Canal at Whaley Bridge initially brought increased traffic onto the canal. Before long, however, the Cromford Canal had to face competition from the railways. By 1849 it had lost much of its traffic to the Manchester, Buxton, Matlock and Midland Junction Railway and after protracted negotiations the canal was finally sold to this railway company. There followed a long but gradual period of decline. In 1944 the canal was finally abandoned as a navigable waterway. Today the Cromford Canal has a new role as a leisure amenity and is popular with walkers, cyclists and bird watchers.

**The Derby Canal** was promoted by a number of local landowners, industrialists, bankers and coal masters as well as representatives of the Derby Navigation Company, the Grand Trunk Company and the Erewash Company. When completed in 1796 the canal ran from Swarkestone to Derby and then on to Little Eaton where a horse-drawn railway ran to Denby. In addition a branch connected Derby with the Erewash canal at Sandiacre. One of the chief reasons why the canal had been built was to bring coal cheaply to Derby but this was not the only cargo carried. Boats on the Sandiacre line in particular carried a whole variety of goods. It was also this line that boats coming from the Erewash Canal proceeded, bringing such things as iron, limestone, paving stones and other goods in addition to coal. On the Swarkestone line cargoes included corn, cement, castings, lead and timber. In addition to the various goods carried the canal also served passengers. For a number of years a market boat equipped with seats and a fireplace left Swarkestone every Friday morning to carry market people to Derby and returned again at the end of the day. For a number of years the canal was a financial and commercial success but competition from a number of railway companies in the 1840s onwards forced the company to reduce its tolls. Attempts were made to sell the canal to the Midland Railway company but negotiations came to nothing and the Canal Company struggled on with decreasing tonnages being carried each year. The Little Eaton line was abandoned in 1935 but it was not until 1964 that the whole canal was finally abandoned.

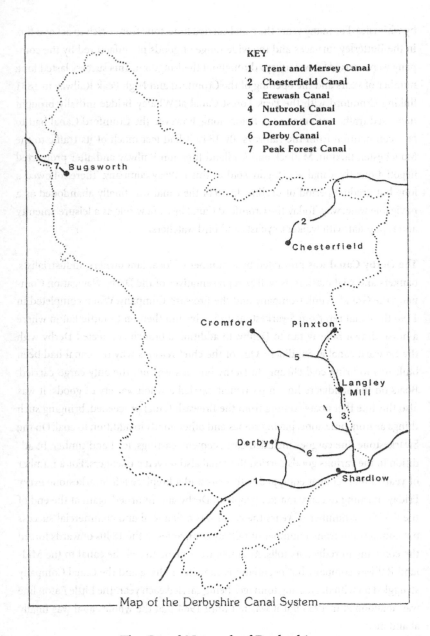

KEY

1 Trent and Mersey Canal
2 Chesterfield Canal
3 Erewash Canal
4 Nutbrook Canal
5 Cromford Canal
6 Derby Canal
7 Peak Forest Canal

Map of the Derbyshire Canal System

*The Canal Network of Derbyshire*

## Rivers

**The River Derwent is** the longest river in Derbyshire. From its source on Bleaklow, east of Glossop, it flows for about fifty miles to Derwent Mouth, near Sawley, where it enters the River Trent. Its course follows the Upper Derwent Valley with its three reservoirs (Howden, Derwent and Ladybower) which provide a water supply for a number of surrounding cities. From here it passes by the village of Bamford where it is joined by the River Noe. Its course then takes it through Hathersage, Grindleford, Calver, Baslow and the Chatsworth Estate. At Rowsley it is joined by the River Wye. After passing through Darley Dale it reaches Matlock and Matlock Bath which developed as a spa and more recently as an inland tourist resort. The river gardens are a popular attraction and rowing boats can be hired here. From the 18th-century the river provided a source of power for a number of textile mills between here and Derby and the area is now recognised as a World Heritage Site. The Derwent flows through the centre of Derby before joining the River Trent at the appropriately named Derwent Mouth.

The name Derwent is Celtic and means 'a valley thick with oaks'

Its tributaries include Bentley Brook, the River Amber, the River Westend, the River Ashop, the River Noe and the River Wye

For half of its course the River Derwent flows through the Peak District

At Matlock Bath an annual festival is held which includes a parade of illuminated boats on the River Derwent

A cable car crosses the River Derwent at Matlock Bath

The River Derwent was made navigable from Derwent Mouth to Derby under an Act of Parliament of 1720 and was opened to navigation in 1721. The river is no-longer considered navigable although the upper river (particularly at Matlock Bath) remains popular with canoeists.

An annual raft race takes place on Boxing day each year from Matlock, through Matlock Bath to Cromford Meadows.

The reservoirs of Howden, Derwent and Ladybower in the upper Derwent Valley supply water to the cities of Sheffield, Derby, Nottingham and Leicester.

**The River Trent** flows through Derbyshire for part of its course. It enters the county just a short distance past Burton-upon-Trent. At Newton Solney it is met by the River Dove and then flows through Willington, Ingleby, Barrow-upon-Trent and Swarkestone. Near Wilden Ferry the canal port of Shardlow was established as a transhipment point between the Trent and Mersey Canal and the River Trent. Here the river becomes fully navigable for the first time and at Cavendish Bridge there is a boatyard and a substantial marina. The river leaves Derbyshire at Trent Lock.

**The River Dove** is an important tributary of the River Trent. It rises on the eastern slope of Axe Edge and drains an area of around 95,000 acres. For the greater part of its course it forms the boundary between Derbyshire and Staffordshire. The river has been described as a 'walkers river' since it is possible to walk along the first twenty miles of its course. After passing Longnor and Hartington the river cuts through a series of dramatic limestone gorges including Beresford Dale, Wolfscote Dale and Milldale. The river continues through Dovedale, which attracts millions of visitors each year. They are attracted by the famous stepping stones as well as caves and limestone formations such as Lionshead Rock, Ilam Rock and Lovers' Leap. An annual cross country race the Dovedale Dash is also held each year along the banks of the river between Ilam and Thorpe. After passing through Dovedale the river emerges into a broad and fertile valley, flows through Rocester and Tutbury (in Staffordshire) and enters the Trent at Newton Solney.

**The River Erewash** marks the boundary between Derbyshire and Nottinghamshire for much of its length. From its source near Kirkby-in-Ashfield in Nottinghamshire it flows westwards to Eastwood and then south through Ilkeston and Sandiacre before joining the River Trent near Long Eaton. The river also gives its name to Erewash Borough Council which was formed in 1974, when the former borough of Ilkeston and the urban district of Long Eaton were united with some of the surrounding rural areas. The River Erewash Foundation was formed a few years ago with the aim of restoring the river to its historic biodiversity.

**The River Wye** is one of the major tributaries of the Derwent. It rises on Axe Edge above Buxton and flows in a south easterly direction for about 15 miles through Buxton, Ashford-in-the-Water and Bakewell. It passes Haddon Hall and is joined by the River Lathkill before flowing into the Derwent at Rowsley. For part of its early course it flows underground, re-emerging in Poole's Cavern to flow into the town centre of Buxton. The Wye is well known for its naturally breeding population of rainbow trout and is popular with fishermen. Brown trout and grayling are also found here and parts of the river are frequently stocked for syndicates, hotels and others who pay handsomely for the fly fishing.

*Bridge over the River Wye at Bakewell*

Other rivers which flow through Derbyshire for all or part of their course include the Amber, the Ashop, the Bradford, the Ecclesbourne, the Goyt, the Hipper, the Lathkill, the Manifold, the Mease, the Noe and the Rother.

# Derbyshire and the Military

## The Army

Normanton Barracks, Derby was the regimental headquarters of the Sherwood Foresters from 1877 until 1966.

**The 95th Derbyshire regiment** was formed in 1823 and saw service in Malta, the Ionian Islands, Cylon and China. In 1854 the regiment was posted to the Crimea where it fought with distinction in the battles of Alma, Inkerman and Sevastapol. The Crimean War was barely over when the 95th was sent to India to help quell the Sepoy Mutiny. Over a period of 16 months the regiment marched over 3,000 miles through jungle and desert and fought in fourteen actions. It was not until 1870 that they returned to England. A little over a decade later the regiment lost its individual identity to become the 2nd Battalion of the Sherwood Foresters.

**The Sherwood Foresters** came into a being as a consequence of the army reforms of 1881. The Derbyshire and Nottinghamshire regiments were merged. The 45th (Nottinghamshire) Regiment became the 1st Battalion and the 95th (Derbyshire) Regiment became the 2nd Battalion of the combined regiment. During the First World War the Sherwood Foresters raised 32 battalions. These fought with great distinction in Flanders, France, Gallipoli and Italy and a total of nine Victoria crosses were awarded to members of the regiment. At the outbreak of the Second World War the 1st battalion was serving in Palestine. The 2nd battalion was sent to France as part of the British Expeditionary Force and was later joined by the 1/5th, 2/5th and 9th battalions. All took part in the fighting leading to Dunkirk. Meanwhile the 8th Battalion took part in the ill-fated Norwegian campaign. Unfortunately the 1/5th Battalion were made prisoners of war after the fall of Singapore. In North Africa the 2nd and 5th Battalions fought with the First Army while the 14th Battalion took part in the Battle of El Alamein. Later in the War all three battalions took part in the fierce fighting of the Italian Campaign. In the post war period the regiment served in Germany, Egypt, Libya, Malaya and Cyprus. In 1971 the Sherwood Foresters was amalgamated with the Worcestershire Regiment. The regiment was again amalgamated on 1 September 2007 and became the 2nd Battalion, the Mercian regiment.

During the First World War the Sherwood Foresters lost 11,409 men. Nine members of the regiment were awarded the Victoria Cross and more than 2,000 received other decorations, honours and distinctions.

In the Second World War a total of 26,940 officers and men served in the Sherwood Foresters, of whom 1,520 were killed or died of wounds and about three times that number were wounded.

The war memorial of the Sherwood Foresters is located in the Derbyshire village of Crich. It takes the form of a lighthouse tower and stands on the summit of a 1,000 ft hill. It was dedicated in 1923 in memory of the 11,409 men of the Sherwood Foresters who gave their lives in the First World War. Later a plaque was added to commemorate the 1,520 men who gave their lives in World War Two.

The Mercian Regiment is an infantry regiment of the British Army which was formed in 2007. It serves as the county regiment of Cheshire, Derbyshire, Nottinghamshire, Staffordshire and Worcestershire. Since its creation the regiment has been regularly deployed to Afghanistan. The Colonel in Chief of the Regiment is HRH Price Charles. The regimental motto is "Stand Firm, Strike Hard".

## The Royal Navy

A number of ships have been named after places in Derbyshire. These include *HMS Buxton, HMS Derby, HMS Chesterfield* and *HMS Derbyshire*. Other Royal Navy ships have over the years been adopted by local communities.

**HMS Buxton** was a town class destroyer purchased from the United States in 1940. Originally the *USS Edwards*, the ship was allocated to the 6th Escort group, Western Approaches Command for the dangerous and vital duty of protecting Britain's supply lanes. In 1943 she was transferred to the Royal Canadian navy as *HMCS Buxton* and served as a training ship. She was finally paid off in 1945.

**HMS Chesterfield** was a town class destroyer purchased from the United States in 1940. Originally the USS Welbourne C. Wood, the ship was employed in convoy duty for most of the war. She was paid off in 1945 as more modern warships became available and was broken up for scrap in 1947.

**HMS Derby** was a Hunt class minesweeper which was launched on the Clyde in August 1918. After a period in the Reserve she joined the East India Station in 1940. Later in the same year the ship was deployed to the Eastern Mediterranean for convoy escort duties and to support military operations. Following a successful Warship Week National Savings Campaign in March 1942 *HMS Derby* was adopted by Bakewell. Later in the War she returned to mine-sweeping duties but was laid up in Reserve in Gibraltar in 1945. The ship was placed on the Disposal list in 1946 and towed from Gibraltar for demolition in Spain later that year.

During the Second World War Derby adopted *HMS Kenya*, a crown colony-class light cruiser which was commissioned in September 1940. The ship took part in the hunt for the *Bismark* in May 1941 and later took part in the sinking of the German supply tanker, *Belchen*. Later in the war she was engaged in escorting Arctic convoys. The ship also saw service in Burma during the closing months of the war and was involved in the Korean War between 1950 and 1951. *HMS Kenya* was finally scrapped in 1962. The original ship's wheel is in Derby Council House and the plaque presented to Derby in 1943 is held by Derby Sea Cadets.

Following a Warship Week, National Savings Campaign in February 1942 *HMS Danae*, a D Class cruiser was adopted by Chesterfield. Launched in 1918, *HMS Danae* was engaged in trade defence and convoy escort duties for most of the Second Wold War. The ship also provided gunfire support during the Normandy landings in June 1944.

**HMS Sovereign**, one of the Royal Navy's fleet submarines, was adopted by Derby in 1975. The propulsion unit for this submarine was designed and developed by Rolls Royce and Associates in Derby. Launched in 1970 and commissioned in 1974 *Sovereign* was a member of the Swiftsure class of submarines and was armed with Spearfish torpedoes, Harpoon missiles and Tomahawk cruise missiles. After a varied career she was decommissioned in September 2006.

*HMS Ambush* is currently Derbyshire's affiliated nuclear submarine. The second of the new Astute class of submarines, it was launched in 2011 and is expected to be commissioned in 2013. Powered by the latest Rolls-Royce reactor, which has been designed to operate for the full life of the submarine it will also be quieter and more difficult to detect than previous nuclear submarines. *HMS Ambush* will be armed with 38 American Tomahawk cruise missiles and an undisclosed number of Spearfish torpedoes.

## The Royal Air Force

There are currently no RAF bases in Derbyshire but during the Second World War the following were operational:

**RAF Ashbourne** was built as a base for bombers with three runways, the longest being 1,700 yards long. Construction began in the spring of 1941 and the airfield opened during the summer of 1942. Ashbourne served as training base throughout its operational life and from 1943 became heavily involved in training for supply dropping and glider towing. After the war the airfield was used for the storage of munitions. This ceased in 1954 and the base was then run down and closed. The site is now an industrial estate, appropriately named Airfield Industrial Estate.

**RAF Burnaston** was opened in June 1939 as Derby Airport, It served as a flying training school for the RAF throughout the Second World War using Magister and Tiger moth aircraft. Training continued here after the war but in March 1947 training was handed over to a civilian company (Air Schools Ltd). The RAF continued to use the airfield alongside its civil owners, Derby Airport until the 1960s.

**RAF Church Broughton** was established in 1942 to train bomber crews. Training was carried out in mainly in Wellington bombers. Development work on the Gloster Meteor, Britain's first jet fighter, was also carried out here in from April 1944 until early 1946.

**RAF Darley Moor** was opened in late 1942. It was used for pilot training using Blenheim bombers. In the Summer of 1943, however, its role changed to airbourne forces pilot training in readiness for D-Day. Horsa gliders towed by Albemarle and

Whitley aircraft were use for training. From May 1945 until August 1954 Hardwick Park was used for the storage of explosives.

## Recipients of the Victoria Cross with connections to Derbyshire

**Fred Greaves** was born on 16 May 1890 at Killamarsh in north-east Derbyshire. After being educated at Bonds Main Council School he went on to work as a miner at Markham Colliery. A keen cyclist, he became the Derbyshire 50 and 100 mile champion. He joined the 9th Battalion The Nottinghamshire and Derbyshire Regiment in 1915 and after training he was posted to Egypt and then to the Dardanelles. After the withdrawal from Gallipoli he was sent with his Battalion to the Western Front. It was here at Poelle Chappelle, near Ypres on 4 October 1917, that he won the Victoria Cross. His platoon was held up by machine gun fire from a concrete pillbox and Corporal Greaves finding that his officers and senior NCOs were casualties, ran through a hail of bullets to capture the enemy stronghold and seize four machine guns. Later in the battle Greaves gathered his comrades to halt a German counter attack. His citation stated that the effect of his conduct on his men throughout the battle could not be overestimated and that those under his command responded gallantly to his example. He was presented with his Victoria Cross personally by King George V at Buckingham Palace. He was promoted to sergeant but at the end of the war returned to Markham Colliery where he worked as a Deputy. He became a member of the colliery's St John's Ambulance Division and was involved in the rescue following the Markham Pit Disaster in 1938. During the Second World War he served in the Home Guard. Fred Greaves died at his home in Brimington, Chesterfield on 11 June 1973 and his body was cremated. His Victoria Cross is displayed at the Sherwood Foresters Museum, Nottingham Castle.

**William Gregg** was born at Heanor on 27 January 1890. He attended Mundy Street School and on leaving started work as a miner at Shipley Colliery. He enlisted in the Rifle Brigade shortly before the outbreak of the First World War and in May 1915 was posted to France. In February 1917 he was awarded the Military Medal for leading a daring reconnaissance raid on German trenches and was promoted to corporal. Later in the same year he was awarded the Distinguished Conduct

Medal for leading a counter attack against the large numbers of German troops. He was promoted to sergeant and only a few months later he was awarded the Victoria Cross for 'the most conspicuous bravery and leadership in action'. On 6 May at Bucquay in France when all his officers had been hit Sergeant Gregg took command and rushed two enemy machine-gun posts. He then started to consolidate his position until driven back by a German counter-attack. With the arrival of reinforcements , however, he led another charge, personally bombing a hostile machine gun position, killing the crew and capturing the gun. When driven back again, he led another successful attack and held on to his position until ordered to withdraw. His citation described how he 'displayed the greatest coolness and contempt for danger, walking about encouraging his men and setting a magnificent example'. He was presented with the Victoria Cross by King George V at Frohen-le-Grand, France on 9 August 1918. He later achieved the rank of Company-sergeant major but at the end of the War he returned to Heanor and resumed work as a miner. During the Second World War he served with the Sherwood Foresters National Defence Company. He died in Heanor Memorial Hospital on 9 August 1969 and was buried with full military honours in the local cemetery. In 2010, following its refurbishment, the local leisure centre was renamed the 'William Gregg VC Leisure Centre'.

**Charles Hudson** was one of Derbyshire's most decorated soldiers and fought in both the First and Second World Wars. Born at Derby on 29 May 1892, he was educated at Sherbourne School, Dorset and the Royal Military College, Sandhurst. He travelled to Ceylon in 1912 where he managed a tea plantation but returned to England at the outbreak of the First World War. He was commissioned as a temporary 2nd Lieutenant into the Nottinghamshire and Derbyshire Regiment and posted to France. His ability and courage were soon noticed and he won swift promotion. His courage was recognised with the award of two DSOs, the MC and the Croix-de-Guerre. He was also mentioned in despatches on four occasions. The award of the Victoria Cross came in the final year of the War. On 15 June 1918, while serving as an acting Lieutenant-Colonel with the 11th battalion of the Sherwood Foresters near Assagio, Italy, he discovered that the front line had been penetrated. Lieutenant Colonel Hudson gathered together a number of headquarters staff including orderlies, servants and runners and led a charge against the enemy. Although severely wounded he continued to give directions for a successful counter attack which resulted in the capture of around 100 prisoners and six-machine guns. The citation stated that 'the high courage and determination displayed by Lieutenant-Colonel Hudson saved a serious situation and had it not been for his quick determination in organising a counter attack a large number of the enemy would have dribbled through, and a counter attack on a large scale would have been necessary to restore the situation.' He was presented with his Victoria Cross by King George V at Buckingham Palace on 18 September 1918 and was also decorated with the Italian Medal for military Valour. From 1938 to 1940 Hudson commanded 2nd Brigade. He fought in the Battle of France and was present at Dunkirk. In 1944 he was appointed Aide-de-camp to the King, a post which he held until his retirement from the Army in 1946. He died on 4 April 1959 and was buried in Denbury Churchyard, near Newton Abbot, Devon.

**Robert Humpston** was born in Derby in 1832 and later enlisted in the 2nd Battalion the Rifle Brigade. He first saw service in the Crimea and was present at the battles of Alma and Inkerman. He received his Victoria Cross in recognition of his actions at Sebastapol where, along with two other riflemen, he charged a Russian rifle pit in broad daylight. He was decorated by Queen Victoria on 26 June 1857 at the first investiture in Hyde Park. He remained in the army and later saw service in India, where he was involved in the suppression of the Indian Mutiny. On his discharge he returned to Derby where he died on 22 December 1884. He was buried four days later in an unmarked grave in Nottingham General Cemetery. The grave remained unmarked for over 100 years but funds were eventually raised for a headstone which was unveiled on 8 September 2007 in the presence of the Lord Mayor of Nottingham and two of Robert Humpston's direct descendents.

**Godfrey Meynell** was born at Meynell Langley in Derbyshire on 30 May 1904. He was educated privately at Norris Hill School before going on to Eton. After passing out from Sandhurst he travelled to India to join the King's Shropshire Light Infantry. He fell in love with the country and in 1926 transferred to Queen Victoria's Corps of Guides where his knowledge of Hindustani and Pashtu proved to be a real advantage. He was awarded the Military Cross in 1933 for his gallantry laying a successful ambush while escorting the Chitral Relief Expedition. Two years later his courage and self-sacrifice was recognised in the award of a posthumous Victoria Cross, While fighting against Mohand tribesmen Captain Meynell and a force of about thirty men fought against overwhelming odds to hold their position. When their Lewis guns were put out of action Captain Meynell and his men continued to engage the enemy in close hand-to-hand fighting. Mortally wounded, it is said that he continued to protect the bodies of his men before he died. The citation stated that the fine example he set his men, coupled with his determination to hold the position to the last, maintained the traditions of the army and reflect the highest credit on the fallen officer and his comrades. His body was later recovered and was buried with full military honours in the Guides Cemetery at Mardan. His Victoria Cross was presented to his widow by King Edward VIII at Buckingham Palace on 14 July 1936. There is a memorial to Captain Meynell VC in Kirk Langley Parish Church.

**Jacob Rivers** was born at Derby on 17 November 1881. He came from a poor family and at the age of eighteen he enlisted in the Royal Scotts Fusiliers. After seven years service in India he was discharged and found employment with the Midland Railway in Derby. Soon after the outbreak of the First World War he re-enlisted, this time joining the Nottinghamshire and Derbyshire Regiment. Because of his previous service he was included in one of the first drafts sent to France where he was involved in much heavy fighting. The award of the Victoria Cross was made following an act of conspicuous bravery on 12 March 1915 at Neuve Chapelle. It was here that Private Rivers, on his own initiative, crept to within a few yards of a very large number of the enemy and hurled bombs on them, forcing their retreat. He was killed later on the same day while engaged in a similar action. His Victoria Cross was presented to his mother by King George V at Buckingham Palace on 29 November 1916. Jacob Rivers' body was never recovered and he has no known grave. His name is however commemorated on the La Tourt Memorial in France.

**John Smith** was born at Ticknall in February 1814. In 1837 he joiuned the Honourable East India Company and after training as an engineer he set sail for India in 1839. In 1841 he was involved in the first Afghan War and later took part in the Punjab Campaign, fightimng in the battles of Sobraon, Mooltan and Googerjerat. A period a relative peace followed during which Smith was employed by the Department of Public Works in the Punjab. The Indian Mutiny brought an end to this period of calm and John Smith, now a sergeant was called upon to help in the recapture of the fortress city of Delhi. An important element of the attack was the destruction of the Kashmir Gate, one of the main entrances to the city. As part of a small group led by two officers Sergeant Smith was responsible for blowing in the Gate . Four members of the group were awarded the Victoria Cross for their part in this action. John Smith's citation read; 'For conspicuous gallantry in conjunction with Lieutenants Home and Salkeld, in the performance of the desperate duty of blowing in the Kashmir Gate of the fortress of Delhi in broad daylight, under a heavy and destructive fire of musketry, on the morning of the 14 September, 1857, preparatory to the assault'. Two years later he was commissioned as an ensign but on 26 June 1864, while on a visit to Jullundur, he died from dysentery. He was buried the following day with full military honours in the Artillery Cemetery there.

**Charles Stone** was born at Street Lane, Denby, near Belper on 4 February 1889. After leaving school he worked as a miner at Denby and Saltwood collieries. He enlisted in the Royal Field Artillery soon after the outbreak of the First World War and after training was posted to France. In October 1917 he was awarded the Military Medal for treating a wounded man without regard for his own safety during a heavy bombardment. Less than six months later on 21 March 1918 at Caponne Farm, France he won the Victoria Cross for an act of outstanding bravery. After working at his gun for six hours under heavy gas and shell fire Gunner Stone was sent back to the rear with a message. He delivered it and then voluntarily returned under heavy fire to assist in holding up the advance of the enemy. First lying in the open and then on the right flank of the two rear guns he held the enemy at bay. At one point he braved heavy machine gun fire to protect the guns. Later he was one of the party which captured a machine gun and four prisoners. The citation stated that Gunner Stone's behaviour throughout the whole day was beyond praise and his magnificent example and fine work through these critical periods undoubtedly kept the guns in action, thereby holding up the enemy on the battle zone at the most crucial moment'. After being decorated by King George V at Buckingham Palace he returned to Belper where he was given a civic reception and presented with a gold watch and chain and £100 worth of war bonds. After his discharge from the army in 1919 he returned to work at Saltwood Colliery, later moving to work at a farm near Ashbourne. He died on 29 August 1952 and was buried with full military honours in Belper Cemetery.

**Sir Henry Wilmot** was born at Chaddesden, Derby on 3 February 1831. He was educated at Rugby School and then joined the 43rd (Oxfordshire and Buckinghamshire) Light Infantry. He transferred to the Rifle Brigade and saw service in the Crimea and India. It was during heavy fighting in and around the besieged city of Lucknow on 11 March 1858 that Henry Wilmot, then a captain won his Victoria Cross. His company was engaged in heavy fighting near the Iron Bridge at Lucknow, when Captain Wilmot found himself with only four men at the end of a street and a large body of the enemy advancing towards them. One of his men was shot in the legs and was carried back by his comrades while Captain Wilmot, under heavy enemy fire covered their retreat using each of the men's rifles in turn. He went on to serve in China in the Second Opium War. After leaving the army he went on to serve as Conservative Member of Parliament for South Derbyshire from 1869 to 1885. Following the death of his brother without heir, Sir Henry was obliged to give up his political career to become the 5th Baron Chaddesden. He became a KCB in 1897 and died in April 1901

# Markers, Malls and Fairs

## Market Days in Derbyshire

Alfreton: Tuesday, Thursday, Friday and Saturday
Ashbourne: Thursday and Saturday
Bakewell: Monday
Belper: Saturday
Buxton: Tuesday and Saturday
Chapel-en-le-Frith: Thursday
Chesterfield: Monday, Friday and Saturday
Clay Cross: Saturday
Derby (Eagle Centre): Monday, Tuesday, Thursday, Friday and Saturday
Derby (Market Hall): Monday to Saturday
Dronfield: Thursday
Eckington: Friday
Glossop: Thursday, Friday and Saturday
Heanor: Friday and Saturday
Ilkeston: Thursday and Saturday
Killamarsh: Thursday
Matlock: Tuesday and Friday
New Mills: Thursday, Friday and Saturday
Ripley: Friday and Saturday
Staveley: Friday
Swadlincote: Tuesday, Friday and Saturday
Wirksworth: Tuesday

Farmers Markets are usually held out of doors in large communal spaces that allow farmers to sell their produce to the general public. Derbyshire has several such markets, most of which adhere to three golden rules:

1. Producers must be local, defined as within a specified radius of the market (normally 30 miles).
2. Producers must sell their own produce. Bakers etc must use a minimum of one local ingredient.
3. The person behind the stall must be the producer, a close family member or an employee directly involved with the product, allowing you to ask questions about how it was produced.

Farmers Markets are known to operate at the following locations within Derbyshire:

Alfreton: Third Saturday of every month
Bakewell: Last Sunday of each month
Belper: Second Saturday of each month
Buxton: First Thursday of the month
Castleton: First Sunday of the month
Chesterfield: Second Wednesday and last Sunday of each month
Derby: Every third Thursday in the month
Hathersage: First Saturday each month
Heanor: Third Saturday of the month
Matlock: Third Saturday of the month

Fixed stalls in Derby's medieval market were often handed down from one generation to the next.

In 1772 Thomas Bott, a farmer, sold his wife for eighteen pence. The transaction took place at Derby Market Place where she was delivered to her purchaser with a halter around her waist.

On 6 April 1954 a fire swept through Derby's Morledge Market causing considerable damage.

Derby's Shrovetide football match traditionally started in the Market Place. The winner of the previous year's game would turn up the ball there before a massive scrum attempted to push the ball towards one of the goals. The first mention of the game in local newspapers was in 1747 though its origins probably date back to the Middle Ages. The game was suppressed in 1847 and has not been played since.

Derby's Market was held in the Market Place until the first half of the 20th-century.

A description of Derby Market place provides the following detailed picture of the area in 1712:

On the East side of the Market Place stands a handsome large pile of building called the Court, which helps to grace it much, as does the cross, under which there is a conduit of good water brought from the Newlands. There is also the Guildhall of the town in the South West corner of the place where the Corporation meet, under which is the Town gaol... Over against it stands a good handsome hall, erected by Mr Crompton, part on the Butchery on the West side of the place, and part on pillars where the market people sell butter, eggs and poultry stand, and behind it part of the Rotten Row... At the upper end of Rotten Row is called the Market Head, where proclamations are usually made and put up, and where the Corporation meet on common matters to assemble, as for visits to judges and the like; at the lower end of Rotten Row is the Corn Market which is very great, where there are several posts set up, about which the several sorts of grain are set and sold.

Derby has a number of retail markets including the Market Hall, Fish Market, Eagle Centre Market and Allenton Market. In addition there is also a cattle market and a wholesale market.

Derby Market Hall was opened on 29 May 1866. When first opened, the Hall contained thirty-eight butcher's shops and around 150 stalls selling a wide range of goods including flowers, fruit, vegetables, books, newspapers, grocery, jewellery, sweets, toys and even sewing machines! On the balcony there were refreshment stalls and a number of drapers. The building was completely refurbished in 1938 but as a consequence many of its original features were covered and the elegant balcony was boarded up. It was closed again in July 1987 for major repairs and renovation. It was reopened two years later by Princess Margaret and is now home to many long established businesses some of whom have traded here for over fifty years.

*Derby Market Hall soon after its opening in 1866*

Derby Fish Market is located in Lock-up Yard, adjacent to the Market Hall. Specialist fishmongers here sell a wide range of seafood ranging from the popular cod, haddock and sea bass to fresh salmon and Whitby crab. Stall holders can also provide advice on fish recipes as well as filleting and gutting the fish for the customer.

The Eagle Centre Market stands on the site of the ancient Cockpit Hill Market.

Allenton Market was the city's first, and until now the only, purpose built local market. This traditional style covered market was opened in 1962.

Derby had a long-established weekly market for cattle, sheep and pigs which for many years was located on the Morledge. It moved to a nearby site on the Holmes (at the rear of the bus Station) in 1861. After trading successfully for over a hundred year it moved to a new purpose built site on Chequers Road in 1970. A traditional livestock market is held here each Thursday and horse sales are held on the second and fourth Saturdays of each month. The market is used for furniture sales on the first and third Saturdays.

Derby Wholesale Market on Chequers Road deals in fresh fruit, flowers and vegetables from all over the world. It is used by traders and is not open to the general public.

Derby's former Corn Exchange Building was opened in 1862 and for many years farmers and merchants traded cereal grains here. In 1897 it became the Palace Theatre of Varieties and later a dance hall. In 1929 the Derby Evening Telegraph took over the building and renamed it Northcliffe House. The newspaper moved to new purpose built premises on Meadow Road in 1981. Today the building is in multiple occupation.

Bakewell is the only market town in the Peak District National Park. The charter for its Monday market was granted by Edward III in 1330. Today the market consists of both domestic stalls and a cattle market.

A guide to Chesterfield published in 1899 described some of the retail establishments in the town. The business of Mr S Hadfield in the Market Place was described as the largest wholesale pork butcher in the town, whose window frontage displayed a tasteful assortment of the choicest joints of dairy fed pork, home cured ham and bacon. He also prepared his own 'Chesterfield sausages', polonies, pork pies, tomato sausages, potted meat and brawn. There were a number of drapers, milliners, shoemakers and general tailors in the town at that time. Mr S Swale, the clothier, outfitter and draper of Vicar Lane, sold 'every article of men's, youth's or boy's outfits from a necktie or a shirt to a suit of ready-made or measured clothing. Cigarettes, cigars, pipe tobacco and snuff were all popular at that time and a number of tobacconists served the needs of smokers. Mr Herbert Green's tobacco and cigar business on Holywell Street stocked a wide range of products and like most tobacconists of the period he also produced his own mixture of tobacco.

The first Co-operative store in Chesterfield opened in 1894 in New Square, selling groceries and provisions. Within ten years the society had expanded to supply a wide range of goods including clothing, drapery, crockery, boots and shoes, ironmongery and coal.

Chesterfield received its first charter in 1204 which allowed weekly market on Tuesdays and Saturdays and an annual fair of eight days at the Feast of the Exaltation of the Holy Cross. The old market lay in the area around the present churchyard

By the Middle Ages most fairs in Derbyshire were held for three days on the vigil, feast and morrow of a particular feast. The longest fair was one of fifteen days at Bakewell and fairs lasting more than seven days took place at Chesterfield, Derby, Melbourne and Sandiacre.

An annual fair was held at Derby during the 11th and 12th centuries during the Feast of St James in July.

William Owen's Book of Fairs, published in 1700 listed fairs at the following places within the county: Alfreton, Ashbourne, Ashover, Bakewell, Belper, Bolsover, Cubley, Chapel-en-le-Frith, Chesterfield, Crich, Derby, Darley Flash, Dronfield, Duffield, Higham, Hope, Matlock, Newhaven, Pleasley, Ripley, Sawley, Tideswell and Wirksworth.

In August 1755 Anne Williamson who had broken out of jail was hanged at Derby for picking pockets at Ashbourne Fair.

For many years Derby was an important centre for the marketing of cheese. The largest fair was held at Michaelmas.

Ilkeston Charter fair is one of the oldest and largest street fairs in Europe. The original charter was granted by Henry III in 1252 for a fair to be held on the Feast of the Assumption in August each year. A statute or hiring fair was later established in the town in October. In 1888 the Assumption Fair and the Statute fair were amalgamated and from that time onwards the event became known as the Charter Fair and was held during the wakes week in October. In 1932 the fair received its first civic opening when Councillor Beardsley became the first Mayor of Ilkeston to officially open the fair. Today the fair combines the latest rides alongside traditional favourites such as gallopers, waltzer and dodgems. The traditional opening ceremony, which includes the reading of the original 1252 charter takes place in front of Ilkeston Town Hall.

In 1952 the 700th anniversary of Ilkeston fair was celebrated by a civic lunch and every school pupil in the town received a souvenir postcard of its charter.

In 1251 Henry III granted a charter to Ripley for one market, one day a week on Wednesday and one fair each year, lasting three days on the Vigil, Day and Morrow of St Helen. Ripley Fair predates the nearby but more famous Goose Fair at Nottingham and is still held in the Market Place each year. The market day was later altered to Saturday with an extra market added on Friday.

Early June each year sees the Peak District fairs for the carnivals at Bakewell and Buxton and also the Well Dressing Fair at Tideswell.

For many years Matlock Green was the centre of one of the biggest cattle fairs and wakes in the district. The fairs were held on the nearest Mondays to 25 February, 2 April, 9 May and 24 October, so many cattle, sheep and pigs were brought for sale here that the fair spread into the surrounding streets. Heavy chains were used to keep the animals off the pavements. The fairs ceased in 1914 following the outbreak of the First World War.

The tiny village of Alstonfield was a thriving market centre in the Middle Ages, having been granted its own market charter in 1308. Annual cattle sales continued here until the early years of the 20th-century.

Glover's History and Directory of Derby, published in 1843 stated that the town's fairs for cattle, horses, sheep, pigs, cheese and pedlary were generally well attended and that the markets were well supplied with corn, butcher's meat, poultry, butter, eggs, fruit and vegetables. The weekly cattle market was described as 'numerously attended and of great importance to the agriculturalists and to the butchers of Derby and the surrounding towns and villages.

Derby Westfield Centre was opened as the Eagle Centre in November 1975. The centre market was rebuilt in 1990 and the entire centre refurbished in 1999. Following a £340 million extension in 2007, it was renamed 'Westfield Derby'. The extension doubled the size of the centre as well as attracting a number of 'blue chip retailers to the site. An 800 seat food court was created as well as a £30 million twelve-screen Cinema de Lux and additional parking facilities. Today the West-field Centre's 227 stores attract over 350,000 shoppers each week. The centre also has a Concierge Desk to provide tourist information, shopping advice, buggy and wheelchair hire and even a shopping minding service!

The Cathedral Quarter was Derby's first Business Improvement District. It was created in 2007 and contains a large range of shops, boutiques, coffee shops and restaurants. Businesses within the Quarter subscribe to a fund which is then used to fund marketing and other activities.

*Irongate in the heart of Derby's Cathedral Quarter*

Bennetts in Derby was established in 1734 and claims to be one of the oldest department store in the country It started life as an ironmongers under the name of Weatherhead Walters and Company. It later extended the range of goods to include agricultural tools, seed and oilcake. By the start of the 20th-century it was selling a full range of goods and could be fully recognised as a department store Today the business sells a wide range of goods including furnishings, fashion, collectables, kitchenware china and stationary. It also contains a delicatessen and a cafe.

Derby Industrial and Co-operative Society, founded in 1850 was only the third co-operative society to be established in this country.

Belper's first annual Cattle and Pig Fair was held on Whit Monday 1851. By the 1860s sales of sheep, horses and farm implements took place along with the annual fair, all then occupying the Butts, Market Place and Coppice.

Chatsworth Country Fair is one of England's most spectacular annual outdoor events, it is held in Chatsworth Park over the August Bank Holiday period and attracts large crowds from all over the country. Attractions include massed pipe and military bands, demonstrations and parades. Over 300 trade stalls sell a wide range of products and other activities include displays by the armed services, ferret racing, archery and sheepdog trials.

# Food and Drink

Ashover Moorland Tart contains a combination of sweet and savoury ingredients including eggs, candied peel, sugar and currents. Encased within a short-crust pastry base it is said to be ideal for lunch on a day out in the Peak District.

The Derbyshire Food and Drink Fair has been held annually since 2001 to celebrate the county's wide range of produce. The event regularly attracts around 10,000 visitors who come to sample the best of Derbyshire food and drink as well as more exotic foods from further afield. In recent years venues have included Bolsover Castle and Hardwick Hall.

The Dome Restaurant, housed in the Devonshire Royal Hospital, now part of the Buxton Campus of Derby University. Opened by top chef Anton Mosimann in 2005, the Dome Restaurant is a regional showcase for excellence in hospitality and catering education. Half of the kitchen is situated in the restaurant, providing a visual cookery theatre where guests watch the food being prepared.

For many years the Royal Forest of the Peak was a source of venison for the King's table. In 1275 instructions were given to Roger Lestrange, the King's bailiff that 'all venison in the King's larder at tydeswell be taken and carried to Westminster to be delivered to the King's larder there'.

Bakewell Pudding is a traditional dish which was first created by accident in 1820 at the Rutland Arms Inn at Bakewell. The cook was instructed to make a strawberry tart but for some reason she poured the mixture of eggs over the strawberry jam rather than mixing it into the pastry. The guests were enthusiastic in their praise of this new dish and it has been popular ever since. A number of shops in the town claim to hold the original recipe.

Ashbourne Gingerbread originated in the early 19th-century when French prisoners held in the town during the Napoleonic Wars shared the recipe with a local baker. It was passed down through the generations and is still made and sold in the town.

The Recipe for Ashbourne Gingerbread is as follows:

Ingredients;
8oz self raising flour,
pinch of salt,
2 tsp ground ginger,
1 tsp golden syrup.

Method – Preheat oven to 350F. Sieve the flour salt and ginger together in a bowl. Cream the syrup, butter and sugar together and then stir in the dried ingredients. Kneed the mixture on a floured surface to a smooth dough. Roll out and cut into the required shape. Place on a greased baking sheet and bake until brown for 10–15 minutes.

Derbyshire Oatcakes are similar to pancakes and can be served with sweet or savoury fillings. They date from the 17th-century as oats grew well in the harsh Peak-land landscape. They are made from a blend of oatmeal flour, milk, yeast, sugar and salt and can still be purchased from various outlets throughout the county.

Pyclets are thick yeast pancakes cooked on a griddle and contained within a metal ring. A typical pyclet is pale, lightly flecked with golden brown and honeycombed with a mass of little holes. The underside is smooth and golden brown in colour. A stall selling pyclets was established at the entrance to Derby Guildhall during the First World War and continued trading until the 1970s.

There are a number of corn mills in Derbyshire producing flour which can be bought by the general public. These include Heage Windmill, Cauldwell's Mill at Rowsley and Stainsby Mill on the Hardwick Hall estate.

Sir Henry Crewe of Calke Abbey wrote, complaining about his beer and his brewer in 1815. 'You never see a drop sparkle in the glass and it tastes thick and sweet', declared Sir Henry. 'What I like is a fine light ale; small beer should be brisk and fresh but not tart'. As to the brewer, he described him as 'the man who has spoiled all my beer for the last three years'.

Thorntons Chocolates is the largest independent chocolate and confectionery company in the UK. For many years the company was based in Belper but in 1985 it moved to a new factory at Alfreton which was opened by HM the Queen.

Stilton Cheese is a traditional blue cheese which can only be made in the three counties of Derbyshire, Nottinghamshire and Leicestershire. Originating in the village of Stilton in the 18th-century there are now only a handful of dairies in the whole world licensed to produce Stilton. The last producer in Derbyshire was the Hartington Creamery which closed down in 2009.

A new Derbyshire cheese was launched in 2012. Franjoy Dairy in Hazelwood produces both cheddar and a Derby cheese called Hazelwood. The cheeses are sold at farmers markets in Belper, Wirksworth, Bakewell and Chesterfield.

Birds the Confectioners was founded at Derby by three brothers; Frank, Thomas and Reginald Bird in 1919. For a number of years its marketing claimed that it never sold a stale cake! Birds now has over fifty retail outlets across the East Midlands which are all supplied by the company's single bakery in Derby.

The Engine Shed is a training restaurant at the Derby College Roundhouse Campus. It is staffed by students and chef lecturers from the College's Hospitality and Culinary Arts Academy and is open to the general public.

The World Peace Cafe is an unusual vegetarian restaurant located in the Tara Buddhist Centre at Ashe Hall, near Etwall. Part of the Kadampa Meditation Centre, all profits are donated to projects dedicated to world peace.

There are a large number of micro-breweries in Derbyshire. One of the earliest was that at the John Thompson Public house at Ingleby where the first pint of JTS XXX was sold in 1977.

The Derby Summer Beer Festival has been held annually since 1977. The event now attracts thousands of people and showcases around 200 different ales. In addition to the real ales on offer visitors can also sample continental beers, ciders and perries as well as a wide choice of hot and cold food. Distinctive beer mugs are produced each year which can be purchased at the venue alongside t shirts and other souvenirs.

Derbyshire once boasted a large number of independent breweries. By the latter years of the 19th-century there were four in Derby and three in Chesterfield as well as others at Melbourne, Woodville, Cromford, Castle Gresley, Hartshorne and Shardlow. The last to survive was Offiler's in Derby which was taken over by Charington United Breweries in 1965.

Offiler's Brewery built three almost identical art deco style pubs in Derby in the 1930s: the Blue Peter in Alvaston, the Blue Boy in Chaddesden and the Blue Pool in Sunnyhill. It was from the Blue Peter on 30 April 1946 that a brightly festooned Offiler's dray conveyed Derby County's victorious FA cup-winning team to a civic reception in Derby.

*The Blue Peter public house at Alvaston*

Capsules for Nestle Dolce Gusto coffee making machines are made at the company's factory at Hatton alongside other products.

Derbyshire Record Office holds a number of early receipe books, some dating back many hundreds of years. Mary Swanwick's handwritten recipe book of 1743 includes over a hundred recipes for poultry, meat, vegetables, puddings, drinks, preserves and savouries. Pastries, pies and pasties also feature and there are instructions on 'how to dress a cod head'.

S & A Foods based in Derby, is a major supplier of international recipe dishes to UK supermarkets and other outlets. The business was founded by Mrs Perween Warsi in 1986, when she started making finger food for a local take-away. The business grew rapidly and after a great deal of perseverance Asda and Safeway gave S & A Foods their first national contracts. The company moved into its first purpose built factory in 1987 and less than ten years later moved into a larger factory on the same site. In 1996 Mrs Warsi was named Woman Entrepreneur of the Year and received the MBE in the 1997 New Year's Honours. In 2001 she was named 'Midlander of the Year' and in 2002 was awarded a CBE in the Jubilee Honours list. Today S & A Foods has a turnover of more than £75 million serving an impressive portfolio of major international customers from its extensive premises in Derby. Its products comprise an extensive range of ethnic cuisine including Indian, Chinese, Caribbean, North African, South East-Asian and Tex-Mex dishes.

Around 40% of all the Christmas Puddings eaten worldwide are made by Matthew Walker & Company in Heanor.

The Newton Wonder apple originates from Derbyshire. Samuel Taylor, the landlord of the Hardinge Arms in Kings Newton discovered a seedling in the roof gutter of his pub and planted it in the garden. It was from this tree that the first Newton Wonder apple was produced in 1870.

Derby Cheese is no longer made in the county. It has a smooth mellow texture similar to Cheshire cheese, with a mild but distinctive flavour which improves significantly as the cheese matures. It was made originally in Derbyshire farm houses and sold in local markets and the annual cheese fairs which were held at places such as Bakewell, Tideswell and Winster. A variation of Derby Cheese is Derby Sage which has a green marbled appearance and a fresh herby flavour that is produced by adding sage juice or finely chopped fresh sage leaves to the curds before the cheese is milled.

Tripe was for many years a popular dish locally, being cheap, nourishing and easily digested. In the 19th-century tripe shops flourished all year round serving piping hot food to be eaten on the spot, or carried home in a basin covered with a cloth. At local fairs, stalls sold hot tripe to the crowds enjoying all the fun of the fair.

Haslet is a dish which which is also served in neighbouring counties. Similar to faggots, it contains pig's liver, belly pork, onions and seasoning. Cooked in the shape of a large bun it is served cold and cut into slices. It was popular until the 1950s when it was often made and sold at specialist pork butchers.

Wakes Cakes are current buns which were made and sold at various fairs and wakes weeks around Derbyshire, The recipe varied slightly from place to place.

A Derbyshire sausage was recently created by Croots Farm Shop at Duffield. This new mutton, herb and lemon sausage was produced to celebrate and support Derbyshire's sheep farming heritage and is the first mutton sausage to be created by Croots.

Henry Stevens, the inventor of the hot dog, was born at Derby in 1856. He emmigrated to the USA in 1890 and made a fortune printing and selling baseball cards before creating and licensing this iconic American snack.

The weekly diet for the inmates at Wirksworth workhouse in 1789 was: Breakfast – Sunday, Wednesday, Friday – Bread and broth; rest of the week – Milk pottage. Dinner – Sunday, Wednesday, Friday – Bread, broth, butcher's meat, potatoes etc; Monday – Baked pudding and treacle sauce. Tuesday, Thursday, Saturday – Bread and milk. Supper – Milk pottage and bread every day.

The diet for inmates at Derby Gaol in 1843 was: Breakfast, a quart of gruel, made from two ounces of oatmeal, and a portion of bread; dinner, one pound of boiled potatoes and a portion of bread; supper, one quart of gruel made from two ounces of oatmeal and a portion of bread. One and a half pound of good wheaten bread a day and one quarter of an ounce of salt per day. Prisoners confined for longer than a period of three calendar months received in addition to their daily allowance two ounces of onions per day. When onions couldn't be procured, a red herring was substituted every second day.

Sudbury's Secret Diner is a restaurant operated by inmates from Sudbury Prison. Standing outside the confines of the prison the restaurant caters for the public and offers a range of dishes. The menu changes regularly and there are daily themes including healthy salads on Summer Wednesdays, curry on Thursday and fish on Fridays.

The Bottle Kiln at West Hallam is an unusual tea room which has won a number of national and regional awards The building was designed around a traditional bottle kiln which still provides an interesting feature of the site.

Rennishaw Hall's vineyard was planted by the late Sir Rearesby Sitwell in 1972 and was for many years the most northerly vineyard in the world. Still and sparkling wine is produced from the grapes which is sold in the Rennishaw Hall shop.

*Renishaw Hall and gardens*

George Stafford's Black Puddings have been famous for over fifty years. Produced originally in George's butchers shop in Stanley Common they won thirteen medals including five gold between 1976 and 1989 at the annual world black pudding championships held at Mortagne-Auperch in France. George himself was awarded the title of Knight of the Black Pudding! After his death in 1997 Richard Chester took over the shop and bought the original hand-written receipt for an undisclosed sum. A mail order service now allows people from around the world to sample this Derbyshire delicacy.

Derbyshire Gooseberry Pudding was for many years the traditional fare for Whit Sunday. This falls fifty days after Easter and is also around the time when gooseberries first come into season. In parts of Derbyshire gooseberries were known as feeberries.

TV show, *The Hairy Bikers' Food Tour of Britain,* visited Derbyshire in 2009. The programme featured three recipes: Loin of venison with blackberry and sloe gin glaze served with clapshot rosti and parsnip crisps by the Hairy Bikers; Slow cooked Derbyshire lamb with oatcake crust, caramalised onion mousse and wild garlic and rosemary jus by Rupert Rowley and Raspberry Bakewell pudding by the Hairy Bikers.

Bradwell's Dairy Ice Cream has been made in the village of Bradwell for over a hundred years. The business was begun in 1899 by Hannah Hall who had ice brought by train from Sheffield and made her legendary ice cream in the front parlour of her home from where she also ran a local newsagents. The company has grown over the years and now supplies ice cream to a number of supermarkets, cafes, shops and restaurants.

The John Thompson Inn at Ingleby was the first pub in the country to be named after the owner and licensee. A microbrewery on the site produces JTS XXX Bitter which is sold on draught in the pub.

A genuine American diner was opened at Church Gresley near Swadlincote in August 2005. Built in the early 1950s it is typical of the railroad-car stainless steel diners of the period. The menu too is typical of 1950s America with fifty different milk shakes, malts, floats, hot dogs, chilli dogs, meat loaf, chowder and steaks.

According to Glover's History and Directory of Derbyshire, published in 1843 the agricultural labourer in Derbyshire had cheese and a little bacon but butcher's meat seldom formed part of his diet.

The Brunswick Inn on Railway Terrace in Derby advertised the following bill of fare in 1843;

Breakfast, plain 1s. 6d.

Ditto, with Meat &c 2s. 0d.

Dinner 2s. 0d.

Tea 1s. 6d.

Supper 1s. 6d.

Wine 5s. Per bottle

# First, Last, Oldest, Biggest, Best

Ilkeston has the largest street fair in Derbyshire. It is held in October each year in the Market Place and Bath Street.

*The Derbyshire Times* is the biggest selling newspaper in the county and is in Britain's top ten for circulation.

The Totley Tunnel, near Grindleford on the on the Sheffield to Manchester Railway is the second longest in England and stretches for a distance of over three miles.

*The Derbyshire Times* made history in 1893 when it became the first weekly newspaper in England to introduce the linotype setting machine.

Derby's first two Members of Parliament were John de la Cornere and Ranulph de Makeneye. They attended Edward I's Parliament in 1295; the first Parliament at which citizens of boroughs were represented.

The first woman to climb Mount Everest was Alison Hargreaves who was born at Belper in 1963. She was killed in a blizzard while climbing K2 in 1995.

Richard Thorley was the last person to be publically executed in Derbyshire. Convicted of the murder of Eliza Morrow, he was hanged outside the new County Gaol at Vernon Street in Derby on Friday 11 April 1862.

The oldest pub in Derby is the Dolphin Inn which was founded in 1530.

The world's first medical flying squad was founded at Derby. The Royal Infirmary Flying Squad was established by Dr John Collins, the Head of the Hospital's casualty department in 1955. The idea was copied by other hospitals across the UK and Dr Collins was eventually awarded the MBE in recognition of his work.

Swarkestone Bridge is the longest bridge in Derbyshire. It has seventeen arches and is almost a mile in length.

Blue John is a type of fluorspar which is found only at Blue John Cavern and Treak Cliff Cavern at Castleton.

The largest object ever made from a single piece of Blue John is the Chatsworth tazza, measuring 20 inches in height

Mrs Elizabeth Petty was the first woman to become Mayor of Derby. She was first elected to the Council for Dale Ward in 1922 and served as Mayor in 1936–7. She became an alderman in the following year.

Councillor Nirmal Singh Dhindsa was the first Asian Mayor of Derby. Elected as a Labour councillor for Sinfin Ward in 1973, he served as mayor for 1994–95.

The first non-stop flight across the Atlantic was made by Alcock and Brown in June 1919, flying in a Vickers Vimy, powered by Rolls-Royce Eagle engines.

The first allied jet fighter aircraft the Gloster Meteor was powered by two Rolls-Royce Welland engines. Rolls-Royce engines also powered later versions of the Comet, the world's first jet airliner.

An experimental Rolls-Royce Trent turboprop engine was flown in 1945 and in July 1950 a Vickers Viscount powered by Rolls-Royce Dart engines became the first turbo-prop airliner in the world to enter service.

Derby County Football Club was one of the twelve founder teams of the Football League. Their first match kicked off on 8 September 1888.

Bennets in Derby is one of the oldest department stores in the country. It was established in 1734.

The first race meeting to be held at Derby Race Course was in 1848.

The Derbyshire Federation of Women's institutes was founded in 1918.

The first children's film matinee performance in Derbyshire took place at Mickleover School on the afternoon of Wednesday 7 February 1900.

Speed cameras were first installed across Derbyshire in February 2003.

Derby's first electric lights were switched on in 1894.

John Logie Baird's Roadshow demonstrated television in Derby for the first time in 1933. The BBC began regular broadcasts in 1936.

Britain's first alpine-style cable car was constructed at Matlock Bath in 1984. Designed and built by the French firm, Pomalgalski, the cable cars ascend to the Heights of Abraham crossing the River Derwent and the main road in the process.

The first cast iron aqueduct in Britain carried the Derby Canal across the Mill Fleam in Derby. Approximately 40ft in length, it was manufactured by the Butterley Company. It was held in storeage for a time by Derby Museum but has since disappeared!

Stone Edge Cupola beside the B5057 near Holymoorside is the oldest free standing chimney in Britain.

The first coke fired blast furnaces in Derbyshire were built at Morley Park towards the end of the 18th-century.

The first fully operational electronic telephone exchange was opened in Ambergate in 1966. This was also the first small to medium electronic exchange in the world

The Ashover Light Railway was the last British narrow guage passenger railway line of any significant length.

Alan Alcott of Dronfield entered the Guiness Book of Records in 2004 in recognition of his putting together the world's largest collection of beer towels.

Alec Tague from New Mills broke the mini-moto speed record on 21 September 2004 at Elvington Airfield, near York. Riding a miniature Italian bike he achieved a speed of 78 mph

Ann Langton from Somercotes entered the Guinness Book of Records in 2012 as the person with the largest number of pig collectables. She started collecting at the age of 17 and now has over 17,000 items ranging from key rings to money boxes.

Vin Cox was awarded a place in the Guinness Book of Records for the fastest circumnavigation of the earth by bicycle. Mr Cox, from Chaddesden finished the ride, which took him through seventeen countries, in 163 days six hours and 57 minutes.

The world's first rotating boat lift was constructed by the Butterley Engineering works in Ripley. The Falkirk Wheel is capable of lifting up to eight boats from the Union Canal to the Forth and Clyde Canal in Scotland.

The first Bishop of Derby was Edmund Pearce. He was appointed in 1927 when the diocese was created.

Chesterfield Bowling club claim that their green is the oldest in the world, dating back to at least the 16th-century.

The first fireproof mill in the country was built at Belper by William Strutt in 1804. North Mill was constructed using a cast iron frame with floors on brick arches and cast iron beams.

Derbyshire County Council is the largest employer in the county.

Derby has claimed the title of being the most haunted city in Britain.

The first history of Derbyshire was written by William Woolley between 1712 and 1715.

The first separate history of Derby was written by William Hutton in 1791.

The first map of Derbyshire was produced by Christopher Saxton in 1577.

Speed's town plan of Derby provides the earliest accurate survey of the town.

The first game of baseball ever witnessed in Derby was played on Saturday 3 May 1890 at Ley's Recreation Ground when the Derby club won a match against the Erdington Club from Birmingham.

Derby elected Richard Bell as its first Labour MP in 1900. He was also one of only two Labour MPs elected nationally, the other being Keir Hardie.

Derby Chamber of Commerce was founded in 1864.

Derby trustee Savings Bank was established in 1818.

Derbyshire's first multi-screen cinema, the Showcase Complex was opened in November 1988.

The legendary Barnum and Bailey's Circus visited Derby for the first time in October 1898.

Public transport in Derby began in 1840. A horse-drawn omnibus provided a link between the newly opened railway station and a number of town centre hotels. The terminus was the Bell Hotel in Sadlergate.

Derby's first tram service was inaugurated in 1880. Electric trams were first introduced in the town in 1903.

'The Restaurant with One Table' at Buckingham's Hotel in Chesterfield claims to be the smallest restaurant in Britain.

Coton in the Elms is the furthest point from the sea in the whole of Britain.

The first open prison in the Midland region was opened at Sudbury in 1948.

The first mass DNA screening of suspects held in Derbyshire was conducted at Buxton in April 1996. More than a hundred people were tested after a 78-year-old woman had been raped. The DNA testing enabled the police to identify the rapist who was jailed for ten years.

The Derby Arboretum was the first public park to be opened in England.

Arkwright's Mill at Cromford was the first water-powered cotton mill in the world.

The prototype of the famous German Second World War fighter aircraft, the Messerschmidt BE 109 was powered by a Rolls Royce engine.

Chatsworth House is the largest stately home in Derbyshire and is sometimes described as the Palace of the Peak.

The deepest cave in England is Oxlow Cavern in the Giant's Hole at Castleton. It is 653 feet deep.

Derby Museum and Art Gallery has the largest collection of Joseph Wright paintings in the world.

The Emperor Fountain in the grounds of Chatsworth House is the world's tallest fountain under pressure. It is capable of reaching a height of 298ft.

The Peak District National Park was the first National Park to be established in the UK. Opened in 1951 it covers an area of 542 square miles of which more than half lies within Derbyshire.

Derbyshire's first newspaper, the *British Spy* or *Derby Postman* was published weekly from 1719 until 1731 at a cost of 2d. It was published by S Hodgkinson of Sadlergate in Derby. The county's first daily newspaper, the *Derby Daily Telegraph* was founded on 28 July 1879.

Buxton is Derbyshire's highest town. Standing at one thousand feet above sea level it is also the second highest market town in England.

In 1881 Chesterfield became the first town in the United Kingdom to install electric street lighting.

Chesterfield claims to have the largest regular open-air market in the country, with around 250 stalls.

Prior Overton's tower at Repton School is the oldest brick building in Derbyshire. Dating from 1437 it is also one of the earliest examples of domestic brick architecture in the UK.

The first customer of Derbyshire Building Society (founded in 1859) was Mr Rivett who paid two shillings as an entrance fee for the first two shares. The first advance of £50 was made to Mr Richard Ashby in December 1859.

The first antiseptic dressings made in the UK were manufactured at Robinson's in Chesterfield in 1889.

High Tor at Matlock Bath is England's highest limestone cliff and stands at about 380 feet high.

The earliest map of Derbyshire was published by Christopher Saxton in 1577. An original copy is on display in Buxton Museum and Art Gallery.

Derbyshire's highest village is Chelmorton and stands at a height of 1,200 feet above sea level.

Derbyshire's first regular bus service operated between Derby and Ashbourne. Commencing in 1913 it was operated by Commercial Car Hirers using a fourteen-seater motor omnibus.

The county's first ever bus service was operated by Bartons and ran from Long Eaton to Nottingham Goose Fair.

The country's first oil refinery was opened at Riddings Ironworks by James Young in 1848. Initially it produced three hundred gallons a day.

Derbyshire's oldest bridge spans the River Wye at Bakewell. Dating from around 1272 it was widened in the early 19th-century in order to allow pedestrians to cross more safely.

The highest stretch of road in Derbyshire is the Snake Pass on the road between Glossop and Sheffield. The road rises to a height of 1,680 feet above sea level and is regularly impassible in Winter.

The character of Ken Barlow played by Derbyshire born William Roache is Britain's and possibly the world's longest serving TV soap-opera character. He has appeared continuously in ITV's *'Coronation Street'* since its inception in 1960. In the first episode he is seen mending his bike in his parent's front room. Since the series began the character has been married five times to four different women.

Ken Edwards of Glossop entered the record books on 5 March 2001 when he ate 36 cockroaches in one minute on TV's Big Breakfast show.

Bryony Balen from Melbourne became the youngest person to ski the full distance to the South Pole. The 21-year-old reached this landmark on 20 January 2012 after skiing 705 miles from the coast.

The Millenium Wall at the National Stone Centre, Wirksworth is a unique collection of vernacular stone walls which was created over the Bank Holiday in 2000 by members of the Dry Stone Walling Association of Great Britain. It forms the most extensive collection of dry stone walls in the UK, showing the variation in geology found in mainland Britain and the skills of the craftsmen and women who build in stone without the use of mortar.

The world's first replica jet engine to be made entirely of Lego bricks was unveiled at the Farnborough International Air Show in 2012 and was later displayed in the Westfield Centre in Derby. The half scale model of the Rolls-Royce Trent 1000 engine was built to inspire young people to pursue careers in science and engineering. Made from 152,455 pieces, the replica was created by professional Lego builders with advice and assistance from a team of graduates and apprentices at Rolls-Royce.

Charlesworth Congregational Church, Glossop claims to be the longest continually worshipping free church in England. An Independent congregation was established here in 1611, making use of a disused medieval chapel. The present church, on the same site, dates from 1797.

Chesterfield hosted the world's first ever gluten-free beer festival in February 2006.

The Barrow Hill Railway roundhouse near Staveley is the oldest operational round house in the world.

*Barrow Hill Roundhouse*

# What's in a Name?

## Place Names

Most settlements in Derbyshire date from before the Norman Conquest. Their names give us some idea of when and why they were first founded and something of the physical environment at the time. Place name elements in Derbyshire are generally the same as those found throughout the Midlands and include the following:

| Origin | Place name ending | Meaning | Example |
|---|---|---|---|
| **Roman** | caster or chester | camp or fortification | Chesterfield, Little Chester |
| **Anglo-Saxon** | borough, bury | fortified settlement | Sudbury, Norbury |
| | bourne or burn | brook or stream | Ashbourne, Bradbourne |
| | ford | crossing place | Brailsford, Ashford |
| | ton | enclosure of land | Alfreton, Burnaston |
| | cot, cote | outlying hut | Hilcote, Hearthcote |
| | field | clearing in wood | Duffield |
| | ley | clearing | Fritchley, Horsley |
| | stow | holy place | Egstow |
| | ton | enclosure of land | Tupton, Osmaston |

| | wich, wick, wike | outlying hut or dairy farm | Parwich, |
|---|---|---|---|
| | dale | Valley | Dovedale |
| | den | hill | Chaddesden |
| | field | Forest clearing | Duffield, Hayfield |
| | ash | ash tree | Monyash |
| | worth | worthy enclosure | Wirksworth, Wingerworth |
| **Scandinavian** | by | settlement or farmstead | Derby, Bretby |
| | thorp(e) | daughter settlement | Cutthorpe, Woodthorpe |
| | toft | homestead | Hardstoft |

### Some place names change over time

Buxworth used to be known as Bugsworth until 1930. A local ballot was held in 1999 to decide whether or not to restore the old name of Bugsworth but this was defeated by a majority of residents.

Until the railway arrived in the early 19th-century Ambergate was known as Toad-moor and consisted of just a few cottages. There is still a Toadmoor Lane in the village.

Woodville was formerly known as Wooden Box, named after the wooden toll booth on the toll road between Ashby-de-la-Zouch and Burton-upon-Trent. Some older residents still talk about going "up Box"!

## Street Names

In Derby and other towns street names sometimes originate with the trades or occupations carried on there in the Middle Ages or earlier. These include:

## In Derby

- **Saddler Gate** was the street of the saddlers.
- **Full Street** near the River Derwent was where the fullers plied their trade.
- **Iron Gate** was originally the street of the smiths. It was here that the medieval iron workers plied their trade.
- **The Corn Market** was the site of a corn market until a corn exchange was built.
- **Friar Gate** was where the Dominicans built a friary in the 13th-century.

## In Chesterfield
- **Glumangate** was the street of the minstrels or gleemen.
- **The Shambles** was where the butchers carried out their trade.
- **Soutergate** was the street of the shoemakers.

Sometimes streets are named after people or significant events. In Derbyshire there are streets, roads, avenues and crescents named after military heroes, writers, poets, inventors, engineers and politicians Many of these streets were named long after the deaths of the people they commemorated but in the Victorian and Edwardian eras when large scale public housing was being developed streets were often named after contemporary heroes or personalities. In Derbyshire streets named after important people or events include the following:

- **Latimer Street** is named after the protestant reformer and martyr who was burned at the stake in 1555.
- **Cromwell Road** and **Fairfax Road** were named after leading Parliamentarians from the English Civil War.
- **Byron Street** is named after the poet who lived at nearby Newstead Abbey in Nottinghamshire.
- **Churchill Street** is named after the famous wartime Prime Minister Winston Churchill.
- **Chaucer Street** is named after Geoffrey Chaucer, who wrote The Canterbury Tales.
- **Garrick Street** was named after the Litchfield born actor of that name.
- **Alma Street** is named after the Battle of Alma, the first major engagement between the British, French and Russians in the Crimean War.

Some streets are named after local Derbyshire personalities and these include the following:

- **Frank Whittle Road** in Derby was named after Sir Frank Whittle, the inventor of the jet engine. It was opened by the man himself in 1985.
- **Flamstead Street** in the Osmaston area of Derby was named after the first Astronomer Royal of that name who came from Derbyshire.
- **John Lombe Drive** is named after John Lombe, the co-founder and first manager of the Derby Silk Mill.
- **Whitehurst Street** is named after John Whitehurst the Derby horologist and scientist who was a founder member of the Lunar Society.
- **Erasmus Street** is named after Erasmus Darwin, the polymath who lived in Derby in the latter part of the 18th-century.
- **Brian Clough Way** is named after the famous manager of both Derby County and Nottingham Forest football clubs.
- **Handyside Street** is named after Andrew Handyside whose engineering firm produced a wide range of constructional and decorative ironwork including Friargate Bridge in Derby.

Several streets in the county are named after saints but this is often because of their proximity to churches with the same dedication. Over two hundred streets in Derbyshire are named after saints. The most popular include streets named after Saint Helen, Saint James, Saint John, Saint Mary and Saint Michael.

Other street names are associated with important buildings such as mills, castles, churches and abbeys. In Derbyshire there are over 200 Church streets, roads or lanes and over seventy mill lanes or streets. Castle streets can be found in over forty different places throughout Derbyshire.

**Street names often change over time.**

**In Derby:**
- **Great Northern Road** was previous known as Dog Kennel Lane.
- **Gower Street** was previously Blood Alley.
- **Macklin Street** used to be known as Cross Lane.
- **Spencer Street** was once known as Gordon Street.

- **Stanford Lane** was originally Stoneyforth Lane.
- **East Street** was first named Bag Lane.
- **Victoria Street** was called Brook Street until the Markeaton Brook was culverted in 1887; the year Queen Victoria came to the throne.

**In Ilkeston:**
- **Albion Place** was previously known as Lee's Yard and Glazier Lee's Yard after the plumber and glazier who bought the land in 1804.
- **Church Street** was formerly known as Botany Bay Road but was renamed in the middle of the 19th-century after the building of church there.

A number of streets on the Pride Park Estate at Derby have names linked to the locomotive and carriage and wagon building works which previously occupied this site. These include Locomotive Way, Roundhouse Road and Brunel Parkway.

**North Street**, Midland Place and Railway Terrace make up the full title of the railway company which built them. Nearby Sheffield Place and Leeds Place were named after two of the company's principal destinations.

**Industrial Street, Co-operative Street and Society Place** make up the name of Derby Industrial and Co-operative Society which was involved in their development in the 19th-century.

**Amen Alley** is probably named because of its proximity to the Cathedral Church of All Saints.

**Vulcan Street** was named after the nearby Vulcan foundry which was built by Sir Francis Lee, the founder of Lee's Malleable castings.

**Green Lane** was a Green area and was the dividing line between St Peter's and St Werburgh's parishes.

Some house builders and developers chose a common theme when naming roads. The Wimpey Estate at Mickleover which was built in the 1950s and 1960s has an Australian theme with names such as Brisbane Road, Murray Road and Tasman Close. Derby's Mackworth Estate has a London theme with names such as Isleworth Drive, Vauxhall Avenue and Cricklewood Road. At Alvaston a number of roads are named after actors and actresses such as Siddons, Garrick and Thorndike.

## Schools

School names reflect a whole range of criteria which have changed over the years. The majority are still named after the village, street or general locality in which they are situated. Church Schools are invariably named after saints and often share the same name as the local parish church. Catholic Secondary Schools which tend to serve a wider catchment area are sometimes given a different name to any of the parishes which they serve. There has been a trend in recent years to name them after Catholic martyrs of the Tudor period. A significant number of schools are named after famous people or local worthies although in recent years there has been a trend away from naming schools after living persons.

Schools named after lesser known saints include the following:

**Ralph Sherwin School** at Derby is named after a Catholic martyr. Born at Rodsley in Derbyshire, he was hanged, drawn and quartered at Tyburn in 1581.

**St Philip Howard R C Comprehensive School** at Glossop is named a Catholic nobleman who refused to renounce his Catholic faith during the reign of Elizabeth I. He was imprisoned in the Tower of London where he died of dysentery in 1595.

**St John Houghton School** at Kirk Hallam is named after a Carthusian monk who refused to take the Oath of Supremacy in the reign of Henry VIII. He was hanged drawn and quartered at Tyburn on 4 May 1535.

**St Thomas More RC High School** is named after the Lord Chancellor to King Henry VIII. He was imprisoned in 1534 for refusing to take the Oath of Supremacy. The following year he was tried for treason and convicted on perjured testimony. He was beheaded on Tower Hill.

Schools named after famous people or local worthies include the following:

**Noel Baker School** at Alvaston, Derby is named after Phillip Noel-Baker, MP for Derby South and the holder of the Nobel Peace Prize.

**Anthony Gell School** at Wirksworth is named after Sir Anthony Gell of Hopton who established and endowed the school in 1576.

**The William Allitt School** at Newhall, near Swadlincote was named after a local councillor of that name. It was the only school in the area to be named after a political figure.

**Arkwright Primary School** at Chesterfield is named after Richard Arkwright, the inventor of the water frame.

**Queen Elizabeth's Grammar School** at Chesterfield was named after Queen Elizabeth I in whose reign the school was founded.

**Walter Evans Primary School** at Darley Abbey is named after the man who built the cotton mills in the village along with houses for the workers and the school itself.

**Mary Howitt Infant School** and the William Howitt Junior School, both at Heanor, are named after two of the 19th-century's most popular and prolific writers. Between them the Howitts produced several hundred works. Mary Howitt was the first person to translate the works of Hans Christian Anderson into English.

**John King Infant School** at Pinxton is named after the inventor of a safety device which could be fitted to the cage which raised and lowered miners.

**Lady Manners School** at Bakewell is named after Grace, Lady Manners of Haddon Hall who founded the school in 1636. It was previously known as Bakewell Grammar School.

**Mundy Junior School** at Heanor is named after the Mundy family who lived at nearby Shipley Hall. They owned a number of coal mines in the area.

**Bishop Pursglove Primary School** at Tideswell is named after Bishop Pursglove who was Bishop of Hull in the reign of Elizabeth I. He was deprived of his office in 1559 for refusing to take the oath of supremacy. He founded a grammar school at Tideswell in the same year.

**Richardson Endowed School** is named after John and Samuel Richardson of Smalley Hall who built the school in 1721 to provide education for boys from Smalley and Horsley.

**Herbert Strutt Primary School** at Belper is named after a member of the Strutt family who developed Belper as a mill town in the 18th and 19th centuries.

## Pub Names

**The Abbey Inn** at Darley Abbey was once part of the Augustinian Abbey. It has been suggested that it may have been the guest house of the abbey.

**The Alma Inn** at Melbourne is named after the famous Battle of Alma fought against the Russians in the Crimean War.

**The Clock Warehouse** in Shardlow was originally a canal warehouse. Narrow boats could sail through an arch and load and unload their cargoes directly into the building.

**The Crewe and Harpur** at Swarkeston is named after two local families. The Harpur-Crewe family resided at Calke Abbey for several generations.

**The Crispin Inn** at Ashover refers to the fact that local men fought in the Battle of Agincourt which was fought on St Crispin's Day in 1415.

The **Sir Nigel Gresley** in Swadlincote is named after the famous engineer who designed the record breaking Mallard steam locomotive.

The **Hardinge Arms** in Kings Newton near Melbourne is named after the Hardinge family who lived in the village.

The **Harrington Arms** in Thurlston takes its name from the Earls of Harrington who lived at nearby Elvaston Castle.

The **Hunters Arms** in Kilburn takes its name from the Hunter family who owned Kilburn Hall and virtually the whole village for 200 years up to 1898.

The **Little John** at Hathersage is named after Robin Hood's second in command who is reputedly buried in the local churchyard.

The **Malt Shovel** at Shardlow was originally a malt house which no doubt served the nearby brewery of Zachariah Smith.

The **New Inn** at Shardlow is close to the Trent and Mersey canal. It was new in the 18th-century when the canal was built.

The **Florence Nightingale** on London Road Derby is named after the famous nursing pioneer of that name. It is close to Derby Community Hospital (formerly the Derby Royal Infirmary).

The **Old Silk Mill** in Derby takes its name from the nearby Silk Mill, the first in Britain which was opened 1722. A mural on the side wall of the inn shows scenes from the famous Silk Mill Lock Out of 1833–4.

The **Saracen's Head** at Shirley takes its name from the coat of arms of the Shirley family.

The **Silver Ghost** at Alvaston is named after the famous Rolls-Royce car of that name which was manufactured in Derby.

**The Standing Order** in Derby takes its name from the fact that the building was originally a branch of the NatWest Bank.

**The Strutt Arms** at Milford is named after Jedediah Strutt who built cotton mills at Belper and Milford (the pub is closed at present).

**The John Thomson Inn** is named after the first landlord and owner, John Thompson. He converted an existing farmhouse into the inn.

**The Vernon Arms** in Sudbury takes its name from the Vernon family who resided at Sudbury Hall and who built the inn.

**The Princess Victoria** in Matlock Bath is named after the princess who became Queen Victoria.

# Epitaphs and Memorials

Epitaphs appear in a variety of forms. Some of those which were originally inscribed on tombstones or church walls have disappeared over time but are still described in old books or documents. Churchyard surveys, individual church histories and antiquarian works are also valuable sources of information.

Titus Cartwright was the village blacksmith at Duffield. His memorial in the local churchyard hints at his occupation.

> My sledge and hammer lie reclined,
> My bellows too have lost their wind:
> My fire's extinct, my forge decayed,
> And in the dust my vice is laid;
> My coal is spent, my irons gone,
> My nails are drove, my work is done;
> My fire-dried corpse lies here at rest,
> My soul, like smoke, is soaring to be blest

In Bolsover Church there is a tombstone dedicated to Thomas Hinde, a watchmaker. The inscription reads: "Here lies in a horizontal position the outside case of Thomas Hinde, clock and watchmaker, who departed this life, wound up in the hope of being taken in hand by his maker. And being thoroughly cleaned, repaired and set a going in the world to come.

This monument to a Parish Clerk was erected in Bakewell churchyard:

> The vocal powers hear let us mark
> Of Philip our late parish clark
> In church non ever heard a layman
> With a clearer voice say Amen
> Who with Hallelujahs sound
> Like him can make the roof rebound
> The choir laments his choral tones
> The town so soon laid here his bones
> Sleep undisturb'd within thy peaceful shrine
> Till angels wake thee with such notes as thine

Other church musicians and choir members also feature in church memorials around the county.

In the church at Ashover a tablet includes the following inscription:

> To the Memory of
> DAVID WALL
> Whose superior performance on the
> Bassoon endeared him to an
> Extensive musical acquaintance
> His social life closed on the
> 4th Dec., 1796 in his 57th year

The following is copied from a gravestone in Stoney Middleton churchyard:

In memory of GEORGE, the son of GEORGE and MARGARET SWIFT, of Stoney Middleton, who departed this life August 21st, 1759, in the 20th year of his age.

> We the Quoir of Singers of this Church have erected this stone
> He's gone from us in more seraphick lays.
> In Heaven to chant the Great Jehovah's praise;
> Again to join him in the courts above
> Lets here exalt God's name with mutual love

Some had more important roles in life such as Anthony Lowe of Alderwasley. He was a Gentleman of the Bedchamber and loyal servant to Kings Henry VII, Henry VIII and Edward VI as well as Queen Mary. He died in 1555 and was buried in the parish church at Wirksworth. His epitaph reads:

Here lyeth Antonye Lowe esquer servant to Kynge Henry the vij
bured mj of deceb ad 1555

Samuel Watson, who was once the chief wood carver at Chatsworth died in 1715. His epitaph in St Lawrence's Church, Heanor read:

Watson is gone, whose skilful Art disploy'd
To 'th' very life whatever nature made
View but his wonderous work at Chatsworth hall
Which were so gazed and admired by all

Robert Plant was a noted clockmaker who came from Stockport to live and work in Tideswell. He died on July 3rd, 1856, at the age of 50. His stone described him thus:

He lived, loved and died lamented. The wisdom of his mind was superior to most men, having a general knowledge of the fine arts in which he studied and laboured with a skilful hand

Eyam churchyard contains a memorial stone to Harry Bagshaw who died in 1924. A cricketer who played for Derbyshire and the MCC, his headstone depicts three wickets being broken by a ball with a finger pointing upwards in the 'out' signal of an umpire. Over the wickets are the words:

Well Played
For when the Great Scorer comes
To write against your name
He writes – not that you won or lost,
But how you played the game

One of Bagshaw's sons designed the headstone. The body was interred wearing an umpire's coat, and with it was placed Bagshaw's favourite cricket ball.

The model village of Edensor was built by the Duke of Devonshire. The church and graveyard contain numerous memorials to the memory of noblemen and their servants. The following are typical examples:

Here lies ye Body of Mr IOHN PHILLIPS some-time Housekeeper of Chatsworth who departed this life on ye 28th May 1735, in ye 28th of May, in ye 73rd year of his age and 60th of his service in ye MOST NOBLE family of His Grace the Duke of Devonshire

The memorial to James Brousard who died in 1762 aged seventy-six states:

Ful forty years as Gardener to ye D of Devonshire
to propagate ye earth with plants it was his ful desire;
but then thy bones alas, brave man, earth did not rest afoard
but now we hope ye are at rest with Jesus Christ our Lord

The gravestone over the remains of William Mather, who died in 1818 indicate a more humble occupation:

When he that day with th' wagon went,
He little thought his Glass was spent;
But had he kept his Plough in Hand,
He might have longer till'd the Land

Some people make varied and considerable contribution to their community as in the case of William Longdon who was buried in St Mary's Churchyard, Ilkeston. His epitaph reads:

Sacred to the memory
of
WILLIAM LONGDON of Cotmanhay farmer,
Sergeant of the East Derbyshire Yeomanry Cavalry
and
many years Guardian of the Poor, Collector and
Assessor of taxes & Constable for the parish of Ilkeston
in his death hastened by his unremitting exertions
his afflicted widow has lost a kind husband
the Shipley troop a trusted yeoman
the parish of Ilkeston, an invaluable officer
and
the whole neighbourhood conservator of the peace
whose name was a terror to evil doers
he died on 17th May 1827
in the 42nd year of his age
& was buried with full military honours
His numerous friends
have caused this monument to be erected
as a testimony of their esteem

Epitaphs frequently make reference to the virtues of the departed as in the following cases:

In Loving Memory of
GEORGE MOON
For many years churchwarden
of Holy trinity Church, MAPPERLEY
a meek and humble Christian;
a kind-hearted neighbour;
a true friend and helper of the young;
and also for conscience sake, a lifelong earnest advocate
of total abstinence
Sincerely mourned
By many sorrowing friends, to whom he left the example
of a godly life fruitful in good works
He entered into rest Nov 9 1881
'Lord I have loved the habitation of thine
Pious, amid the place where thine honour dwelleth'

Joshua Needham of Great Hucklow died in 1791, aged 70 and was buried at Tideswell. His epitaph read:

Always a friend to truth, a soul sincere,
In action faithful and, in honour clear;
Who broke no promise, served no private end,
Who gained no title, and who lost no friend

Not all inscriptions are not quite so positive. The following epitaph (also from Tideswell) was dedicated to the second wife of William Booker, who died in 1881. It was erased as being irreverent by a former Vicar of the Parish:

> Sarah Booker, here she lies
> Nobody laughs and nobody cries,
> Where she's gone to and how she fares,
> Nobody knows and nobody cares

The church at Ault Hicknall contains a memorial to a keeper of Hardwick Park who died in 1703. The inscription reads:

> Long had he chased
> The Red and fallow deer
> But death's cold dart
> At last fixed him here

A more unusual, and potentially more dangerous occupation is described in the following memorial tablet in the Parish Church of St James, Taxal:

'Underneath lyeth the body of Michael Heathcote Esq.,Gentleman of the Pantry and Yeoman of the Mouth to his late King George the Second, who died June 22nd 1768 aged 75 years,

Michael Heathcote was in fact the King's food taster!

An unusual monument in Bakewell church manages to mention business, loyalty and religion

To the memory of MATTHEW STRUTT, of this town, farrier, long famed in these parts for vetinary skill. A good neighbour and a staunch friend to Church and King. Being Churchwarden at the time the present peal of bells were hung, through zeal for the house of God and unremitting attention to the airy business of the belfry, he caught a cold, which terminated his existence, May 25, 1798, in the 68th year of his age.

Accidental deaths are also recorded on tombstones. The following are typical examples:

In
Memory of
WILLIAM JARVIS
Who was killed at the
Somercotes Ironworks
June 16 1865
Aged 32 years
(In St Michael and All Angels Church, Stanton-by-Dale)

In Loving Memory of
JAMES
The beloved husband of
CAROLINE L BOWLEY
Who was accidentally killed
By the premature explosion of a shot
At the WEST HALLAM Colliery on January 13th 1904
Aged 47 years
The cup was bitter the shock severe
To part with one we loved so dear
It was God's will it should be so
At his command we all must go
This stone was erected by his friends & relations
April 23rd 1905

The following tells of the tragic accidental death of a young boy:

In
Affectionate Remembrance
of
JOHN HALL
Who met his death at MAPPERLEY POND
by bathing
June 30th 1866
Aged 10 years & 1 month
Farewell my dear parents
The Lord bid me come
Farewell my dear sisters
I'm now taken home
Farewell my dear brother
I shall see you no more
Till I meet you again
On Canaan's bright shore

Violent deaths are also sometimes recorded as in the case of this headstone in the churchyard at Repton:

In
Memory of
SAMUEL MARSHALL
BAKER
Aged 21
Who unfortunately fell victim to a barbarous assassin on the 4th February 1786
By murd'rous hand my thread of life was broke;
Dreadful the hour and terrible the stroke.
Repent, thou wicked spoiler of my youth;
Behold me here, consider parents both:
See from thy bloody hand, what woes arise
While calls for vengeance pierce the lofty skies:
Thou too must suffer, though thou scape the laws
for God is just and will avenge my cause

George Sheldon, who was the village Constable at Tideswell lost his life in 1805 on the open moors in a snowstorm. His epitaph read:

> By depth of snow and stormy day,
> He was bewildered in his way.
> No mortal aid did come him nigh;
> Upon the snow he then did lie.
> Helpless being worn out with strife,
> Death soon deprived him of his life;
> But hope he found a better way
> To the regions of eternal day.

Husbands frequently outlived their wives in the 18th and 19th centuries and commonly remarried. A tombstone in the churchyard at Bakewell contains a long inscription to the memory of John Fale, barber-surgeon and his two wives, Elizabeth Foljambe and Sarah Bloodworth. It ends with the following words:

> Know posterity, that on the 8th of April, in the year of grace 1757, the rambling remains of the above JOHN DALE were in the 86th yeare of his pilgrimage laid upon his two wives
> This thing in life might raise some jealousy,
> Here all three lie together lovingly
> But from embraces here no pleasure flows,
> Alike are here all human joys and woes;
> Here Sarah's chiding John no longer hears,
> And old john's rambling Sarah no more fears;
> A period's come to all their toylsome lives,
> The good man's quiet; still are both his wives

Not all monuments are to be found in churchyards. A monument to Steve Bloomer stands in Lock-up Yard close to Fish Market. It reads:

Steve Bloomer, the first king of English football goalscorers entered the 20th-century with his fame as Derby County's outstanding marksman already established.

As the next century beckoned - when this monument was erected in 1996 - his rams' all games record of 332 games was still unsurpassed.

His 353 Football League goals for Derby County and Middlesborough was a record until near his death in 1938 at 64.

Bloomer's 28 goals in 23 games gave him a then unique average of 1.21 per cap.

The son of a Midland's blacksmith, Bloomer was a pupil at St James' School in Derby.

He was described as a 'Working Class Hero by Nottingham Trent University student Jonathan Belshaw in his 1990's study of Victorian Social Changes.

The monument erected through the auction of Bloomer's England caps plus family.

Contributions, has been presented to Derby City Council by his descendants.

Not all epitaphs are inscribed in stone or bronze. James Brindley's death was noted in the Chester Courant of 1ˢᵗ December 1771 in the following terms:

James Brindley lies amongst these Rocks,
He made Canals, Bridges and Locks
To convey water he made Tunnels
for Barges, Boats and Air Vessels;
He erected several Banks,
Mills, Pumps, machines, with Wheels and cranks:
He was famous t'invent Engines,
Calculated for working Mines;
He knew Water, its Weight and Strength,
Turn'd Brooks, made Soughs to a great length;
While he used the Miners Blast,
He stopp'd Currents from running too fast;
There ne'er was paid such Attention
As he did to Navigation
But while busy with Pit or Well,
His Spirits sunk below level;
And, when too late his Doctor found,
Water sent him to the ground.

Perhaps the last word on epitaphs should be given to Brian Clough who said; 'I want no epitaphs of profound history. I contributed. I hope they would say that, and I hope somebody liked me'.

# Government and Politics

## Local Government

With the exception of the City of Derby, Derbyshire has a two tier system of local government comprising the county council and eight district/borough councils.

Derbyshire County Council is a first tier local authority. In 2012–13 it spent £530.8 million in providing services for approximately 750,000 residents. The Government grant provides funding for 47% of the services provided other than schools which are fully funded by a direct grant. This means that the Council Tax provides 53% of the money required to provide services such as:

Homes for old people
Meals on Wheels
Children's Homes
Social workers
Libraries
Roads and street lighting
Waste and recycling
Country parks
Trading standards
Registrars of births, deaths and marriages
Community safety
Emergency management
Youth offending service
Welfare rights

Derbyshire Fire Authority oversees the work of Derbyshire Fire and Rescue Service. It provides strategic leadership, monitors the cost incurred and sets the budget. The Authority consists of sixteen councillors; twelve from Derbyshire County Council and four from Derby City Council. A substantial part of the funds required to operate are generated from a direct charge on the Council tax payer, the remainder coming from a government grant and income generated by the Authority.

## District Councils

There are eight district/borough councils in Derbyshire. These are:

Amber Valley Borough Council
Bolsover District Council
Chesterfield Borough Council
Derbyshire Dales District Council
Erewash Borough Council
High Peak Borough Council
North East Derbyshire District Council
South Derbyshire District Council.

These Borough/District councils are responsible for a wide range of services including housing, council tax collection, pest control, refuse collection, parking, entertainment and leisure services.

Amber Valley Borough Council was created in April 1974 by the merger of a number of urban and rural district councils and was awarded borough status in 1988. It covers an area of 102.5 square miles and has a population of approximately 123,000 people. The administrative headquarters are at Ripley but the Borough also includes the towns of Alfreton, Belper and Heanor. Elections to the Borough Council are held in three out of every four years with one third of the 45 seats being contested at each election.

Bolsover District Council covers an area of 61.9 square miles and has a population of around 75,900. It was created in 1974 following the merger of Bolsover Urban District with Barlborough Rural District and Clowne Rural District. The Council is run by 37 democratically elected members. Each councillor is elected for four years with the next election scheduled for May 2015. The Council has a strategic alliance with North East Derbyshire District Council with a joint chief executive and four other joint directorates. The District Council has four contact centres at Bolsover, Clowne, Shirebrook and South Normanton.

Chesterfield Borough Council covers the areas of Chesterfield, Staveley and Brimington. The council comprises 48 councillors each representing a single electoral division. Elections to the whole council take place every four years. The Mayor, who, is elected each year by the councillors, chairs meetings of the full council and carries out a range of civic ceremonial duties.

The Derbyshire Dales District includes the towns of Ashbourne, Bakewell, Matlock and Wirksworth as well as over fifty villages. It covers an area of 305.9 square miles and has a population of 71,000 people. Derbyshire Dales District Council is composed of 39 councillors who are elected every four years. In order to give local people a greater say in council affairs there are three area community forums. These cover the Northern, Southern and Central areas of the District and are intended to act as a focus point for mutual communication and consultation between the local community, stakeholders and councillors from all local councillors in their area. They are held in public at various venues throughout the District. The District Council has its headquarters at Matlock.

*Ilkeston Town Hall. Council meetings alternate between here and Long Eaton*

Erewash Borough covers an area of 42.3 square miles and has a population of around 112,000 people. The Borough Council's headquarters functions are divided between the main urban areas of Long Eaton and Ilkeston and Council meetings are held at both venues. Elections to the 51 places on the Borough Council are held every four years. Full Council meetings are chaired by the Mayor who also carries out a range of ceremonial and civic duties.

The Borough of High Peak District covers an area of 208.2 square miles and has a population of around 100,000 residents. The five main areas of settlement in the Borough are centred around the towns of Buxton, New Mills, Glossop, Whaley Bridge and Chapel-en-le-Frith. The Borough is administered jointly from Buxton and Glossop and has a strategic alliance with Staffordshire Moorlands District Council. Elections to the Borough Council, comprising 43 councillors, take place every four years.

North East Derbyshire District Council was created in 1974 and was formed by the merger of the former Clay Cross and Dronfield urban districts and all the parishes of the former Chesterfield Rural District except one (Brimington). The District comprises around 107 square miles, and almost entirely encircles Chesterfield where the District Council offices are located. The two main centres of population are at Dronfield and Clay Cross. The Council formed a strategic alliance with Bolsover District Council in 2011. The two councils share a chief executive and aim to save money by joint procurement, sharing assets and providing some joint services.

South Derbyshire District Council was formed on 1 April 1974 following the merger of Swadlincote Urban District, Repton Rural District and part of South East Derbyshire Rural District. It covers an area of 130.5 square miles and has a population of around 95,000. It claims to be one of the fastest growing districts in the country. Swadlincote is the principal town and the administrative headquarters of the District Council. Other substantial settlements include Chellaston, Etwall, Hatton, Hilton, Melbourne, Repton and Shardlow. South Derbyshire District Council is made up of 36 locally elected councillors. Elections to the whole council take place every four years.

**Derby City Council**

Derby City Council is a unitary authority which provides all local government services to its residents. The Council is composed of 51 councillors who represent 17 three-member wards, with one third elected three years in four.

**Town Mayors**

A number of Derbyshire towns have Mayors. A number of district councils in Derbyshire have a mayor who acts as Chair of the Council as well as performing a range of civic and ceremonial duties.

**Town and Parish Councils**

Town and Parish councils make up the third tier of local government in some areas of the county. Their functions include recreation facilities, parks and open spaces, cemeteries, public conveniences, car parks and village halls and community facilities.

**Parliamentary Constituencies**

There are 11 parliamentary constituencies in Derbyshire. They are Amber Valley, Bolsover, Chesterfield, Derby North, Derby South, Derbyshire Dales, Erewash, High Peak, Mid Derbyshire, North East Derbyshire and South Derbyshire.

Amber Valley Constituency was created in 1983. It includes the market towns of Alfreton, Ripley and Heanor as well as their surrounding areas. Belper which was previously part of the constituency was moved to the new Mid Derbyshire constituency in 2010. Members of Parliament have included:

1983 Phillip Oppenheim Conservative

1997 Judy Mallaber Labour

2010 Nigel Mills Conservative

Bolsover Constituency was created in 1950. Originally it comprised the urban district of Bolsover and the rural districts of Blackwell and Clowne. Minor boundary changes took place in 1983 and 2010 when on both occasions parts of North East Derbyshire were transferred to the Constituency. It has been a Labour stronghold since its creation. Members of Parliament have included:

1950 Harold Neal Labour

1970 Dennis Skinner Labour

Chesterfield Constituency was created in 1885. Its current boundaries include most of the town of Chesterfield but the areas of Staveley and Barrow fall within the neighbouring constituency of North East Derbyshire. It was for many years a

Labour stronghold but is now a marginal seat. Members of Parliament have included:

1964 Eric Varley Labour

1984 Tony Benn Labour

2001 Paul Holmes Liberal Democrat

2010 Toby Perkins Labour

Derby North Constituency was created in 1950. It is a fairly compact constituency covering a large residential area in the northern half of the city. It includes both inner-city areas and more affluent suburbs. Members of Parliament have included:

1962 Niall MacDermot Labour

1970 Phillip Whitehead Labour

1983 Greg Knight Conservative

1997 Robert Laxton Labour

2010 Chris Williamson Labour

Derby South Constituency was created in 1950 when the former two seat constituency of Derby was split into two single-member seats. At the last election it had an electorate of 72,046. The constituency includes some socially deprived inner-city areas as well as more affluent suburbs. Members of Parliament have included:

1950 Phillip Noel-Baker Labour

1970 Walter Johnson Labour

1983 Margaret Beckett Labour

Derbyshire Dales Constituency was created after a review by the Boundary Commission and was contested for the first time in the 2010 General Election. It covers a large area including parts of Amber valley and the whole of the Derbyshire Dales district after which the constituency was named, It is represented by Patrick McLoughlan (Conservative).

Erewash Constituency was created in 1983 and covers the towns of Long Eaton and Ilkston and their surrounding areas. The boundaries of the constituency were changed for the 2010 general Election with some areas being transferred to a new Mid Derbyshire constituency. It is a relatively small constituency with an electorate of a little over 70,000. Members of Parliament have included:

1983 Peter Rost Conservative

1992 Angela Knight Conservative

1997 Liz Blackman Labour

2010 Jessica Lee Conservative

High Peak Constituency was created in 1885. It has undergone some boundary changes over the years and now covers an area in the north of the county including the towns of Buxton, Chapel-en-le-Frith and Glossop. Members of Parliament have included:

1939 Hugh Molson Conservative

1961 David Walder Conservative

1966 Peter Jackson Labour

1970 Spencer Le Marchant Conservative

1983 Christopher Hawkins Conservative

1992 Charles Hendry Conservative

1997 Tom Levitt Labour

2010 Andrew Bingham Conservative

Mid Derbyshire is a new constituency created in 2010. It includes areas which were previously parts of Derby North, West Derbyshire, Erewash and Amber Valley. It is a relatively small constituency with an electorate of less than 67,000. Pauline Latham (Conservative) was elected as the first Member of Parliament with a considerable majority.

North-east Derbyshire Constituency was created in 1885, Following recent boundary changes it now covers the north eastern part of Derbyshire surrounding Chesterfield on three sides. The constituency includes a number of former mining villages as well as the towns of Staveley and Dronfield. Members of Parliament have included:

1935 Frank Lee Labour

1942 Henry White Labour

1959 Tom Swain Labour

1979 Raymond Ellis Labour

1987 Harry Barnes Labour

2005 Natasha Engels Labour

South Derbyshire Constituency was created in 1983 and at the 2010 general election had an electorate of 71,326. A number of boundary changes have taken place since its creation and the constituency now covers the whole of the South Derbyshire district, having lost parts of the city of Derby. Members of Parliament have included:

1983 Edwina Currie Conservative

1997 Mark Todd Labour

2010 Heather Wheeler Conservative

**European Parliament**

Derbyshire is part of the East Midlands Region of the European Parliament. MEPs are elected by a system of proportional representation and serve for five years. The last elections to the European Parliament were held on 4 June 2009 when the following MEPs were elected:

Roger Helmer Conservative

Emma McClarkin Conservative

Glenis Wilmot Labour

Derek Clerk UK Independence Party

Bill Newton Dunn Liberal Democrats

The total number of votes cast for each party was as follows:

British National Party 106,319

Christian Party 'Proclaiming Christ's lordship' 17,907

Conservative Party 370,275

English Democrats Party 28,498

Jury Team 7,362

Liberal Democrats 151,428

No2EU:Yes to Democracy 564

Pro democracy;libertas.eu 7,882

Socialist Labour Party 13,590

The Green Party 83,939

The Labour Party 206,494

United Kingdom First 20,561

United Kingdom Independence Party 201,984

Turnout 1,228,065
Electorate 3,312,944
Percentage Turnout 37 per cent

## Political Personalities

**Margaret Becket** was elected as Member of Parliament for Derby South in 1983 having previously been MP for Lincoln from 1974 until 1979. After Labour's landslide victory in the 1997 general election she entered the cabinet as President of the Board of Trade and Secretary of Trade for Trade and Industry. In 1998 she became President of the Privy Council and Leader of the House of Commons. Three years later she was appointed Secretary of State for the Environment, Food and Rural Affairs. In 2006 she became the first ever woman to be appointed Foreign Secretary.

**Tony Benn** was Labour MP for Chesterfield from 1984 to 2001. He was elected to Parliament as MP for Bristol South East but had to resign when he inherited the title of Viscount Stansgate from his father. Following a change in the law he was able to renounce his peerage and return to the House of Commons as MP for Bristol South once again. The constituency was abolished in 1983 but he returned to the House of Commons as MP for Chesterfield following a bye-election in March 1984. During his long parliamentary career he held a number of important posts including Secretary of State for Energy, Secretary of State for Industry, Minister of Technology and Postmaster General.

**Dennis Skinner** was born at Clay Cross in 1932 and later won a scholarship to Tupton Hall Grammar school. At the age of 16 he left school and went to work as a coal miner. He joined the NUM and by the age of 33 became County President. He became involved in local government and became a County Councillor in 1966. When the local Member of Parliament decided to retire Dennis was invited to put his name forward to the selection committee. He was elected to parliament in 1970 and has been the MP for Bolsover ever since. He has remained a backbencher throughout that time and has won a reputation as a rebel and a wit. He is said to be proud of his nick name as the 'Beast of Bolsover'.

**Philip Noel-Baker** was a Member of Parliament for Derby from 1936 to 1950 and for Derby South from 1950 until 1970. A Quaker and a pacifist, he played an important role in the formation of both the League of Nations and the United Nations Organisation and in 1946 he was appointed to the British delegation to the United Nations. He held a number of posts in the post-war Labour government but continued to campaign for disarmament. He was awarded the Nobel Peace Prize in 1959.

# Royal Derbyshire

**Repton** was the capital of the Saxon Kingdom of Mercia. It was the burial place of a number of Mercian kings and the crypt at St Wystan's Church was a royal mausoleum.

**Edward the Elder** advanced into Derbyshire during his campaign against the Danes and established a fortified burgh at Bakewell.

**King Canute** visited Repton at some point during his reign. He was so impressed with the tales of the martyred Saint Wystan that he transferred his relics to the great Abbey of Evesham.

**Henry II** received the submission of King Malcolm of Scotland at Peverel Castle in 1157. There are records of other visits here in 1158 and 1164.

**King John** made several visits to Derbyshire. In 1200 he was at Derby and Bolsover in March and at Melbourne in November. He also spent some time at Horsley Castle in 1209.

**Henry III** visited Derbyshire in 1264 and lodged for a time at Peverel Castle following the subjugation of Nottingham.

**Edward I** visited Derbyshire in 1275, stopping at both Ashbourne and Tideswell when on his way to North Wales. In 1293 he made a Royal Progress through the county staying at a number of places including Codnor Castle. He also made frequent visits to the county to hunt in Duffield Frith.

**Edward II** stayed briefly at Codnor castle in 1322 as the guest of Richard, Lord Grey, one of his most ardent supporters. He spent some time in the county again in 1325 and visited Derby during the Christmas period in 1326.

**Henry IV** made frequent visits to Derbyshire. It was from here in 1403 that he rallied his troops before marching to victory against a rebel army at Shrewsbury.

**Mary Queen of Scots** was held prisoner in Derbyshire for a number of years. She was lodged in a number of places including Wingfield Manor and Chatsworth Old Hall. She also visited Buxton to take the waters and hunted in Peak Forest. It was during her time at Wingfield Manor that the Babington plot was hatched. The plotters, led by Sir Anthony Babington planned to overthrow Elizabeth I and place Mary on the throne. She also stayed for one night at Babington Hall in Derby on her way to incarceration at Tutbury Castle.

**King James I** visited Derby in August 1619 on his way from Nottingham to Tutbury Castle. Records indicate that he kept court at Derby in August 1624 when he knighted Sir Roger Cooper of Thurgarton in Nottinghamshire.

**King Charles I** was entertained by the Earl of Newcastle at Bolsover Castle on three occasions; 1632, 1633 and 1634. On the last occasion he was accompanied by Queen Henrietta Maia. The expense of the visit was said to have reached the vast sum of £15,000 and included a performance of Ben Johnson's masque of *Loves Welcome to Bolsover.*

**King Charles I** visited Derby in 1635 and slept at the Great House in the Market Place. The Corporation and the townsmen gave the Duke of Newcastle a fat ox, a calf, six fat sheep and a purse of gold to enable him to keep hospitality In 1641 he passed through the county again and visited Derby on 11 August. At the start of the Civil War in September 1642 he lodged briefly at Derby on his way from Nottingham to Shrewsbury.

**William Cavendish** was one of the four young noblemen who carried the train of King Charles II at his coronation in 1661.

**William Cavendish** the Earl of Cavendish was involved in the plot which led to the 'Glorious Revolution' of 1688. Not surprisingly he was generously rewarded by his new sovereign. The Earl was made Lord Lieutenant of Derbyshire in 1689 and shortly afterwards created Duke of Devonshire and Marquis of Hartington. Surprisingly there is no evidence that either King William or Queen Mary visited Derbyshire at any time during their reigns.

Derbyshire played a significant part in the **Jacobite rebellion** of 1745. The highland army led by 'Bonnie Prince Charlie' arrived at Ashbourne on 3 December 1745. The following day it arrived in Derby and assembled in the Market Place where the Prince was proclaimed Regent to this father, James III. When Charles arrived he was provided with accommodation at Exeter House in Full Street. Other senior officers were accommodated in houses around the Market Place and the soldiers were billeted at inns and houses elsewhere in the town. The artillery was parked on Nun's green and the advance guard marched on to secure Swarkestone Bridge. On 5 December a Catholic Mass was performed at All Saint's Church (now the Cathedral). That night a council of war was held at Exeter House and Charles was persuaded that there was not sufficient support to continue their march towards London. The retreat began early on 6 December. The Jacobite army was finally defeated at the battle of Culloden on 16 April 1746. Bonnie Prince Charlie escaped but spent the rest of his life wandering around Europe. He died in Rome in 1788. A statue of Bonnie Prince Charlie stands on Cathedral Green, not far from the site of Exeter House.

**The Dowager Queen Adelaide** (widow of King William IV) resided at Sudbury Hall in the early 1840s. It was here that she wrote instructions for her funeral during an illness in 1841.

**Queen Victoria** and **Prince Albert** made a number of unofficial visits to Derby. They passed through Derby on their way to Chatsworth in 1843 and also stayed at the Midland Hotel, near the railway station in 1849 and 1852.

**Edward, Prince of Wales** (the future Edward VII) visited Derby in 1881 to attend the Royal Show at Osmaston Park. He travelled by train and was lavishly entertained by the Mayor, Alderman Abraham Woodiwisse.

In 1891 **Queen Victoria** made an official visit to Derby to lay the foundation stone for the Derbyshire Royal Infirmary. During her visit she knighted the Mayor, Sir Alfred Haslam.

**Edward VII** was also a frequent visitor to the county. He was a keen shooter of game and was a regular visitor to Chatsworth both as Prince of Wales and later as King. He visited Derby in 1906 to open the Royal Show. On his way from a reception in the Market Place to the showground he stopped at the Spot to unveil a statue of his mother, presented to the town by Sir Alfred Haslam, Mayor at the time of Queen Victoria's 1891 visit.

**King George V** and **Queen Mary** visited the Industrial Exhibition at Derby on 10 December 1913. The King was at Derby again in June 1921 to visit the Royal Show.

**Princess Mary,** daughter of King George V and Queen Mary visited Buxton on 29 October 1921.

**The Prince of Wales** (later Edward VIII) gave royal patronage to Ashbourne's Shrovetide Football match for the first time in 1928. After 'turning up' the ball on Shaw Croft, the Prince travelled to Derby for an official lunch. In the afternoon he went on to visit Rolls Royce and the LMS carriage and wagon and locomotive works. On 3 June 1932 he made a royal visit to Holloway to lay the foundation stone of the Florence Nightingale Memorial Hall.

**The Duke of York** (later King George VI) visited a number of factories in Derbyshire in his role as President of the Industrial Welfare Society. On 2 May 1933 he visited Stanton Iron Works and Lea Mills. The following day he toured Leys Malleable Castings in Derby.

**The Duke of Kent** was the fourth son of King George V. He was known as the 'Ambassador of the Workless' and towards the end of 1935 he made a three day tour of Derbyshire to visit unemployed occupational centres. On 17 December he visited Belper and received a baby chair made in oak for his young son. He returned to Derby on 6 March 1941 when he inspected bomb damage, met members of the Home Guard and visited a number of factories.

**King George VI** and **Queen Mary** made a morale raising visit to Derby during the First World War. After being met at the railway station by the Mayor, Alderman Arthur Neil, they drove to Osmaston to inspect troops before spending over an hour at the Rolls-Royce factory.

**The Princess Royal**, sister of King George VI and the Duke of Kent made several wartime visits to Derbyshire. As Controller-Commandant of the ATS she made two visits to inspect servicewomen and in 1945 visited Derbyshire Royal infirmary to meet wounded soldiers.

**Queen Elizabeth** the **Queen Mother** opened Derby Assembly Rooms on 9 November 1997. She attended a concert by the Royal Philharmonic Orchestra at which she was presented with a Royal Crown Derby loving cup, by the Mayor. The following day she opened the new buildings of St Christopher's Railway Children's Home. Previous visits by the Queen Mother included tours of the Guildhall, Cathedral and Royal Crown Derby.

**Princess Margaret** officially opened new premises for the Royal School for the Deaf on Ashbourne Road, Derby on 28 June 1973. She also visited the Rycote Centre on Kedleston Road. She had previously visited the town on a number of occasions and was back again in 1984 when she visited Derby to promote the work of the NSPCC. At a service in Derby Cathedral she personally thanked many youngsters as they handed over donations totalling £45,000 for the Derbyshire NSPCC appeal.

**Princess Anne** has visited several different places in the county including Derby, Chesterfield, Ilkeston and Buxton. In September 2011 during a whirlwind tour of the county she visited a number of local firms including Denby Pottery, Deb, Thornton's Chocolates and David Nieper.

**Prince Charles** has also been a frequent visitor to Derbyshire. In February 1981, in a whirlwind six hour tour of Derby, he visited a Sikh temple, the Madeley Centre, the Ukranian Club, Polish Club and the Serbian Orthodox Church. He has returned to the county on a number of occasions and in 2003 he started the Ashbourne Shrove Football match by turning up the ball. More recently, in February 2012, he came to Derby to visit Rolls-Royce and Bombardier. His visit to the county also included a tour of Haddon Hall and Gardens, where he viewed restoration work and met supporters and volunteers.

**Queen Elizabeth II** has visited Derbyshire on a number of occasions. The following are some of the highlights:

As Princess Elizabeth, accompanied by the Duke of Edinburgh, she visited Derby on 27 June 1949 to officially open the new Council House. After their arrival in the town the royal couple visited the Royal Crown Derby china works and Rolls-Royce. After the official opening ceremony and tea at the Council House, the Princess went on to lay the foundation stone of the war memorial village for disabled servicemen at Allenton.

The Queen made her first official visit to Derbyshire as sovereign on 28 March 1957. After arriving at Sudbury railway station at 10am the Queen and the Duke of Edinburgh fulfilled a number of engagements before arriving at Repton School for lunch and an afternoon of tours and ceremonies. Later in the day she arrived at Derby where, after inspecting a guard of honour, she went on to make a number of visits. The Royal couple were entertained to tea at the Council House where the Corporation presented them with a Royal Crown Derby dinner service.

In 1977 the Queen visited Derby as part of the Silver Jubilee celebrations. She presented Letters Patent to the Mayor conferring city status on Derby. During her visit to the county she also opened the newly-extended Derbyshire police headquarters at Butterley Hall.

In March 1985 the Queen's visit to Derbyshire included the official opening of the new Thornton's factory near Swanwick. She also visited Queen Elizabeth's Grammar School to mark its 400th anniversary.

In 1992 the Queen's tour of the county included the official opening of Carsington Water as well as visits to Matlock and Wirksworth. At Derby she viewed the newly refurbished Queen's Leisure centre and met consultants at the Derby Royal Infirmary.

In 1997 the Queen came to Derby to open the Pride Park Stadium; the first time she had ever opened a football ground! On this occasion she also visited the Royal School for the Deaf and the Derbyshire Children's Hospital.

The Queen returned to Pride Park Stadium in 2002 as part of her Golden Jubilee celebrations. The city of Derby laid on a pageant entitled 'Derbyshire Celebrates' which was attended by around 27,000 people.

The Queen chose Derby Cathedral to host the annual Maundy Thursday service on Thursday 1 April 2010. During the service she presented specially minted coins to 84 men and 84 women (representing the age of the Queen). After the ceremony she had lunch at the Cathedral Quarter Hotel before going on to open the new Derby Royal Hospital.

# Derbyshire on Film and Television

The 1980s TV series *Boon* starring Michael Elphick was filmed at a number of locations in the Midlands including Ilkeston Market Place and the Scala Cinema, which featured in the opening title sequence of Series 7.

Ken Russell's 1969 adaptation of D. H. Lawrence's novel, *Women in Love*, featured a number of Derbyshire locations including Kedleston Hall, Matlock and the Crich Tramway Museum. 'Shortlands' the home of Gerald Crich (Oliver Reed) where the young lovers drown during a party is Elvaston Castle. The famous naked wrestling scene was filmed in the Gothic Hall there.

The 1954 black and white film, *The Dam Busters* starred Michael Redgrave as Barnes Wallis (the inventor of the bouncing bomb) and Richard Todd as Wing Commander Guy Gibson. It was filmed over the Upper Derwent Valley, an area that was used for training for the actual raid.

Ridley Scott's 2010 film *Robin Hood*, starring Russell Crowe includes a scene filmed at Dovedale.

The 1970 film adaptation of *The Virgin and the Gypsy* starring Christopher Miles, Franco Nero and Honor Blackman used a number of Derbyshire locations including Matlock, Youlgreave, Beeley Moor and Derwent Dam.

*Starlings*, a TV sitcom first broadcast on Sky 1 in 2012, follows the life of a typical working class family who live in Matlock and was filmed in and around the town. It was written by Matt King and Steve Edge and produced by Steve Coogan.

The 2010 film *The Wolfman* was partly filmed at Kedleston Hall which was transformed by adding weeds, dead grass and ivy to parts of the exterior.

*Peak Practice*, the long running TV series was filmed in and around the village of Crich which featured as Cardale. Other Derbyshire locations included Kirk Ireton (the setting for Jack and Beth's wedding), Belper Mill (which became the police station in later episodes) and Wirksworth (where Will and Sara visited the local bank). Filming also took place at Derby, South Wingfield and Fritchley.

Codnor Castle featured in an episode of the *Time Team* first broadcast in November 2008. In addition to the spectacular find of a Henry V gold noble coin, the team also discovered three phases of construction of the castle including the great hall and the drawbridge.

*Sweet Medicine* was an ITV drama series broadcast in 2003 about a family doctor's surgery in the Peak District. The majority of filming took place in Wirksworth which provided the setting for the fictional Derbyshire town of Stoneford. It was intended as a replacement for Peak Practice but failed to achieve the expected viewing figures. Only one ten-episode series was produced.

The 2002 TV series *Stig of the Dump* (based on the book by Clive King and starring Robert Tannion, Geoffrey Palmer and Phyllida Law)) was filmed partly in Derbyshire. The quarry where much of the series was set is Duke's Quarry in Whatstandwell. Other locations include Darley Dale and Alderwasley, where the pub featured is actually the Bear Inn.

Vernon Street, close to the centre of Derby was used as a setting in the 1980s series *Nanny*, starring Wendy Craig. The Choir of St Oswald's Church, Ashbourne, also featured in the series.

The National Tramway Museum at Crich has been used in the making of a number of films and TV series but it has also featured in Blue Peter and Anneka Rice's *Treasure Hunt*.

Red House stables at Darley Dale near Matlock has provide carriages and other horsed draw vehicles for a number of productions filmed in Derbyshire and elsewhere.

The exterior of Repton School was used to represent Brookfield School in both the 1939 and 1969 films, *Goodbye, Mr Chips*; and in the 1984 BBC TV drama of the story originally written by James Hilton. The 1939 version starred Robert Donat as Mr Chipping and around 200 Repton boys stayed at the school over the holidays in order to appear as extras in the film.

Ecclesbourne Valley Railway, near Wirksworth has been used as a location for a number of TV dramas. An episode of *Casualty* was filmed here in 2007. Wirksworth Station was dressed to represent a modern station and was painted in a contemporary colour scheme and equipped with real time monitors.

Stanage Edge is a very long gritstone edge and a popular beauty spot near Hathersage. It has featured in a number of film and TV dramas including *Pride and Prejudice*, and *Jane Eyre*.

Calver Mill was used for the exterior shots of the TV drama, *Colditz*. The series featured a number of well known actors including David McCallum and Robert Wagner.

Chesterfield Football Club's home ground appeared in a number of guises in the making of *The Damned United* (a film following the career of Brian Clough). It feature as Wembley Stadium in the film and repainted it also became the Baseball Ground, Carrow Road and Bloomfield Road.

The TV series, *The League of Gentlemen* was filmed at Hadfield, which doubled as the fictional town of RoystonVasey. In the film spin-off, *The League of Gentlemen Apocalypse*, Hadfield appears as itself when the characters from the series enter the real world through a portal beneath the church.

The film, *The Full Monty* was shot mainly in and around Sheffield but some scenes were filmed at the former colliery site at Shirebrook.

The 1980s BBC version of *The Chronicles of Narnia* featured a number of Derbyshire locations including Wingfield Manor. The crypt there was transformed into the witch's palace for filming but the slabs laid by the production company had to be removed on the insistence of English Heritage.

D. H. Lawerence's novel, *The Rainbow* was adapted for television by the BBC in 1988. Starring Imogen Stubbs, Tom Bell, Kate Buffrey and Jon Finch, locations included the Midland Railway Centre at Butterley and Hardwick Hall.

The 2006 BBC TV four-part adaptation of *Jane Eyre* was filmed exclusively on location in Derbyshire and the Peak District. Bolsover Castle featured as Lowood School where Jane spent her early years. The Riding School at the Castle was transformed into a dormitory. Haddon Hall represented Mr Rochester's house and when the special effects department lit the Hall to simulate the fire, the local fire brigade received almost a hundred calls! Hathersage and Stanage were used for the moorland scenes, and Dovedale features in the first episode where Rochester looms out of the mist in a black stallion and meets Jane for the first time. Other locations used in the film include Kedleston Hall, Ilam Youth Hostel and Wingfield Manor.

Chatsworth House was the subject of a three-part documentary broadcast by BBC television in 2012. Narrated by Max Bealey, *Chatsworth* charted the working of Chatsworth House over the course of the year. It included interviews with the Duke and Duchess of Devonshire as well as a several members of staff.

Sudbury Hall was used by the BBC as the location for the interior scenes of Pemberley House in the 1995 adaptation of *Pride and Prejudice*, starring Colin Firth and Jennifer Ehle. In one scene the camera follows Elizabeth Bennett and the Gardiners through the long gallery and a series of elegant rooms as they are guided round the house.

*The Duchess*, starring Keira Knightly and Ralph Feinnes was filmed at a number of locations including Chatsworth House (the real-life home of Georgiana, Duchess of Devonshire) and Kedleston Hall. During the filming, Kedleston Hall was used to depict Althorp Hall (the Spencer family home), Devonshire House in London and a rented villa in Bath. Following the release of the film in 2008 exhibitions of some of the costumes and props used in the film were staged at both Kedleston and Chatsworth.

Jim Broadbent and Colin Firth starred in the 2007 film, *And When Did You Last see Your Father?* It tells the story of writer, Blake Morrison (Colin Firth) as he tries to understand, forgive, know and love his dying father, played by Jim Broadbent. The film includes a number of Derbyshire locations including Kedleston Hall, Cromford, the Snake Pass and the Lathkill Hotel at Over Haddon.

*The Other Boleyn Girl*, directed by Justin Chadwick and starring Scarlett Johansson and Natalie Portman was filmed at a number of locations throughout the country. In Derbyshire, filming took place at North Lees Hall, Haddon Hall and Dovedale. Several members of the cast and crews stayed at the Peacock Hotel at Rowsley whilst filming.

The BBC television current affairs programme *Question Time* was broadcast from Derby on Thursday 5 July 2012. Chaired by David Dimbleby the panellists included the Energy and Climate Change Secretary, Ed Davy MP, former Home Secretary Alan Johnson MP, Conservative MP Louise Mensch, Sunday Times and Independent columnist Dominic Lawson and John Lydon, former lead singer of the Sex Pistols and founder of the band Public Image UK.

The BBC TV series *Restoration* was broadcast over three seasons, from 2003 to 2005, with the aim of publicising and saving neglected buildings of historic importance throughout Britain. Cromford Mill featured in one of the programmes in the first series alongside a coffin factory in Birmingham and Bethesda Chapel at Stoke-on-Trent.

The BBC *Countryfile* programme has made several visits to Derbyshire. In November 2011 Matt Baker toured the Derwent Valley reservoirs on a mountain bike. More recently the programme came to film at Rennishaw Hall to look at work being done in the gardens and the vineyard

A Derbyshire murder featured in the 2004 BBC drama, *In Denial of Murder*. The case involved the conviction and imprisonment in 1974 of a 17-year-old council worker, Stephen Downey for the murder of a 32 year old legal secretary in Bakewell. His conviction was overturned in 2002.

The television series *Most Haunted* investigates paranormal activity at locations throughout the UK and abroad. Among the places it has investigated in Derbyshire are Derby Gaol, Elvaston Castle, Tissington Hall and Matlock Bath Pavilion.

Architectural historian Dan Cruickshank selected Hardwick Hall as one of five choices for the 2001 BBC television documentary series, *Britain's Best Building*.

Hardwick Hall was used to film the exterior scenes of Malfoy Manor in the most recent Harry Potter films. It also featured in the TV series Mastercraft, episode 6 on stonemasonry where trainees vied to create fitting sundials for the gardens there.

A television production of *The Roses of Eyam* based on the events in the Plague Village of Eyam between September 1665 and December 1666 was broadcast on BBC 2 in June 1973.

The BBC television programme *Homes Under the Hammer,* hosted by Martin Roberts and Lucy Alexander featured a property in Derbyshire during an episode first broadcast on Wednesday 26 September 2012.

Haddon Hall is probably the most filmed location in Derbyshire. Over the past thirty years over forty films and television programmes have been shot here. Well known films shot partly at Haddon Hall include :

1985  – *Lady Jane Grey* – Featuring Helena Bonham Carter
1986  – *The Princess Bride* – Now a cult classic
1989  – *The Lady and the Highwayman* – Starring Oliver Reed
1994  – *Dragon World* – Featuring Alistair Mackenzie and Brittney Powell
1995  – *Jane Eyre* – Directed by Franco Zefferilli
1996  – *The Prince and the Pauper* – Starring Keith Michell
1998  – *Elizabeth* – Featuring Kate Blanchett, Geoffrey Rush and Joseph Feinnes
2004  – *Pride and Prejudice* – Featuring Keira Knightley
2006  – *The Other Boleyn Girl* – Starring Scarlett Johansson and Natalie Portman
2010  – *Jane Eyre* – Featuring Dame Judi Dench

Popular TV series to have used the Hall as a location have included *Sherlock Holmes, Moll Flanders, The Inspector Linley Mysteries.* Countless individual dramas and documentaries have been filmed here and over the years Haddon Hall has also featured in *Travels with Pevsner, Top Gear, The Holiday Programme, Flog It, Bargain Hunt, Gardeners' World* and *Songs of Praise!*

# This and That

Bradbourne is the only 'Thankful Village' in Derbyshire. These are villages from which all the young man who went to fight in the Great War, returned safely. Eighteen men went from Bradbourne and eighteen returned.

Daimler was the Luftwaffe code name for Derby during the Second World war. With Rolls Royce and a number of other engineering firms based in the town, Derby was a prime target for the German air force.

Derby's Sikh community take to the streets each year to celebrate the Vaisakhi. This is the most important day in the Sikh calendar and is both a harvest festival and the Sikh new year. It also commemorates 1699, the year Sikhism was founded in its current form by Guru Gobind Singh. The parade, through the Normanton area of the city, is lead by a drummer and a group of women sweeping the road with brooms. This is because the Sikh holy book, the Guru Granth Sahib has a place of honour at the head of the parade and the way has to be kept clear and clean for it. In recent years the parade has attracted as many as 15,000 people.

Cherry Blossom shoe polish is made in Derbyshire. Alfreton firm, Granger's bought the iconic brand in 1990 and started to manufacture the shoe-care range in the town four years later. The company also produces its own brand shoe polish. About two million tins per year now leave the Clover Nook Industrial Estate factory as well as creams, waxes and aerosols also manufactured by the company.

Derby was named the Real Ale Capital of the UK by the Campaign for Real Ale in 2012. At the time of writing the city boasted seven breweries; Mr Grundy's Brewery, Derby Brewing Company, Dancing Duck Brewery, Derventio Brewery, Brunswick Brewery, Falstaff Brewery and Middle Earth Brewery. The Derby branch of CAMRA also hosts two beer festivals each year; the winter festival is held at Derby College's Roundhouse, while the Summer one takes place at the Assembly rooms in the Market Place.

The Bakewell Show takes place on the first Wednesday and Thursday in August on land adjoining the Agricultural Centre. The first Bakewell Show, very much a local affair, took place in 1819 but it is now a major national agricultural and horticultural event with a wide range of animals being shown as well as show jumping and exhibitions of local crafts and produce.

The steel ribbed umbrella was invented by Samuel Fox of Bradwell in 1852.

Winster Morris Men have been performing since at least 1863. Their dances are their own and are exclusive to the village. A full team comprises sixteen dancers accompanied by the King, the Queen, the Jester and the Witch, all played by men.

At one time almost every village had a set of stocks. Today they can still be seen in a handful of places including Sudbury, Chapel-en-le-Frith, Uppertown and Eyam.

The Melbourne Festival is held in September each year when shops, offices and people's homes are opened up to display the work of a wide range of artists and craftsmen including artists, photographers, potters and jewellery makers. In addition the festival organisers also stage a programme of music and drama in local venues. Other similar arts festivals are held in Derbyshire at places such as Wirksworth and Ashbourne.

Motor cars were manufactured on a small scale in Derbyshire at the beginning of the 20th-century. First came the Simplex Pefecta from Normanton in 1900, followed by the short-lived Repton three wheeler from the village of that name in 1904.

Jane Austin is said to have stayed at the Rutland Arms Hotel in Bakewell whilst writing *Pride and Prejudice*. The town of Bakewell has been identified as Lambton.

The railway station at Duffield was once known as a 'Top Hat' station because several of the senior managers and directors of the railway lived there.

Evans Concrete Products of Somercotes provided all thirteen access bridges for London's Olympic Park.

Repton School is one of the foremost public schools in the country. Founded in 1557 as a result of the will of Sir John Port from nearby Etwall, the school took over some of the buildings of the recently dissolved Repton Priory.

A Derby man took part in Captain Scott's ill-fated expedition to the South Pole in 1911. George Clarke Simpson remained at base Camp and was later part of the team that discovered the bodies of Scott and his companions.

A lifeboat named 'The Spirit of Derbyshire' has served Ilfracombe lifeboat station for more than twenty years. It was given its name in recognition of the county's significant fund raising efforts. In 1989 the 23 branches of the RNLI across Derbyshire started a campaign to raise the £360,000 needed to buy one of the new Mersey lifeboats for the station almost 240 miles away. In the space of a year the people of Derbyshire raised a total of £412,000 and the lifeboat was officially placed at Ilfracombe in July 1990. Since then it has been launched almost 300 times and has rescued around 400 people. The boat will be retired in 2014 and replaced one of the latest Shannon class lifeboats.

Derbyshire Heritage Awards are presented each year to celebrate the county's museums and heritage sites. Awards are presented in five categories and the winner of each goes forward for the Museum of the Year Award. This was won by Erewash Museum in 2011 and 2012.

Hundreds of people in Derbyshire died in the 1918 influenza epidemic.

The American Adventure Theme Park near Shipley was officially opened in July 1987. It claimed to be Britain's first purpose-built theme park. It closed in 2006.

There are over 300 acres of open space in the city of Derby.

Devastating storms struck Derbyshire in October 2002. Rail services and power lines across the county were severely damaged by gale force winds and accompanying rain. Railway lines across the whole county were closed at one point and more than 24,000 homes were without power.

One of the first Advanced Passenger Trains was named City of Derby, in recognition of the research, design and production carried out in Derby. The naming ceremony took place in June 1978

Around 80 motor cars took part in a grand procession through Derby on 27 April 1900 as part of the Automobile Club's 1,000 mile tour of Great Britain.

Lara Croft, the world famous computer game and animated film character was created by Core Design in Derby in 1996. In 2006 Lara Croft was inducted into the Walk of Game and the Guinness Book of Records has recognised her as the 'Most Successful Human Game Heroine'. A road named after her, Lara Croft Way, was opened in Derby in 2010.

The village of Repton was once the capital of the Saxon kingdom of Mercia. Several Kings of Mercia were buried here.

The weather vane on the top of Derby's Railway Roundhouse depicts an early steam locomotive.

Spider Bridge on the Derby ring road at Allenton was so named because of its shape. It is in fact a series of pedestrian bridges constructed over a busy road junction and island.

Crich Tramway Museum has a collection of over sixty electric and horse-drawn trams from all over Britain as well some from overseas. Local examples include an early horse drawn tram from Chesterfield and a double-decker electric tram from Derby.

A £43,000 science garden featuring a human sundial and concrete planets was opened at Alvaston Park in January 2012. It was built by volunteers and local schools using a National Lottery grant. At the centre of the garden is a sun mosaic orbited by concrete sculptures of Mercury, Venus, Earth and Mars. The distance between each planet was calculated to scale with one metre representing a million kilometres in space.

The War Memorial Village at Allenton, Derby is a cluster of over thirty homes provided with special facilities needed by disabled people. The foundation stone was laid by the then Princess Elizabeth and the Duke of Edinburgh and the first home was occupied in May 1950.

A winged horse by Damien Hurst was one of a number of monumental sculptures exhibited at Chatsworth House between September and October 2011.

The world's first tilting train was developed and built in Derby in the 1970s. Starting life as an experimental high-speed train capable of travelling at speeds up to 155 mph, it was withdrawn from service only four days after its first public run because of problems with the tilt mechanism as well as other factors.

Da Vinci Community College in Derby became the region's first co-op school in 2012. Under the new structure pupils, parents, teachers and the wider community will officially own it.

Leicester Square's famous Swiss Glockenspiel was recently replaced by clockmaker, Smiths of Derby. The original was removed when the Swiss Centre was demolished in 2008 but the Derby firm was able to design and build a replacement which has now been installed as a free-standing unit.

Derby's Caribbean Carnival is a two-day event which takes place every year in July at various locations around the city. The event, which is organised by Derby West Indian Community Association, includes live music, processions, food and craft stalls and general entertainment indigenous to the Caribbean and West Indies.

Sudbury Open Prison is a Category D open prison for males. It has over 580 inmates who are offered a range of academic and vocational courses to prepare them for life after their release.

The Peel Monument in Dronfield was built in 1854 as a tribute to Sir Robert Peel to commemorate his repeal of the Corn Laws in 1846.

Hawks and a falcon were brought in to reduce the number of pigeons at Royal Derby Hospital in 2011. A male and female Harris hawk and a pere seke falcon were released at the hospital twice a week to scare away the pigeons.

The Archbishop of Canterbury made a three day visit to Derbyshire in September 2011. Beginning with a tour of Derby University multi-faith Centre the Archbishop's itinerary also included a walk-about on Normanton Road and a debate at Pride Park Stadium. Elsewhere in the county he also visited Bakewell, Ashbourne and Chesterfield.

Wings and Wheels is the name given to a nine foot high sculpture created by Rachel Carter and placed at the Derby Road/Market Street junction in Heanor. The steel structure, which cost £20,000 was inspired by the history of textile manufacturing and the logo of the former knitwear factory I & R Morley forms part of the design.

A mural in Babington Lane, Derby depicts a number of prominent local people including Jeddediah Strutt, Richard Arkwright and Joseph Wright. Also featured are the Rolls-Royce Merlin engine, the Silk Mill and the Quad. The mural was created by Mel Holmes and is part of the Derby City Council's Art in the City project.

Following a pilot scheme at Bolsover in 2009 self-service check-outs have been installed in most of Derbyshire's busiest libraries.

Derby Corporation operated a trolley-bus service in the town from 1932 until 1967.

In 1999 a Crime Scheme Management Manual developed by Derbyshire Constabulary was adopted by police forces throughout Europe.

The village of Higham once had 23 wells. Only three remain today.

The stone pillar box in French lane, Horsley is unique in Derbyshire and possibly in England. It is no longer used by the Royal Mail.

Lullington has several times been awarded the Best Kept Village in Derbyshire (of under 500 population). It has also been the winner of the Britain in Bloom competition.

Lea Green, near Holloway, is an outdoor learning and personal development centre operated by Derbyshire County Council. Situated on a 25 acre site on the border of the Peak National Park, it provides a range of courses for young people and adults which aim to be challenging, thought provoking and fun.

Two fragrances named after the Amber Valley area of Derbyshire (Amber Valley Pour Homme and Pour Femme) were created by Claire Hollinghurst in 2012. The perfume was made using Blue Box which lets people choose their favourite scents to create their personal programme.

At the time of writing it had been decided to create a National Police Air Service. Ripley has been chosen as the base for one of these helicopters.

Swarfega the world famous hand cleaner was invented by Audley Bowdler Williamson of Heanor.

More than 1,800 people were caught watching TV without a license in Derby in 2011. In the same year more than 5,100 people in Derbyshire were caught out along with 390,000 across the whole of the UK.

Annual wakes were a popular feature of village life in Derbyshire until recent years. The following rhyme casts light on some of these activities in earlier times:

> At Winster Wakes, there's ale and cakes,
> At Elton Wakes there's quenchers,
> At Bircher Wakes there's knives and forks,
> At Wensley Wakes there's wenches!

# Select Bibliography

Becket, J.V. The East Midlands from AD1000, London, 1988

Brighton, T. The Discovery of the Peak District, Chichester, 2004

Cooper B. Transformation of a Valley, London, 1983

Cooper, R. The Book of Chesterfield, Chesham, 1987

Davidson, A.W. Derby: Its Rise and Progress, Derby, 1906

Drury, G. The East Midlands and the Peak, London, 1963

Hadfield, C. The Canals of the East Midlands, Newton Abbott, 1981

Harris, H. Industrial Archaeology of the Peak District, Newton Abbott, 1971

Heath, J. The Illustrated History of Derby, Buckingham, 1982

Hey, D. Derbyshire a History, Lancaster, 2008

Hoskins, W.G. The Making of the English Landscape, Harmondsworth, 1985

Mee. A. (ed.) The King's England - Derbyshire,

Morgan, P.(ed.) Domesday Book, Phillimore Series Vol. XXVII Derbys., Chichester, 1978

Nixon, F. Industrial Archaeology of Derbyshire, Newton Abbot, 1969

Pevsner, N. The Buildings of Derbyshire, London, 1953

Richardson, A.R. Citizens Derby, London, 1949

Rippon, A. The Book of Derby, Derby, 1980

Rippon, N. Derby Our City, Derby, 2001

Sadler, G. History and Guide Chesterfield, Stroud, 2001

Smith, D. The Industrial Archaeology of the East Midlands, Dawlish, 1965

Smith, M.E. Industrial Derbyshire, Derby, 2008

Stocker, D. England's landscape The East Midlands, London, 2006

Turbett, G. A History of Derbyshire, Whitchurch, 1999

In conducting my research I also made use of a wide range of primary sources as well as newspapers, magazines and journals. A number of websites yielded useful information and local museums gave me valuable insights into a number of topics

Printed by Primatrace, United Kingdom

Printed by Printforce, United Kingdom